THE SOCIAL HISTORY OF PALESTINE
IN THE HERODIAN PERIOD

The Land Is Mine

THE SOCIAL HISTORY OF PALESTINE

IN THE HERODIAN PERIOD

The Land Is Mine

David A. Fiensy

Studies in the Bible and Early Christianity
Volume 20

The Edwin Mellen Press
Lewiston/Queenston/Lampeter

Library of Congress Cataloging-in-Publication Data

Fiensy, David A.
    The social history of Palestine in the Herodian period : the land
is mine / David Fiensy.
        p.   cm.   -- (Studies in the Bible and early Christianity ; v.
20)
    Includes bibliographical references.
    ISBN 0-88946-272-0
    1. Land tenure--Palestine--History. 2. Palestine--History--To 70
A.D. 3. Social classes--Palestine--History.   I. Title.
II. Series.
HD129.F54   1991
333.3'095694--dc20   90-22673
                                                                          CIP

This is volume 20 in the continuing series
Studies in the Bible & Early Christianity
Volume 20 ISBN 0-88946-272-0
SBEC Series ISBN 0-88946-913-X

A CIP catalog record for this book
is available from the British Library.

The Edwin Mellen Press   The Edwin Mellen Press
Box 450   Box 67
Lewiston, New York   Queenston, Ontario
USA 14092   CANADA L0S 1L0

The Edwin Mellen Press, Ltd.
Lampeter, Dyfed, Wales
UNITED KINGDOM SA48 7DY

Printed in the United States of America

DEDICATION

TO MY WIFE MOLLY

TABLE OF CONTENTS

MAPS, PLANS and TABLES

ACKNOWLEDGEMENTS

The idea for this monograph arose during a National Endowment for the Humanities Summer Seminar in 1986. The manuscript itself was written during my two year term as Institute Scholar in Tübingen, West Germany at the Institut zur Erforschung des Urchristentums. I owe a great debt of thanks to the Institut for its consistent commitment throughout the past twenty eight years to research related to early Christianity. I also want to thank our many concerned Christian friends in the United States whose financial support made this work possible.

I also want to express my gratitude to those in West Germany who gave me advice from time to time concerning this project. Professor Martin Hengel of the Institutum Judaicum offered rich bibliographic suggestions as did the staff of the Archäologisches Institut in Tübingen. Professor Gerd Theissen of the University of Heidelberg was also most gracious and helpful. Professor Eric Myers of Duke University in America also read a chapter and offered bibliography.

Finally, I wish to thank my best helpers in this whole endeavor: my wife Molly and my children Amanda and Jeannie.

ABBREVIATIONS

A	Josephus, *Antiquities of the Jews*
ANRW	*Aufstieg und Niedergang der römischen Welt*
B	Josephus, *Jewish War*
BA	*Biblical Archaeologist*
BAG	Bauer, Arndt and Gingrich, *Greek Lexicon*
BAR	*Biblical Archaeology Review*
BASOR	*Bulletin of the American Schools of Oriental Research*
BDB	Brown, Driver and Briggs, *A Hebrew and English Lexicon*
CAH	*Cambridge Ancient History*
CBQ	*Catholic Biblical Quarterly*
CIJ	Frey, *Corpus Inscriptionum Iudaicarum*
Compendia	Safrai and Stern, *The Jewish People in the First Century. Compendia Rerum Iudaicarum.*
CPJ	Tcherikover and Fuks, *Corpus Papyrorum Iudaicarum*
Danby	Danby, *The Mishnah*
DJD II	Benoit, Milik and de Vaux, *Les Grottes de Murabaat: Discoveries in the Judean Desert II.*
Epstein, *BT*	Epstein, ed. *The Babylonian Talmud*
HUCA	*Hebrew Union College Annual*
IDB	Buttrick, ed. *Interpreters Dictionary of the Bible*
IEJ	*Israel Exploration Journal*
Jastrow	Jastrow, *Dictionary*
JE	Singer, ed. *Jewish Encyclopedia*
JQR	*Jewish Quarterly Review*
JRS	*Journal of Roman Studies*
LCL	Loeb Classical Library
LSJM	Liddel, Scott, Jones and McKenzie, *Greek Lexicon*
Neusner	Neusner, *The Tosephta*
NTS	*New Testament Studies*
OCD	Hammond, ed. *Oxford Classical Dictionary*
PEQ	*Palestine Exploration Quarterly*

POT	Charlesworth, ed. *The Pseudepigrapha of the Old Testament*
P.S.I.	*Papiri Greci e Latini: Pubblicazioni Della Societa Italiana*
Schwab, *TJ*	Schwab, *Le Talmud de Jerusalem*
SVM	Schürer, Vermes, and Miller, *The History of the Jewish People in the Age of Jesus Christ*
TDNT	Kittel, ed. *Theological Dictionary of the New Testament*
V	Josephus, *Vita*
WHJP	*World History of the Jewish People.* Volume VI edited by Schalit. Volume VII edited by Avi-Yonah
ZNW	*Zeitschrift für die neutestamentliche Wissenschaft*

Rabbinic Works:

b.	Babylonian Talmud
j.	Jerusalem Talmud
t.	Tosephta

All rabbinic tractates are abbreviated according to Danby. All biblical, apocryphal and pseudepigraphical books are abbreviated according to *POT.* All scripture is quoted from the Revised Standard Version.

INTRODUCTION

This monograph has to do in general with the social history of Palestine during the Herodian period and specifically with the rural peasants over against the socially and economically powerful urban elite. As G. Alföldy wrote a few years ago in his *Die römische Gesellschaft:*

> Doubtless the most important change in the study of history that our generation has witnessed is the formulation of sociological questions and the use of sociological methods within the discipline.[1]

Indeed asking sociological questions and using sociological methods of inquiry in the field of ancient history is now widely recognized as necessary to understand the past. Thus many classical scholars--often building on the excellent foundation laid by M. Rostovtzeff and A. H. M. Jones--are deeply involved in the search to recover ancient Greco-Roman life among the common folk.[2]

Biblical scholars have also given attention to sociology and anthropology in the past ten years. Scholars in Germany, Great Britain, North America, and Australia have followed the lead of classical historians in asking new questions of the texts in order to understand events such as the Jewish war of A.D. 66.[3] H. Kreissig echoes the critique which this group of scholars would have of the earlier attempts to understand Palestinian Judaism. Kreissig complains of earlier efforts which fail to distinguish Jews both religiously and socially "as if they had been a homogeneous mass who lived only from religion."[4]

What is needed, these scholars seem to be saying, is a new look at Palestinian society, asking new questions. Since historians would almost universally agree that Palestine in the Herodian period was an agrarian society composed of mostly peasant farmers, the obvious way to understand this society best is to understand the peasantry and its relationship to other social and economic classes.

S. Freyne has, therefore, produced a description of Galilee from Alexander to Hadrian which seeks to understand it as a peasant society. R. Horsley and J. S. Hanson – as did H. Kreissig fifteen years earlier – have attempted to understand the Jewish rebellion as at least partly a class-conflict between the rural peasants and the urban elite. S. Applebaum, A. Ben-David, and D. S. Oakman emphasize the economic plight of the agricultural worker. B. Malina has described peasant categories and values in New Testament period Palestine to make us aware of the otherness of this society.[5]

The chapters of this work also investigate the lower classes of Palestinian society. They describe mostly the economic and social conditions of those common people who followed Jesus of Nazareth as well as a host of would-be prophets and messiahs. Many of these rural people were either killed or enslaved in the rebellions of A.D. 66 and 132. From their class came most of the bandits, beggars and other undesirables of Palestinian society. They are the nameless masses that history has usually ignored.

Any investigation into the peasantry of Palestine must begin with a working definition. We shall formulate our working definition of peasantry by adapting that given by de Ste. Croix:

1) Peasants are subsistence farmers who provide their own maintenance from their own labor.

2) They may be freeholders, tenants, day laborers, or agricultural slaves.

3) They ideally work their holdings as family units (except for day laborers and slaves).

4) They produce collectively more than is necessary for their own subsistence and with this surplus support the elite class (landlords, government leaders) to whom they are in some way in subjection.[6]

First of all then, peasants work their land for a subsistence. They are not agricultural business people farming for profit, and land is not capital or commodity. Rather "the land and (the peasant) are parts of one thing, one old-established body of relationships...."[7] Peasants do not view land as an investment and farming as a business. Farming is their way of life and the land their inherited means of life.

Second, peasants in this monograph will include not only freeholders and tenants, but also day laborers and slaves. The latter two types of workers do not appear in de Ste. Croix's definition. We think of work on the common folk of Palestine must include all four categories, however.

Third, peasants normally work their land as a family unit (nuclear or extended). The entire family must work together to provide a subsistence for itself. In the case of day laborers, however, the laborer works for wages usually apart from his family. Agricultural slaves may have had no families.

Finally, all peasant societies are marked by a radical bifurcation in which a small group of aristocrats stands over against the mass of agriculturalists. The latter must surrender their surplus to the former. "Peasants...are rural cultivators whose surpluses are transferred to a dominant group of rulers."[8]

Our investigation of Palestinian peasant society is difficult because of the nature of the sources. First, no peasant from Palestine has expressed himself in a surviving document on his social plight. Second, most of our literary sources of any kind were written by the urban elite class which had often little sympathy and less understanding for the rural peoples. What was true of the classical world in general was also true of Herodian Palestine. As Rostovtzeff noted thirty years ago:

> The cities have told us their story, the country always remained silent and reserved. What we know of the country we know mostly through the men of the cities, for whom the men of the country, the peasants, were sometimes targets of jokes...sometimes a foil to set off the wickedness of city life...The voice of the country population is rarely heard.[9]

We are not totally at a loss, however, in investigating this theme. First of all we can begin asking new questions of the old sources. Works such as those by Kreissig and Horsley and Hanson, for example, have given us some very useful results in restudying the familiar sources. Secondly, we can, where possible utilize the results of archaeology. Peasants have left us very few documents in Palestine, but they have left objects (e.g. houses, pottery, tombs, and even their own skeletal remains.). Surely our fund of knowledge about Palestinian peasants can be increased by examining the material remains. Third, as MacMullen points out,[10] we can look at comparable societies. He suggests we consider data from more recent peasant societies about which we know more, to understand common phenomena in ancient society such as overpopulation or the use of day laborers. Finally, as MacMullen again suggests, we may employ sociology and anthropology "to humanize" the people we are studying.[11] Anthropology in particular can be a preventative against ethnocentrism, a mistake all too easily made when undertaking a study such as this. On the other hand we shall be careful to allow social theory to illumine the historical picture but not to reduce history merely to a combination of social forces.

Throughout the following chapters runs a common thread: the effect of changing land tenure on the lives of the peasant class. We begin the investigation by describing the land-tenure ideal in Palestinian society. Next we summarize the changes in land tenure brought about by the Hellenistic and Roman periods, namely, the growth of the large estates. We then detail the effect of these changes on the economic standard of living of the peasant (Chapter 3) and the various social units of the peasant sub-society (Chapter 4). Finally, we construct a broad social overview of the structures of Palestinian life.

The time framework we have chosen to concentrate upon is termed by archaeologists the Herodian period (37 B.C.- A.D. 70). It will be obvious to the reader that this time period was chosen because Jesus of Nazareth lived within it. This work is in a sense, then, an attempt to illumine partly the life of the historical Jesus. Naturally, however, we cannot conduct historical investigation in a vacuum. Therefore, we shall to some extent also describe the Hellenistic and Hasmonean periods which came before our era of concern and the Mishnaic period which comes after it.

ENDNOTES

1.   Alföldy, 1986, p. 1.

2.   P. Brunt, 1971a and 1971b; G. E. M. de Ste. Croix, 1981; R. MacMullen, 1974; P. Garnsey, 1980; K. D. White 1970 and 1977.

3.   See D. J. Harrington, "Social Concepts in the Early Church: A Decade of Research" *Theological Studies* 41 (1980) 181-190; *idem.*, "Second Testament Exegesis and the Social Sciences: A Bibliography" *Biblical Theology Bulletin* 18 (1988) 77-85; R. Scroggs, "The Sociological Interpretation of the New Testament: The Present State of Research" *NTS* 26 (1980) 164-179; T. Best, "The Sociological Study of the New Testament: Promise and Peril of a New Discipline" *Scottish Journal of Theology* 36 (1983) 181-194; B. Malina, "The Social Sciences and Biblical Interpretation" *Interpretation* 37 (1982) 229-242.

4.   Kreissig, 1970, p. 89.

5.   S. Freyne, 1980; R. Horsley and J. S. Hanson, 1985; H. Kreissig, 1969 and 1970; S. Applebaum, 1976 and 1977; D. S. Oakman, 1986; B. Malina, 1981; and A. Ben-David, 1974.

6.   De Ste. Croix, 1981, pp. 210f.

7.   Redfield, 1956, pp. 27f.

8.   Wolf, 1966, pp. 3f.

9.   Rostovtzeff, 1957, p. 192. *Cf.* L. White, *Medieval Technology and Social Change* (Oxford: Clarendon, 1962) p. 39.

10.   MacMullen "Peasants, during the Principate" *ANRW* II. 1 (1974) 253-261, esp. p. 251.

11.   *Ibid.*, p. 257.

CHAPTER 1

PEASANT NOTIONS CONCERNING
THE LAND OF ISRAEL

There can be little doubt that Palestine in the Herodian period was an agrarian society with a population mostly of peasant farmers eking out a subsistence from the land either as free peasants, tenants, day laborers, or agricultural slaves. Historians almost universally describe the Greco-Roman world in such terms[1] and the evidence for Palestine is similar.[2] Land, therefore, was not only very important economically but also important conceptually. Land was life. The way one regards land and thinks about land will to a great extent determine how one uses the land both of himself and of his fellow. We must, then, begin our examination of the social history of Palestine in the Herodian period with a discussion of peasant beliefs, traditions, and expectations regarding the land.

H. G. Kippenberg writes of the clash during this period between two ideologies regarding the land, the traditional Old Testament conception and the new Greco-Roman conception:

> The sources describing the social history (of Palestine) in the Roman period testify to the oppression...of the free peasants under the system of the appropriation of surplus. The important institutions of the older era which arose as resistance against class formation...are no longer in force in the Roman period...The erection of an economy of profit was a contradiction to the egalitarian religious traditions. This social change was an emancipation from the tradition...[3]

Kippenberg suggests, then, that there was a peasant notion (based on the Old Testament "tradition") which emphasized individual independence and economic equality, and a new ideology, standing in stark contrast to the tradition, which emphasized profit and which intensified social class differences.

More recently, D. E. Oakman has pointed out that two general ideas of land tenure existed side by side in antiquity, that of the elites who in one way or another controlled and profited from most of the land, and that of the peasants most of whom in one way or another had to serve the elites.[4]

R. Redfield[5] described peasant culture in general as a half-culture and a half-society. The other half of culture in an agrarian society is high culture or learned culture, which Redfield termed the "Great Tradition." The Great Tradition is the tradition of the reflective few, cultivated in schools and temples, the tradition of the philosopher, theologian, or literary man. This tradition is consciously cultivated and handed down. On the other hand the culture of the masses in nondeveloped societies is termed by Redfield the "Little Tradition." The Little Tradition is low culture, folk culture, or popular tradition which is passed on among the unlettered of the village community.

The Great Tradition "works its way down" to the peasants and becomes a part of the Little Tradition, but this process is both slow and always incomplete. Because the process is slow the Little Tradition will always appear outdated to the bearers of the Great Tradition (usually the urban elite). In other words peasants appear to be old fashioned. But the uneducated can also never fully appropriate the culture of the Great Tradition, but rather only a simplified version of it, or a version of the Great Tradition that has been filtered through custom and folk tradition.

What we shall attempt to sketch below is intended to be approximately the beliefs, assumptions, and values regarding the land of Israel as these would have been known in the Little Tradition. We want to see the land through the eyes of the Palestinian Jewish peasant. Unfortunately, no peasant in Palestine ever wrote anything of any length that has survived. We know, therefore, little directly about their views on the land. We can, however, piece together a broad picture based on texts that would have been important to and representative of peasants – namely the Old Testament and related texts – and based on peasant behavior.

The Little Tradition must have been a tradition that still clung to the old idea that the land belonged ultimately to Yahweh and was given in trust to Israel as inalienable family farm plots. Land is not capital to be exploited but the God-given means to subsist.

We must bear in mind the important theological significance of the land of Israel for Jews of antiquity. W. D. Davies[6] has rightly instructed us concerning the religious meaning of the land of Israel. He lists two important Old Testament conceptions concerning the land. First of all, the land of Palestine is the promised land. God promised the land to the patriarchs (Gen. 12:1-3, 15:1-6, 15:17-21, 17:44) and although the land belonged earlier to the Canaanites, God has given it over to the Israelites (Josh. 1:2f, 11, 15, 9:24, 10:42, 14:9, Dt. 9:24-29). This same notion appears also in Judaism in the Hellenistic period (Jubilees 13:3, Testament/Assumption of Moses 2:1, Sirach 46:8). Thus the land belongs to Israel as a promised gift of Yahweh and is Israel's inheritance.

The second claim[7] the Old Testament makes about the land is that the land belongs exclusively to Yahweh. Lev. 25:23 states: "The land shall not be sold in perpetuity, for the land is mine, for you are strangers and sojourners with me." G. von Rad[8] maintained that this conception of the land as Yahweh's is very old and is the theological basis of all Israelite land rights.

If the land is Yahweh's, then Yahweh is the landlord and the Israelites his serfs or tenants.[9] A number of scholars have tried to demonstrate that several practices relating to the land have their basis in this concept. First, the assignment of land by lot (Num. 26:55, Micah. 2:5) rests on this principle.[10] Assigning land by lot "was a confession that Yahweh owned it," wrote von Rad.[11] Second are the laws about the harvest and providing for the poor, for example: gleanings must be left to the poor (Lev. 19:9-10, 23:22, Dt. 24:19-21), passers-by may satisfy their hunger from a field (Dt. 23:25-26), annual tithes and first fruits must be paid to Yahweh (Ex. 21:29, Lev. 27:30-32), and a tithe must be given to the poor every third year (Dt. 14:28-29, 26:12-15).[12] Third, are the laws which state that the land must keep the Sabbath and lie fallow every seventh year (Lev. 25:2-7, Ex. 23:10-11), and the laws of Jubilee (Lev. 25:10-17, 28, 30, 40) in which all property reverts back to its original owner every fifty years. We shall return to these two laws below.[13] Fourth, the concept of the land of Israel as Holy Land rests on the ideas that the land is Yahweh's, that He dwells there (Num 35:34) and thus the land is consecrated to Him.[14]

The non-canonical sources show that this same belief in the land as Yahweh's – and the corresponding implications which arose from this doctrine – continued into the Hellenistic and Roman periods. Most importantly the land is called the Lord's land:

> 4 Ezra 9:7f: "and it shall be that everyone who will be saved and will be able to escape...will see my salvation in my land and within my borders which I have sanctified for myself from the beginning. (See also 4 Ezra 12:34, 13:48, 2 Baruch 40:2, 1 Enoch 90:20).[15]

A passage in the Babylonian Talmud illustrates the theological link between the law of the Sabbatical year and the notion that the land is the Lord's:

> Sanhedrin 39a: The Holy One, blessed be He, said to Israel, sow your seed six years but omit the seventh, that ye may know that the earth is mine.[16]

Furthermore, the land is called "Holy Land" or the "Good Land" in texts widely distributed from the second century B.C. to the second century A.D. (Jubilees 13:2,6, Sibylline Oracles 3.266f, Wisdom of Solomon 13:3,4,7, Tobit 14:4,5, 2 Baruch 65:10, 71:1, 1 Enoch 89:40, Kelim 1:6-9, Mekilta Pisha I).[17]

Finally, the agricultural laws are widely attested not only in the Mishnah,[18] but also in the New Testament, and Josephus.[19]

Of particular importance for our purposes are the laws concerning Sabbatical rest and Jubilee, both of which have to do with the seven year cycle, are based on a concept of restoration to a previous status, and were somewhat fused together both in the Old Testament and later Judaism. The Sabbatical rest laws (Ex. 21:2-6, 23:10-11, Lev. 25:2-7, Dt. 15:1-18) command that every seventh year the land must lie fallow, all debts must be forgiven and all Hebrew slaves released. That these laws were not always observed can be seen from Lev. 26:34-35, Jer. 34:14, and Neh. 10:31. The last passage also demonstrates an attempt to reestablish this legislation.

B. Z. Wacholder's impressive list of references to the seventh year has shown us that the Sabbatical year laws seem to have been observed to some degree in the Second Temple period.[20] 1 Macc. 6:49, 53, *A* 13.234 and 14.475 refer to the hardships caused by letting the land lie fallow during the seventh year. The Mishnah, especially the tractate Shebiith, devotes a great amount of space to the Sabbatical year. We read in later rabbinic works of Jews being mocked in Caesarea for keeping the Sabbath year,[21] and some of the contracts found at Wadi Murabaat dating to the time of Bar Cochba refer to the year of release.[22] Tacitus (*Hist.* 5.4) writing in the early second century also alludes to the Jews observing the Sabbatical year. Yet it is also clear that some ignored this legislation and sowed their land as usual.[23]

For our purposes, however, it is more important that the other elements of the Sabbatical year legislation were ignored. First of all, we know of no references to release of Hebrew slaves during the Sabbatical year. Some scholars assume that the release still took place but there is no evidence for this assumption.[24] The only reference to freeing slaves is Simon bar Giora's liberation during the Jewish war (*B* 4.508). This event would argue that Hebrew slaves would not still be manumitted in the Sabbatical year. One could argue that these slaves were Gentiles, but why then would Simon free them and why would they have joined the rebellion if they were Gentiles?

Further, another element in the Sabbatical year legislation, the release of debts, was definitely abrogated at least by the time of the great Hillel (contemporaneous with Herod the Great[25]) in the first century B.C. The new law created by Hillel was called the *prozbul*[26] and allowed for the debt to be carried through the seventh year and beyond by a legal fiction which assigned the loan to the court to collect the debt. Mishnah Shebiit 10:3 reads:

> A loan secured by prozbul is not cancelled by the seventh year. This is one of the things that Hillel the elder ordained.[27]

A papyrus text has been found at Wadi Murabaat dating from A.D. 55/56[28] which may reflect the prozbul. This document, which is a contract of indebtedness reads as follows:

> [The ye]ar two of emperor Nero.[] At Siwaya, Absalom, son of Hannin, from Siwaya, has declared in my presence that there is on account with me, me Zechariah, son of Yohanan, son of H. [], living at Cheaslon, the sum of twe[nt]y zuzin. The sum I am to rep[ay] b[y but if] I have not paid (?) by this time, I will reimburse you with (interest of) a fifth and will settle in en[tirety], even if this is the year of release רשבת שממה דה And if I do not do so, indem[nity] for you (will be) from my possessions, and whatever I acquire (will be) at your disposal.[29]

The Aramaic word for "release" in the papyrus שממה is the same root as in Dt. 15:1, thus there can be little doubt that the contract is referring to the Sabbatical year.

E. Koffmahn translates the phrase רשבת שממה דה "in this year of release" instead of "even if this is the year of release" as J. T. Milik followed by J. Fitzmyer and D. Harrington did. Both K. Beyer and Wacholder follow Koffmahn. Wacholder denies, therefore, that the text is alluding to the prozbul. It simply states that the contract was made in the Sabbatical year and not that the payment must be made even though it may be the sabbatical year.[30] But even if the text should be translated "in this year of release," the contract seems to indicate that the release of debts was no longer practiced since the document lists the penalty for not paying the debt, as if there could be no other alternative. Therefore this text may witness to the prozbul in the first century A.D.

The Sabbatical year legislation regarding cancellation of debts and perhaps release of slaves was largely ignored or abrogated in the late Second Temple period. What had stood as a legal safeguard against impoverishment in perpetuity was now largely removed.

The law of Jubilee is given in Lev. 25:8-55. It allowed both for the restitution of land, sold probably under economic duress (vs. 25), and the release of slaves every fifty (or 49?) years:

> (vs. 10)...and you shall hallow the fiftieth year, and proclaim liberty דרור throughout the land to all its inhabitants; it shall be a Jubilee יובל for you, when each of you shall return to his property, and each of you shall return to his family...(vs. 23) The land shall not be sold in perpetuity for the land is mine

and you are strangers and sojourners with me. (See also vss.
39-41)

The Jubilee is also referred to in Isa 61:1f where "liberty" דרור is
proclaimed for the captives.

Some have maintained that this legislation may stem from as late as
the exile,[31] and that it was never observed.[32] Without settling those issues,
we can still learn from the law of Jubilee very important notions current in
the Jewish mind-set in the Herodian period.

The theology of the Jubilee is, since the land is the Lord's and the
Israelites His tenants or serfs, the land is not theirs to sell in perpetuity. The
land is not a mere economic commodity but a sacred trust.

This concept had strong socioeconomic implications attached to it.
The first one was that one's inherited farm plot, his patrimony should be
inalienable.[33] Philo also saw this implication clearly:

> (Spec. Leg. 2.111) He (Moses) considers that alienated estates
> ought to be restored to their original possessors in order that
> the apportionments should be secured to the families and that
> no-one to whom they had been allotted should be altogether
> deprived of the grant.[34]

The notion that one's inherited plot was inalienable is not only
ancient in Israel but is also well attested for most peasant societies, where
land is more "a family heirloom" than an economic commodity.[35] Ideally
everyone would sit "under his vine and under his fig tree" (Micah 4:41, Zech.
3:10), in other words on his own small farm, raising his subsistence crops with
the help of his family.[36]

The classic statement of the idea of inalienable patrimony is the story
of Ahab and Naboth. When Ahab asked to buy Naboth's vineyard, the latter
replied, "the Lord forbid that I should give you the inheritance of my fathers"
(2 Kgs. 21:3). Naboth's strong refusal underlines the importance of keeping
one's inheritance.

Rabbinic literature attests that this attitude toward the ancestral farm
plot persisted through the Second Temple period and beyond both among
the halakic sages and among the peasants:

> (Sifra, Behar 5) A man has no right to sell his ancestral field so
> that he can get ready capital wherewith to buy cattle, or
> mobilia, or slaves, or to raise sheep and goats, or even to

conduct business therewith. The only circumstances in which it is permitted is-if he has become penniless.[37]

j. Ketuboth 2.10: It was taught: We have eaten of the qesisah of soandso. What is meant by qesisah? When a man sold off the field of his holding, his relatives would fill barrels with roasted grain and nuts and would crack them in front of the children. The children would gather them up, chanting: soandso has been broken off (niqsas) from his holding.[38]

The first passage, a halakic ruling, demonstrates the strong feeling for the ancestral piece of land as inalienable. One may only sell his land in dire economic straits. Viewing land as merely capital or as a means to make money, that is, as an investment, is in this halacah prohibited.

The second passage, an haggadic section of the Jerusalem talmud demonstrates the folk custom regarding one who has sold his land. The relatives seem to express by the ritual of the grain and the nut cracking that that was a significant event for the extended family. Perhaps the children's chant is intended to be mocking,[39] in which case the extended family is reprimanding him. Whether this story should be dated to before the destruction of the temple or not[40] is of no consequence for our purposes since such customs tend to persist a very long time and reflect very old sentiments.

The inalienability of one's inherited plot is also reflected in the gô'el customs (Lev. 25:25) in which a man would buy his kinsman's ground when he had come into economic straits, thereby keeping the land in the possession of the clan. Thus, Jeremiah (Jer. 32:6-9) and Boaz (Ruth 4:9) bought the property of their kinsmen, exercising their prior right of purchase. If a man could not keep his patrimony, the clan should have it.[41] This custom probably also stands behind the interesting little story in Numbers 36 in which the daughters of a certain Zelophehad must marry their kinsmen to keep their inheritance within the tribe.[42]

The second socioeconomic implication of the Jubilee legislation was that the land should be approximately evenly distributed with no one becoming wealthy to the impoverishment of others.[43] This notion surfaces in the eighth-century B.C. prophetic condemnation of "adding field to field" (Isa: 5:8, Micah 2:2) where it does not appear that the fields are acquired illegally.[44] The problem is that poor people through indebtedness or famine must sell their patrimony in perpetuity to survive. Such a state of affairs contradicts the ideal.

A similar problem and its concomitant condemnation arose during the late fifth century in the time of Nehemiah (Neh. 5:1-13). The small farm plot owners complained because they were having to mortgage their fields to buy grain and pay the Persian king's tax in a time of famine, while the "nobles and officials" were acquiring the mortgaged land and building up large estates. Nehemiah "became very angry when (he) heard the outcry" because these nobles and officials were not walking "in the fear of our God." He demanded the fields be returned to their original owners. This "agrarian reform," as V. Tcherikover[45] termed it, preserved the Israelite ideal for a while of every man sitting under his own vine and fig tree, all about equal in amount of land. At least the degree of difference between the wealthier class and the ordinary peasant was kept to a minimum.

Interestingly, testimony concerning the social attitude of the Palestinian Jews is found in Hecataeus of Abdera (300 B.C.) who is quoted in Diodorus Siculus (XL.3.7). Hecataeus writes that Moses:

> After annexing much land apportioned it out, assigning equal allotments to private citizens and greater ones to priests...The common citizens were forbidden to sell their individual plots, lest there be some who for their own advantage should buy them up, and by oppressing the poorer classes bring on a scarcity of manpower.[46]

The Jewish belief that the land should remain equally distributed was obvious enough to impress a pagan observer in the early third century B.C.

Thus the Jubilee legislation protected against the permanent alienation of ones patrimony and against amassing large tracts of land by a few people. The ideal was rough equality.

One is forced to conclude however that the Jubilee was probably rarely kept in the Second Temple period. The so called "Book of Jubilees" (second century B.C.) organizes all world history around the Jubilees (e.g.45:13), but this does not prove that anyone was observing the Jubilee then. The Qumran Community Rule (1QS 10:8) alludes to a דרור ("liberty"), the same word as Lev. 25:10, and from the context apparently is talking about the Jubilee.[47] But again, the Jubilee is only a time indicator and we have no way of knowing if anyone actually observed this year of liberty and restitution or not. Philo refers to the Jubilee (*Spec Leg* 2.104-107, 110-111, 115, *Virtues* 99) but he merely explains the legislation without indicating whether anyone practised it.

A passage in Josephus is of special importance in this regard:

> A 3.282:...the fiftieth year is called by the Hebrews Jobel; at that season debtors are absolved from their debts and slaves are set at liberty, that is to say those who are members of the race and having transgressed some requirement of the law have by it been punished by reduction to a servile condition...Now too he restores estates (ἀγροί) to their original owners....[48]

Josephus in the first place merges the sabbatical year practice of debt cancellation with the Jubilee. Leviticus says nothing about cancelling debts in the Jubilee year. Second, Josephus describes the slaves released as being punished whereas Leviticus indicates the servitude is the result of poverty (Lev. 25:39).[49]

Even more troublesome is the confused description that follows, which describes how lands are restored to their original owners in the Jubilee (*A* 3.283). Josephus describes a reckoning-up of the products over the years the buyer has "owned" the land. Then follow three hypothetical cases:

1) If the proceeds over the years exceed the expenses (evidently for the price of the land, the raising and harvesting of the crops, etc.) then the seller may have his land back.

2) If the expenses are more than the proceeds, the seller must pay a sum equal to the difference or else he forfeits his property (for good?).

3) If the costs equal the expenses the seller also in this case recovers his property.

This process of calculation is also additional to the text of Leviticus but may be based on Lev. 25:25-28. The process makes the seller in effect responsible for the buyer's successful harvest. If the harvest is not a success, the seller must pay for it, an unlikely prospect since the seller probably would have sold his land in the first place only out of economic necessity. This description in Josephus looks too much like an attempt to justify not practising the Jubilee legislation regarding restitution of land. It is interesting in this connection to note that Josephus himself came from a wealthy and prestigious priestly family that owned large tracts of land in the hills around Jerusalem (V420). His family obviously did not observe the Jubilee.

We find actually very little evidence that anyone observed the law of Jubilee in the Second Temple period. R. North's[50] citation of A3.317 in which Josephus claims there is not a single Hebrew who does not obey the laws of Moses, proves nothing. This obvious exaggeration is not only patently false, Josephus was not even referring to the Jubilee here but the Mosaic legislation in general. On the other hand, we read about too many landless people – bandits, day laborers and tenant farmers[51] – to conclude that this legislation was generally observed.

In addition, texts from both Talmuds (j.Sheb. 10.4; b.Arak 32b-33a) and from a Tannaitic midrash (Sifra, Behar Sinai 7.1)[52] affirm that the Jubilee was not observed in the second temple period:

j. Sheb 10.4: Why did the Jubilee cease after the exile?

b. Arakin 32b: But did they count the years of release and Jubilees after the return from Babylon? If even after the tribe of Reuben, the tribe of Gad and the half-tribe of Manasseh went into exile, the Jubilees were abolished, should Ezra...have counted them?[53]

Kippenberg has also noted that one of the sales documents from Wadi Murabaat (26.9-11), from the Bar Cochba era, implies the Jubilee is not observed:

The above named buyers have the claim to this piece of ground forever, as also their heirs. They can keep it or sell it or do with it whatever they want as can their heirs from today and forever.[54]

A similar document from the same period of time comes from the Nahal Hever finds (HevC).[55]

On the other hand we find evidence that many Jews, poor peasants included, longed for the Jubilee-Sabbatical year laws to be enforced. We would expect that the Little Tradition would be less likely to adopt the relatively new Greco-Roman conceptions of the land. But in addition to this general consideration three lines of evidence combine to indicate that the Jews of Palestine in the Herodian period longed for a just and humane society in terms of the Jubilee. This evidence is found in the Qumran document known as 11Q Melchizedek, in the preaching of Jesus, and the actions of the Jewish dissidents and rebels in the first century A.D.

The fragments of the Melchizedek document have been dated by A. S. van der Woude, by paleographical indications to the Herodian period, specifically to the first half of the first century A.D.[56] E. Puech more recently dates the document to the second half of the second century B.C.[57]

According to this document, Melchizedek will be an eschatological, heavenly redeemer figure who will call home the people of the diaspora during the tenth Jubilee. Evidently the author is alluding to Daniel's "seventy weeks" (9:24-27). Since the Jubilee will occur at the same time as the Sabbatical year the author quotes at the beginning of the text both Lev. 25:13 and Dt. 15:2 and later writes that this time of deliverance was previously announced in Isa 61:1f. Melchizedek will also exact judgment upon Belial and his condemned angels. He is God's agent of judgment.[58]

The significant feature of this document for our purposes is the association of the time of deliverance with the Jubilee-Sabbatical year. This Old Testament social ideal has become an eschatological hope. Whether we date the document to the late second century B.C. or to the early first century A.D., we should nevertheless conclude that at least by the first century there was a longing for the enactment of the social measures of that legislation.[59]

Jesus' preaching also indicates that Jews in the Herodian period longed for the enactment of the Jubilee. A. Trocmé, followed by J. H. Yoder and J. A. Sanders,[60] suggests that Jesus saw the kingdom of God in terms of the Jubilee and that he therefore proclaimed the arrival of Jubilee (Lk. 4:14-21, 12:30-33, 6:20-26). The account of Jesus in his home town of Nazareth is especially important (Lk. 4:14-21) because Jesus applied the Jubilee text from Isa 61:1f to himself.

More recently S. H. Ringe has argued for this hypothesis. She defends the historicity of Luke 4 by the following arguments: 1) The internal coherence and logic of the pericope as it now stands indicates that the passage is based on an authentic event. 2) The appearance in this passage of midrashic techniques typical of Jesus' teaching point toward historicity. 3) The non-Lukan vocabulary leads to the conclusion that this story is not a free composition but based on tradition.[61]

Ringe suggests that Jesus' words in Mt. 11:2-6 = Lk. 7:18-23 are also based on Isa. 61 and explains the two main Jubilee themes in Jesus' preaching as good news for the poor and a proclamation of release or forgiveness.[62]

Whether Jesus was calling for a literal Jubilee or merely using the vocabulary and concepts related to the Jubilee to frame his teaching on the kingdom of God, we cannot settle here. We should, however, conclude that the notions of Jubilee played a role in his theology.

Finally, we have the actions of the Jewish peasants involved in the rebellions of A.D. 6 and 66. The process of both Hellenization and later Romanization led to revolts and protests almost universally,[63] and Palestine was no exception. But was the protest in Palestine based at least in part on a perceived challenge to the Old Testament concept of egalitarianism and right to patrimony which rested in turn on the belief that the land belonged to Yahweh? We cannot be as certain with this evidence, but the events are certainly suggestive.

M. Hengel[64] has speculated that the uprising in A.D.6 over the property evaluation of Quirinius (A18.1-5, B2.118, Acts 5:37) stemmed from the feeling that Caesar was usurping God as owner of the land. Quirinius as governor was to make an "assessment of the property of the Jews"[65] (ἀποτιμησόμενὸς τε αὐτῶν τὰς οὐσίας) or a registration of property (ἀπογραφή).[66] This shocked the Jews generally, and one "sophist" in particular, named Judas, called this assessment the equivalent of slavery. Hengel maintains that the Jewish outrage was because the Romans seemed to abrogate Leviticus 25 and Deuteronomy 15.

Even more interesting is the account given by Josephus of the behavior of the Sicarii in A.D. 66 who broke into and burned down the building in Jerusalem where the public archives (ἀρχεῖα) and records of indebtedness were kept. (B 2.427). It is also important that the Galileans held a strong hatred for the city of Sepphoris (V 375) the capital of Galilee when the war broke out where debt records were also kept (V 38) and that the Galileans too tried to burn down the city (V 375). The socioeconomic reasons for such action have long been recognized by historians.[67] But is there also a connection to the biblical tradition of Jubilee? Was this an announcement of a messianic Jubilee/Sabbatical Year in which the prozbul would no longer be valid? The association of the cancellation of debts with the Sabbatical year suggests that the Old Testament ideal played some role in their actions.

The activity of Simon bar Giora is also reminiscent of Jubilee concepts. He appears to have attempted to bring about a new social order of egalitarianism.[68] He not only attacked the houses of the wealthy (*B* 2.652), but freed all slaves (*B* 4.510). Was Simon, then, attempting to enforce the Sabbatical year and Jubilee legislation concerning the release of Hebrew slaves? We have no way of knowing, of course, whether these were actually Hebrew slaves he liberated, but their subsequent participation in the rebellion might indicate that they were. Also, why would Simon free them if they were Gentile slaves?

We also have all the other references to the wealthy, aristocratic, sometimes High Priestly, citizens being attacked which indicates that the peasants felt unjustly impoverished. We must bear in mind that since Palestine was an agrarian society, wealth was probably acquired from land, that the more land one owned the wealthier he would be, and that to acquire large tracks of land probably meant that many other people had to lose their land.

During the procuratorship of Felix (A.D. 52-60) certain bands of would-be messiahs and bandits went about looting the houses of the nobles and killing their owners (*B* 2.264). Once the war broke out in A.D. 66 a full scale campaign against the wealthy began by the Sicarii, Zealots, and the followers of Simon bar Giora. The Sicarii burned the palace of Agrippa II and the High Priest and pursued other wealthy Jews through the city sewers of Jerusalem (*B* 2.426-428). The Zealots killed many prominent citizens (*B* 4.140-145, 5.439-441) including Chief Priests (*B* 4.315, 327, 335, 358, 5. 527-532). Simon attacked the houses of the wealthy large landowners and in general disliked the rich intensely (*B* 2.652, 5.309).

Such actions make the Jewish war appear, at least in part, to have been a class war.[70] We would suggest that these events were influenced, if not directly by Jubilee theology, at least by the egalitarian traditions associated with it. In a society where class distinctions are so marked some few people must be controlling a disproportionate amount of land to the impoverishment of the rest of the population. The egalitarian ideal, according to which everyone sits under his own vine and fig tree, has been abrogated. Instead some have acquired large estates while others have either lost their land or are deeply in debt. We should probably imagine a situation not unlike that at the time of Nehemiah. This time, however, there was no Nehemiah to reverse the trend.

Land then is a sacred gift from God which remains ultimately God's. Land is the "precondition of all life, the source of all production and not a commodity." It is the means of subsistence not mere capital to be bought and sold.[71] Land is especially not something which the rich and powerful should take away from the poor and weak, certainly not in perpetuity. Ownership is more of a sacred tenancy with God as the landlord than absolute ownership. Theology and socioeconomics were then intertwined in the biblical world as they are in most contemporary undeveloped societies, and theology was supposed to inform socioeconomics.

ENDNOTES

1.   Finley, 1973, p. 97; Jones, 1940, p. 265; Brunt, 1971a, p. 87; de Ste. Croix, 1981, p. 10; Rostovtzeff, 1957, p. 343; D. J. Thompson in Wacher, 1987, p. 555.

2.   Ben-David, 1969, p. 49; Schalit, 1969, p. 322, Finkelstein, 1929, p. 189; Klausner in Avi-Yonah, *The Herodian Period*, WHJP Vol. 7, p. 179.

3.   H. G. Kippenberg, *Religion und Klassenbildung im antiken Judäa* (Göttingen: Vandenhoeck and Ruprecht, 1978) pp. 154ff.

4.   Oakman, *Jesus and the Economic Questions of His Day* (Lewiston/Queenston: The Edwin Mellen Press, 1986) p. 38. Cf. B. Malina, "Wealth and Poverty in the New Testament and its World," *Interpretation* 41 (1987) p. 361.

5.   Redfield, *Peasant Society and Culture* (Chicago: University of Chicago Press, 1956) pp. 68-84. Cf. G. M. Foster, "What is a Peasant?" in J. M. Potter, M. N. Diaz and G. M. Goster, eds., *Peasant Society: a Reader* (Boston: Little, Brown and Co., 1967) pp. 2-14; and B. Malina, *The New Testament World: Insights from Cultural Anthropology* (Atlanta: John Knox, 1981) pp. 73-75.

6.   Davies, *The Gospel and the Land* (Berkeley: University of California 1974) pp. 15-53. See also G. von Rad, *Theologie des alten Testaments* (München: Kaiser, 1961, vol. I, pp. 298f; R. de Vaux, *Ancient Israel*, trans. J. McHugh (London: Darton, Longman and Todd, 1961) pp. 164-77; W. Brueggemann, *The Land* (Philadelphia: Fortress, 1977) p. 3.

7.   Davies, 1974, pp. 24-29.

8.   Von Rad, 1961, p. 298.

9.   A. van Selms "Jubilee" *IDB*, II; de Vaux, 1961, p. 165.

10.   Davies, 1974, p. 27; von Rad, 1961, p. 298; de Vaux, 1961, p. 165. Note Ezek. 45:1 and 47:22 looks towards new allotment.

11.   Von Rad, 1961, p. 298.

12.   Davies, 1974, p. 28; de Vaux, 1961, p. 165.

13.   De Vaux, 1961, p. 165.

14.   Davies, 1974, pp. 29-33.

15.   Translation by B. Metzger in *POT*, I. Metzger accepts a date of A.D. 100 for 4 Ezra.

16.   Translation by J. Shachter in Epstein, *BT*.

17.   See Davies, 1974, pp. 49, 58, 61.

18.   "It is no accident that one-third of the Mishnah...is connected with the land." Davies, 1974, p. 56. See especially the first order of the Mishnah, Zeraim.

19. Mt. 12:1, 23:23, *V* 63, 80, *A* 12.378, 13.234, 14.475.

20. B. Z. Wacholder "The Calendar of Sabbatical Cycles during the Second Temple and the Early Rabbinic Period" *HUCA* 44 (1973) 153-196.

21. Lamentations Rabbah, Proem. See A. Oppenheimer, *The Am Haaretz*, trans. I. H. Levine (Leiden: Brill, 1977) p. 16.

22. Wacholder, 1973, pp. 176-179.

23. Oppenheimer, 1977, p. 82; Kreissig, 1969, p. 248; Büchler, 1906, 220-37. See Demai 3:6, Kilaim 7:5, Sanh. 3:3, Maaseroth 5:3, t. Terumoth 5:15.

24. Klausner, 1975, p. 193 and J. H. Heinemann "The Status of the Labourer in Jewish Law and Society in the Tannaitic Period" *HUCA* 25 (1954) 263-325, esp. pp. 268f.

25. G. F. Moore, *Judaism* (Cambridge: Harvard University Press, 1954) Vol. I, p. 77.

26. See L. E. Newman, *The Sanctity of the Seventh Year: A Study of Mishnah Tractate Shebiit* (Chico, CA: Scholars Press, 1983) p. 206. On the prozbul as an institution and the origin of the term see M. Jastrow; D. Correns, *Die Mischna: Schebiit* (Giessen/Berlin: Töpelmann, 1960); Moore, 1954, vol. III, p. 80. The word probably comes from the Greek term προσβολή (though Jastrow argues for προς βουλῆ βουλευτῶν) and means "to bring to" (Correns) i.e., to bring a declaration to the court. J. Neusner suggests quite plausibly that the prozbul existed before Hillel and that Hillel only gave it his endorsment. See *From Politics to Piety* (Englewood Cliffs, New Jersey: Prentice Hall, 1973) pp. 14-17.

27. Translation in Danby. See also Sifre Dt 113.

28. The date was assigned by P. Benoit, J. T. Milik and R. de Vaux, *Les Grottes de Murabaat* (Oxford: Clarendon, 1961; *DJDII*) p. 100 based on the text's own assertion, and followed by both K. Beyer and J. A. Fitzmyer/D. J. Harrington. See Beyer, Die *Aramäischen Texte vom Toten Meer* (Göttingen: Vandenhoeck and Rüprecht, 1984) p. 306; and Fitzmyer and Harrington, *A Manual of Palestinian Aramaic Texts* (Rome: Biblical Institute, 1978) p. 210. E. Koffmahn, *Die Doppelurkunden aus der Wüste Juda* (Leiden: Brill 1968) p. 41 and M. R. Lehmann "Studies in the Murabaat and Nahal Hever Documents" *Revue de Qumran* 13 (1963) 56f date the document to A.D. 54/55.

29. Translation by Fitzmyer and Harrington, 1978, pp. 137-139.

30. Koffmhan, 1968, p. 81; Milik, *DJD* II, p. 102; Wacholder, 1973, pp. 170f; Beyer, 1984, p. 307.

31. E. Kutsch, "Jobeljahr" *Religion in Geschichte und Gegenwart* (Tübingen: Mohr, 1959) Vol. III, cols. 799-800. P. Heinisch on the other hand, followed by G. Lambert, argued for a composit text of basically four sections ranging in date from the Mosaic era to the time of Solomon. See Heinisch, *Das Buch Leviticus* (Bonn: Hanstein, 1935); and G. Lambert "Jubilé Hebrue et Jubilé Chrétien" *Nouvelle Revue Theologique* 72 (1950) 234-251. A. Jirku, *Von Jerusalem nach Ugarit* (Graz: Akademische, 1966) pp. 321f, says the Jubilee is an old tradition going back to the conquest. See

18

further the discussion in R. North, The *Sociology of the Biblical Jubilee* (Rome: Pontifical Institute, 1954) pp. 191-212.

32. Kutsch, 1959, cols. 799-800; North, 1954, p. 87; de Vaux, 1961, p. 177. But how does one prove it was never observed?

33. North, 1954, pp. 39f.

34. Translation by F. H. Colson in LCL.

35. E. R. Wolf, *Peasant Wars of the Twentieth Century* (New York: Harper and Row, 1969) p. 277.

36. De Vaux, 1961, p. 166. Cf. S. Dar, 1986, p. 74: "The family holding, however small, was regarded as a possession and a symbol, which must never be given up."

37. Translation by G. Alon, *The Jews in their Land in the Talmudic Age* (Jerusalem: Magnes, 1980) Vol. I, p. 154f. Cf. also t. Arak 5:6.

38. *Ibid.*, p. 155.

39. Safrai, *Encyclopedia Judaica*, vol. XIV, col. 581, says this ceremony "took place in order to shame a person who sold his patrimony."

40. Alon, 1980, I. p. 155.

41. North, 1954, p. 36; de Vaux, 1961, p. 167; J. Pedersen, *Israel: Its Life and Culture* (London: Oxford University Press, 1926) vol. 1/2, pp. 390-92.

42. See A. Damaschke, *Bibel und Bodenreform* (Berlin: Mann, 1924) pp. 3f.

43. Kutsch, 1959, cols. 799f; van Selms, *IDB*, II; North 1954, p. 214.

44. North, 1954, p. 39.

45. V. Tcherikover, *Hellenistic Civilization and the Jews* (New York: Atheneum, 1975) p. 121.

46. Translation by F. R. Walton in LCL. See the comments on the text by M. Stern, *Greek and Latin Authors on Jews and Judaism* (Jerusalem: Israel Academy of Sciences and Humanities, 1974) vol. I, pp. 28-35; and H. G. Kippenberg and G. A. Wewers, *Textbuch zur neutestamentlichen Zeitgeschichte* (Göttingen: Vandenhoeck and Ruprecht, 1979) pp. 79f. The T. Moses 2:2 may also reflect this idea. See Priest's translation in *POT*, vol. I.

47. As G. Vermes, *The Dead Sea Scrolls in English* (New York: Penguin, 1975) p. 89, translates it.

48. Translation by H. St. J. Thackeray, LCL.

49. See Thackeray's footnotes in LCL at this point.

50. North, 1954, p. 85.

51. For bandits see e.g. *B* 1.204, 305-313; *V* 77-79; and M. Hengel, *Die Zeloten* (Leiden: Brill, 1961) pp. 25-47, R. A. Horsley, "Ancient Jewish Banditry and the Revolt against Rome" *Catholic Biblical Quarterly* 43 (1981) 409-32. For tenant farmers and day laborers see Chapter 3.

52. See J. D. Eisenstein, "Sabbatical Year and Jubilee" *JE*, vol 10, pp. 605-609; Safrai, *Encyc. J.*, vol. 14, col. 580; Wacholder, *HUCA* 1973, 154; S. Krauss, *Talmudische Archäologie* (Hildesheim: Georg Olms, 1966) vol. II, pp. 98, 491, 497.

53. Epstein, *BT*.

54. Kippenberg's translation, 1978, p. 145.

55. See Fitzmyer and Harrington, 1978, pp. 156-159.

56. A. S. van der Woude "Melchizedek als himmlische Erlösergestalt in den neugefundenen eschatologischen Midraschim aus Qumran Höhle XI" *Oudtestamentische Studien* 14 (1965) 354-373. For text and translations also see: M. de Jonge and van der Woude, "11Q Melchizedek and the New Testament" *NTS* 12 (1966) 301-326; J. Fitzmyer, *Essays on the Semitic Background of the New Testament* (London: Chapman, 1971 pp. 245-267; E. Puech "Notes sur le manuscrit de 11Q Melkisedeq" *Revue de Qumran* 12 (1987) 483-513.

57. Puech, 1987, 483-513.

58. See de Jong and van der Woude, 1966, pp. 304ff; Fitzmyer, 1971, pp. 251-267; Puech, 1987, pp. 510-513; Y. Yadin "A Note on Melchizedek and Qumran" *IEJ* 15 (1965) 152-154.

59. The suggestion made by W. H. Brownlee "Messianic Motifs of Qumran and the New Testament" *NTS* 3 (1956-57) 202-205, and followed to some extent by S. H. Ringe, *The Jubilee Proclamation in the Ministry of Jesus: A Tradition Critical Study in the Synoptic Gospels and Acts* (Union Theological Seminary, New York: Ph.D., 1981) p. 110, that 1QS 10:4-8 refers to the Jubilee and Sabbatical year in eschatological terms remains problematic. See P. Wernberg-Møller, *The Manual of Discipline* (Leiden: Brill, 1957) pp. 142f.

60. A. Trocmé, *Jesús et la Révolution Non-violente* (Geneva: Editions Labor et Fides, 1961) pp. 22-36; J. H. Yoder, *The Politics of Jesus* (Grand Rapids, Michigan: Eerdmans, 1972) pp. 34-77; J. A. Sanders "From Isaiah 61 to Luke 4" in J. Neusner, ed. *Christianity, Judaism and other Greco-Roman Cults* (Leiden: Brill, 1975) vol. I, pp. 75-106.

61. Ringe, 1981, pp. 149-152.

62. *Ibid.*, pp. 164-258. See also P. Hollenbach, "Liberating Jesus for Social Involvement" *Biblical Theology Bulletin* 15 (1985) 151-157.

63. See S. K. Eddy, *The King is Dead* (Lincoln, Nebraska: University of Nebraska, 1961) pp. 324-328; S. L. Dyson, "Native Revolt Patterns in the Roman Empire" *ANRW* II. 3 (1975) pp. 138-175.

64. Hengel, 1961, p. 138.

65. Text and translation by L. H. Feldman in LCL.

66. (ἀπογραφή) can mean a list of property or a register of persons subject to taxation. See LSJM.

20

67.   E. Meyer, *Ursprung und Anfänge des Christentums* (Stuttgart/Berlin: Cotta, 1921) vol. III, p. 74, n. 2; Hengel, 1961, p. 342; S. Applebaum, "The Zealots: the Case for Reevaluation" *JRS* 61 (1971) 155-170; G. Baumbach, "Zeloten und Sikarier" *Theologische Literaturzeitung* 90 (1965) 727-739; R. A. Horsley and J. S. Hanson, *Bandits, Prophets, and Messiahs* (Minneapolis: Winston Press, 1985) pp. 211f; G. Cornfeld, *Josephus: The Jewish War* (Grand Rapids: Zondervan, 1982) p. 186; P. Brunt, "Josephus on Social Conflicts in Roman Judaea" *Klio* 59 (1977) 149-153, G. Theissen, 1978, pp. 33-46.

68.   Applebaum, 1971, pp. 155-170 and Cornfeld, 1982, p. 376.

69.   Cornfeld, 1982, p. 302.

70.   See especially Applebaum, 1971, pp. 155-170; Hengel, "Das Gleichnis von den Weingärtnern Mc 12:1-12 im Licht der Zenonpapyri und der rabbinischen Gleichnisse" *ZNW* 59 (1968) p. 24; G. E. M. de Ste. Croix, *The Class Struggle in the Ancient Greek World* (Ithaca, N.Y.: Cornell University Press, 1981) p. 442; and H. Kreissig, "Die Landwirtschaftliche Situation in Palästina vor dem Judäischen Krieg" *Acta Antiqua* 17 (1969) 223; idem. *Die sozialen Zusammenhänge des jüdäischen Krieges* (Berlin: Akademie, 1970) pp. 88-109.

71.   Damaschke, 1924, p. 4. For a similar statement on the view of land among peasants in general see Redfield, 1956, pp. 27f and J. H. Kautsky, *The 7.*

Politics of Aristocratic Empires (Chapel Hill, NC: University of North Carolina, 1982) p. 273; and Wolf, 1969, p. 277.

CHAPTER 2

LARGE ESTATES IN PALESTINE
IN THE HERODIAN PERIOD

The peasants of post-exilic Palestine lived their lives as peasants everywhere, as an endless cycle of planting and harvesting. Always for them there was God, the family, and the land. They earned their subsistence by the sweat of their brow with the help of their children, and in special needs with the help of their extended family members. Most were about equal in wealth and satisfied with what they had. But then the Hellenists came.

We must not of course over emphasize the changing economic conditions under the Hellenists. There were large estates during the Old Testament monarchy and the Persian periods, and the Persian king also demanded taxes.[1] The difference is the degree of intensity and efficiency in which the Hellenists, beginning with the Ptolemies and later the Seleucids, exploited their subject territories. That exploitative efficiency was a challenge of Jewish peasant values – and probably of the values of some in the upper classes as well – of the land.

The Ptolemies inherited the belief in Egypt that all the land belonged to the Pharaoh as the deified human personification of Horus-Ra.[2] Thus land tenure in Ptolemaic Palestine began with the notion that all land was the personal possession of Ptolemy, as heir to the Pharaohs, to be administered as he saw fit.[3] Ptolemy I Soter (304-283) and Ptolemy II Philadelphus (282-246) divided all land into royal land (γῆ βασιλική) which was leased to tenants who paid a share of the crop; and release land or grant land (γῆ ἐν ἀφεσει) which was given over to temples, to soldiers, or to private persons,[4] but which still belonged to the king and could be recalled.[5] The Seleucids adopted about the same system. All land was either royal land, the property of a Greek city, or land given to various institutions (e.g. temples) or individuals.[6]

The land in Egypt was organized administratively for tax purposes along the lines of the ancient divisions, called "nomes." Each nome was divided into toparchies, with the smallest administrative unit being the village. Palestine had a similar organization.[7] Each large administrative unit had both a military and economic overseer, and the smaller units had probably only one administrator.[8] Over the entire administrative complex stood the second most powerful man in Ptolemaic Egypt, the Dioiketes, whose job was to oversee all the finances of the king, both his private estates and his tax revenues.[9]

Such organizational efficiency had one overriding purpose: to wring every cent possible from both the land and the people who worked the land. M. Hengel's quotation of W. W. Tarn, who described the economic organization of Ptolemaic Egypt as "a money making machine," is an apt one. [10] The Ptolemies engaged in a more intensive exploitation of the land and people than the native Egyptian fellahin had ever known.[11] Agriculture now became "agrabusiness."[12] The same system and mentality was also applied in Palestine by the Ptolemies and later by the Seleucids.

But did this situation change later? H. Kreissig[13] maintains that the Hasmonean period gave a respite to the Jewish peasant, and prevented the rural areas from being (γῆ βασιλικη). But we must not forget that the Hasmoneans also had large estates and seem as a matter of fact simply to have taken over the estates of the Seleucids (see below).[14] Certainly, at any rate, later Herod the Great regarded the land as his. He possessed large tracts of land by the time of his death and is known to have confiscated land at will. His economic "reign of terror" with high taxes and direct expropriation of land "horrified" his chroniclers.[15]

The Palestinian Jewish peasants then endured an economic system beginning with the Ptolemies that was harsher, more efficient, more burdensome, more exploitative than they had ever known. The Ptolemies combined the oriental concept of the divinely sanctioned power of the king with Greek competence in organization and ran their kingdom as if it were one large private estate or οἶκος.[16] Under the Seleucids, and the Herods this organized skimming-off-the-surplus remained intact. They and their aristocratic friends maintained lucrative large estates, levied heavy taxes, and could expropriate more land as they saw fit. According to the Great Tradition, all land in principle and the best land in fact belonged to the elites.

But Palestine endured a second challenge to its traditional ideal of land tenure in the Herodian period which began in the first century B.C. in the western part of the Roman empire. This was the movement, which soon spread throughout the empire, toward concentrating more land into the hands of a few entrepreneurs so that, increasingly, "fewer had more."[17] This tendency was not based on the notion of the right of the monarch to all the best land, but solely on entrepreneurship and investment. The Roman sources attest to the fact that Italy, Greece, North Africa and Egypt contained some enormous estates in the first century B.C. and later.[18] For example, in 49 B.C. Lucius Domitius Ahenobarbus offered to an army, which P. A. Brunt estimates to have been 10,000 men, 40 iugera a piece in Spain. He thus needed to own a tract of land or a series of estates which totalled at least 400,000 iugera or 270,000 acres.[19] Since it is doubtful that Ahenobarbus gave away his entire land holdings to his veterans, he must have owned considerably more than that. A freedman named Isodorus in A.D. 8 boasted that he owned 3,600 pairs of oxen. They would have been enough to plough 360,000 iugera or 226,000 acres.[20] Pliny the Elder[21] in the first century A.D. claimed that six landlords owned half of Africa. Finally M. I. Finley describes a text that refers to a family in Egypt that allegedly owned an estate of 75,000 acres.[22] From the reported income of other estates we can reason that these owners also must have had immense agricultural empires.[23]

Most of the larger estates in the empire, however, were not so enormous, but averaged around 100 acres, still enough, apparently, for a gentleman to live comfortably with tenants, day laborers, or slaves and a bailiff to do the work.[24] H. Dohr[25] placed the land holdings in the Roman empire into three categories:

1) Small holdings (10-80 iugera = ca. 6-50 acres).
2) Medium-sized estates (80-500 iugera = ca. 50-315 acres).
3) Large estates (over 500 iugera = over 315 acres).

We shall be dealing below with both the medium and large estates of Palestine, and we should expect that the situation in Palestine was similar to that of the empire in general, with most gentlemen landowners owning medium-sized estates. The royal estates on the other hand were much larger, though given the small size of Palestine, certainly were never as large as some of those listed above.

More and more the owners of these medium and large estates were absentee landlords, living in cities and hiring overseers, bailiffs,[25a] to run their farms. Some owners seldom visited their lands at all, but devoted themselves rather to city life with its cultural and political interests and worried only about the income they would receive from their estates.[26]

We shall attempt to demonstrate below that these two ideas of land tenure, the Ptolemaic and the more recent Roman conception, in which land was respectively the property of the king by divine right and in which land was capital, the means of enrichment and thus to be amassed if at all possible – in other words the conceptions of land tenure according to the Great Tradition – existed also in Palestine in the Herodian period. Fewer and fewer people owned more and more in Palestine. The ruling monarchs and their friends and officials owned estates ranging in size from medium to large (see below). The land was not the Lord's then, but first and foremost the monarch's (and his family's and friends') and second any other enterprising person's who could by influence, social standing, force, or dishonesty acquire it. First we shall survey the royal lands, then, attempt to locate private estates.

Royal Estates

As A. Schalit[27] observed, although the conquerors of Palestine accepted the theoretical notion that all the land and everything in it belonged to them, as victors, as a private possession, in practice they tended to expropriate first and foremost the estates of the conquered king since these were the best lands. As we shall see, then, large estates are inherited by the succeeding dynasty whether, Seleucid, Hasmonean, Herodian, or Roman. This chain of possession can both be demonstrated literarily in many cases, and also archaeologically.[28]

Jericho Region

This area which also included Engedi and later Phasaelis and Archelais was in antiquity a date palm and balsam plantation. The products from this estate were world famous as was the wealth derived from them. The balsam trees only grew here in Palestine and in Egypt and were thus a rare and very sought-after commodity. The dates from this region were regarded as some of the finest in the world.[29]

Theophrastus (372-288 B.C.) first referred to the plantation when he wrote (in the Ptolemaic period) of two (παράδεισοι) in Syria where balsam grows.[30] (παράδεισος) is a Persian loan word which commonly indicates during the Hellenistic period that an older Persian estate has been taken over by a Hellenistic king.[31] Pliny the Elder maintained that these two "gardens" (horti) were earlier – evidently in the Persian period – quite small (one was about 20 iugera or 13 acres and the other less), but that the plantation was later enlarged.[32]

We have no testimony about the estate under the Ptolemies and Seleucids. We can assume, however, that they would have at least maintained the existing estate. Hengel[33] suggests, based on what is known in general of the Ptolemies, that they began to expand the size of the estate. Strabo claimed the date palm grove alone in his time (first century B.C.) was 100 stadia (somewhat over 11 miles) long and Pompeius Trogus (late first century B.C. to early first century A.D.) said the balsam plantation was 200 iugera (128 acres).[34] The plantation by the Herodian period was, then, a large estate and must have been enormously profitable.

MAP 1: ROYAL ESTATES

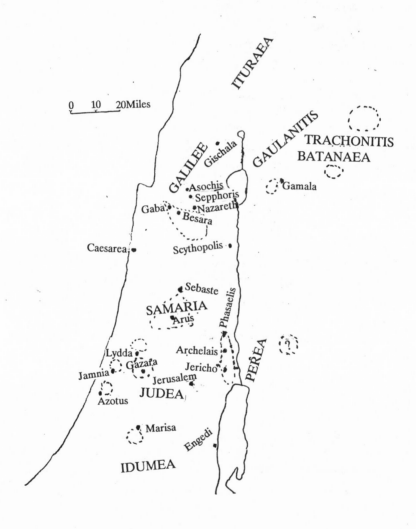

Likewise we have no direct evidence about the Hasmonean period. We assume again that they continued to work this plantation in a similar way. First the non-Jewish historians of the first century B.C. such as Strabo, Dioscorides, and Diodorus Siculus write as if the plantation still existed.[35] Second, Herod inherited the plantation from the Hasmoneans although he then had to turn it over to Cleopatra.[36] Thus the estate was being operated before Herod's time. Finally, archaeologists have discovered a Hasmonean winter palace at Jericho.[37] This discovery does not prove that the Hasmoneans maintained the plantation, but it is reasonable that they would have a palace near their large estates. The evidence taken together certainly points in the direction of a Hasmonean era in the history of this plantation.

Josephus relates that Mark Antony expropriated the lucrative palm and balsam groves of Jericho and gave them to Cleopatra. Herod then in turn leased the plantation from Cleopatra.[38] Herod evidently received these lands back after the death of Antony because we later find Archelaus rebuilding the royal palace at Jericho and developing another field of palm trees at Archelais.[39] Herod himself developed a new palm plantation north of Jericho in his newly founded city of Phasaelis.[40] Probably Jericho became Augustus' private estate after Archelaus was banished in A.D. 6.[41]

During the Jewish war the insurrectionists attempted to destroy the plantation. Pliny relates, perhaps sarcastically, that there were "pitched battles in defense of a shrub."[42] It is interesting to note that seventy years earlier during another Jewish revolution insurrectionists led by the deluded Simon, one of Herod's slaves, vented their anger by attacking the royal palace at Jericho and burning it to the ground.[43] The wealth gained from this estate seems especially to have enraged the Jewish lower classes.

The estate was saved from the rebels in A.D. 66, however, and just five years after the defeat of the Jews the plantation was returning once again a handsome profit in the service of Vespasian.[44]

Thus the Jericho plantation in the Herodian period was a large domain belonging to Herod as a private possession, but later to Rome. This estate had been passed down from conqueror to conqueror from the Persian period until the Roman. The area stretched eleven miles plus the plantations at Phasaelis and Engedi (see map 1). The size of the estate, the salty soil, the easy irrigation from nearby springs, the climate, and above all the fact that Palestine had a near monopoly on balsam made this estate extremely profitable. The lower classes that rebelled both at the death of Herod in 4 B.C. and later in A.D. 66 perhaps saw this estate as a symbol of exploitation by the wealthy.

The Plain of Esdraelon

A. Alt[45] was the first scholar to trace the history of the Great Plain or Plain of Esdraelon as a large private domain. Our knowledge of this region begins with the decree of the Roman senate in 44 B.C. which reaffirmed the right of the Hasmoneans to private ownership of the Plain:

> As for the villages in the Great Plain, which Hyrcanus and his forefathers before him possessed, it is the pleasure of the Senate that Hyrcanus and the Jews shall retain them with the same rights as they formerly had...[46]

As Alt reasoned, since the Hasmoneans in the year 44 B.C. and their forefathers "possessed"[47] the villages of the Plain, evidently the ownership extends back at least to the early first century B.C. and perhaps beyond. But the only way to account for the fact that the Hasmoneans would take over so large a tract of land is that it was formerly a Seleucid private domain and probably prior to that Ptolemaic. Thus it appears quite reasonable to conclude that the entire Great Plain was a private estate of Ptolemy which was taken over by the Seleucids and later by the Hasmoneans.

This conclusion is supported by the clear inscriptional evidence that the eastern part of the Plain, around Beth Shean (Scythopolis) was a large domain given over as grant land to a high official of Antiochus III, named Ptolemy.

The so-called Hefzibah inscription, a limestone stele 77 x 47 cm, was found four miles northwest of Beth Shean in 1960.[48] The stele contains eight documents, six letters from Antiochus III to Ptolemy the Strategos of this district and two "memoranda"[49] from Ptolemy. J. E. Taylor dates this correspondence from 201-195 B.C.

Ptolemy the Strategos was governor of the Plain of Jericho and an extremely wealthy man according to 1 Macc. 16:11. The Hefzibah inscriptions show that at least part of his wealth was obtained from his estates near Beth Shean. In one of the earliest documents, number 4,[50] Ptolemy writes about the things (ἐν ταῖς κώμαις [μου]) "in my villages." In document 1 Antiochus writes (ἐν [ταῖς] ὑπαρχούσαις [σοι κώμαις]) "in the villages belonging to you (i.e. Ptolemy)," and in number 7 (ἐν ταῖς κώμα[ις] αὐτοῦ) "in his (i.e. Ptolmey's) villages." That the references are not simply to Ptolmey's administrative responsibility but to his personal estates in seen in document 2 where the villages (referred to as "things assigned by (Antiochus)" (τὰ καταγ [εγραμένα παρ ἡμῶν]) are called "property" (κτή[σει]); and especially in document 6 where Ptolemy speaks of "the villages belonging to me as property" (ἐν κτήσει), "inheritable" (εἰς [τ]ὸ πα[τ]ρικόν), "which you yourself ordered to assign (?) to me? (εἰς [ἃς] σὺ προ[σ]έταξας καταγράψ[αι]).[51]

Thus, clearly the villages belong to Ptolemy as possessions (κτῆσις). This word often refers to lands or estates.[52] Landau,[53] on the basis of document 6 suggested that Ptolemy owned some villages (and lands connected with them) outright, but administered others in hereditary lease (πατρικόν), while having yet a different relationship to a third group of lands and villages. Taylor[54] rightly saw no reason for distinguishing three kinds of tenure arrangements and concluded that the three designations were all descriptive of the same thing.

How can someone "own" villages? The practice was not uncommon under the Hellenistic monarchs.[54a] Their private estates included not only vast tracts of land, but also in some sense the people called (λάοι) living in the villages who would work the land. The (λάοι) were not slaves but were apparently dependent at least economically on the landlord.[55] Ptolemy also calls his villagers (λάοι) in document 4. They evidently worked his lands as tenant farmers, paying him a share of their harvest.

Antiochus had then given Ptolemy the Strategos grant lands from his own royal estates. Presumably, these were first royal estates of the Ptolemies of Egypt which passed later to the Seleucids.[56] Granting a high administrator large tracts of lands certainly has precedent and was the usual way of rewarding loyal officials.[57]

We can assume, then, that the Ptolemies and later the Seleucids owned the lands and villages in the entire Great Plain in the same sense that the Hefzibah inscription indicates that Antiochus III owned the eastern part around Scythopolis.[58] The archaeological survey team of Isaac and Roll have identified seven Hellenistic settlements scattered throughout the Plain which they surmise belonged to the royal domains of the Ptolemies and Seleucids.[58a]

Herod of course did not later inherit the lands in the eastern part of the Plain around Scythopolis/Beth Shean since this city had under the Seleucids become a full-fledged polis with its own administration.[59]

Herod the Great's handling of the lands in the western part of the plain, demonstrates that he considered this region, however, his to do with as he pleased. In 25 B.C. he settled his cavalry veterans giving each of them a plot of ground, in a place called Gaba in the western edge of the Plain. This settlement is reminiscent of the Ptolemaic practice of granting a cleruchy to veterans.[60]

Berenice, the sister of Agrippa II, seems to have inherited as least part of these lands in spite of the fact that Galilee was under Roman jurisdiction after the death of Agrippa I in A.D. 44. Josephus during the Jewish war confiscated "a large quantity" of grain stored in Besara (about 2.4 miles east of Gaba) which belonged to Queen Berenice.[61] Thus Besara[62] would seem to have been the central village of Berenice's estate where she stored her surplus grain.[62a]

The extent of Berenice's estate is unclear. Avi-Yonah[63] concluded that the Great Plain was a royal (later a Roman imperial) estate whose produce was always stored at Besara. That would mean that Berenice had control of all of the plain (with the exception of the territory belonging to Scythopolis) instead of only the western edge of the Great Plain. Alt[64] believed Agrippa II also owned lands there based on the story in Josephus (*V* 126=*B* 2.595) of the wife of Agrippa's official being assaulted in the Plain. Since this woman was traveling at the time, however, she was not necessarily on Agrippa's land.[65] One would reasonably expect that Agrippa II did own land in the Plain, but this story does not prove that.

One later reference from Josephus may point to the Plain as a large domain or perhaps a series of large domains. Josephus himself was given land by Vespasian in the "Plain" after the war (*V* 422). Assuming this plain was the Great Plain that could mean that much of it is now the personal property of Vespasian as conqueror of Palestine.

After the Bar Cochba war, the Sixth Roman Legion constructed a camp in the Great Plain near Megiddo. The camp, called Legio,[66] existed until almost two hundred years later at the time of Diocletian, it was elevated to the status of a polis and renamed Maximianopolis. The legionnaires during this period were given according to Alt and Avi-Yonah the usufruct from the lands of the Great Plain which was now called the Plain of Legio.[67] Thus, as Alt argued, the Great Plain or Plain of Legio was simply expropriated by the empire from a previous native owner (whom Alt assumed to be one of the Herods).

Unfortunately, one looks in vain for any real evidence that the Legion actually expropriated the Plain. Evidently the change of the name itself convinced Alt and Avi-Yonah that the military had owned the ground. B. Isaac and I. Roll maintain, however, that this conclusion is only speculation and that there is no evidence the Roman military ever owned territory in Palestine.[68] Their criticism should urge caution in assuming the Plain passed into Roman hands. Quite possibly it remained the possession of the Herod family.

Thus we can trace a large estate as it was passed on from the Hasmoneans to the Herods and possibly to the Romans. Further, Alt's argument, that the Hasmoneans probably took this domain over from the Seleucids who in turn probably continued what had been a Ptolemaic private estate, seems valid especially in light of the Hefzibah inscription. Once again, then, a large estate has passed from the Ptolemies to the Herods in an unbroken line.

Estates in Western Samaria

a) The Field Towers. The survey team led by S. Dar has rendered a valuable contribution to our investigation in their examination of western

Samaria.[69]   The survey was conducted from 1971-1981 and examined agricultural and village sites. One of the most pervasive phenomena which the team discovered were the so-called "field towers." The team surveyed 962 towers (and excavated 45) which were scattered from Mt. Gilboa in the north to the Nablat stream bed in the southwest (see map 2).

Dar lists six categories of towers based on shape, size and other special features. All the towers were built of "rather large" quarried stones without mortar to an average exterior height of 2.3m to 3.7m for a one storey tower (most of the towers were one storey) an and exterior height of 4.1m for a two storey tower. The average tower had walls 3-4m square and .7-.8m thick. The total weight of a tower ranged from 100-150 tons. The inside of the tower was approximately 30% of the exterior measurements.   The excavation of the 45 towers revealed that they were erected in the Hellenistic period (third to second century B.C..) based on pottery findings, but that they still functioned in the Herodian period and on into the second century A.D. Y. Mintzker estimated that each tower required about 300-400 days of labor (by a single person?) to be built.[70] Thus in the Hellenistic period from the middle third century on a large number of stone towers were built in various places in Samaria and Judea requiring an enormous amount of labor and expense.

Who built these towers and why? Dar argues strongly that the towers indicate they were a planned, government project. All the towers are attached to a plot of ground and the settlement pattern of these plots "shows that a single planning agency determined the division of the fields." Further, the large amount of labor required a "trained professional team" (or one should probably say "teams") to build the tower.[71]
This is a reasonable conclusion and would mean that the Ptolemies in the third century built most if not all of the towers in order to support an intensive agricultural enterprise. Such a program certainly accords well with what we know about Ptolemaic economic planning.

33

Map 2

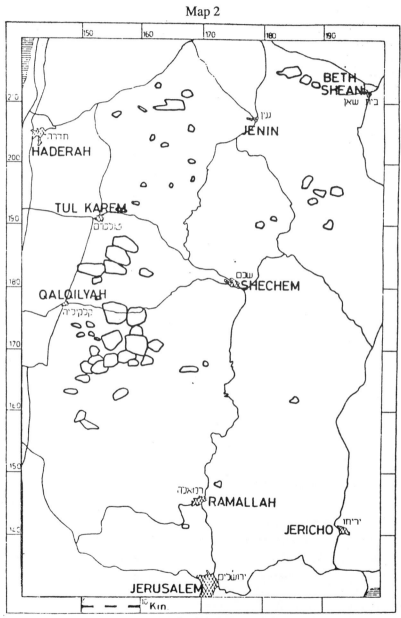

*Dar. Figure 64. Distribution map of the towers.

The function of the towers is less clear. S. Applebaum had suggested the towers were temporary residences for workers who farmed a plot removed from their village.[72] But Dar maintains that very few of these towers could have been lived in. He also denies that they could have been defensive towers or observation towers since very few of them had observation points on the roof or even windows. Dar, therefore surmises that the towers were fermentation buildings and were thus connected to vineyards. Wine needs a dark, cool, ventilated, place to ferment. After measuring the temperature inside the towers and examining other data, Dar declared the towers perfect for wine production.[73]

Thus if Dar is correct, the towers attest to an aggressive, burgeoning business in wine production in the Ptolemaic era of Palestine. Dar's theory is compelling and should be accepted until something better is proposed. Whatever their precise function, however, the towers were certainly used in agriculture, and from the expense involved we may be certain that the Ptolemies expected a large profit in return.

This leads to a second observation. Large areas of Samaria were evidently part of the Ptolemaic private domains. Furthermore, since the pottery indicates use of the towers through the first century A.D. and into the second, we can once again conclude that these lands were continued as large estates and handed down from monarch to monarch and from conqueror to conqueror. We shall attempt below to identify some of the later owners of these estates.

b.) Beth Anath. The Zenon papyri, part of which were written in Palestine in 259-258 B.C., to Apollonius the Dioiketes of Ptolemy II, attest to an estate at (βαιτανατος) (Beth Anath). This estate is, according to Tcherikover. royal land which has been given to Apollonius as (γῆ ἐν δωρεᾷ) or grant land. From the crops referred to in these papyri we know the estate raised grain, had orchards, and also vineyards which produced "Syrian wine."[74] The vineyards consisted of 80,000 vines which according to Hengel[75] would have required around "17 hectares" or 40 acres and a work force of 25 workers or "a small village." From a papyrus describing a contention between the peasants and an official called Melas we learn that they were tenant farmers who were required to pay a portion of their crop to Apollonius. Melas, according to this papyrus, has demanded payment, but the peasants petition for a reduction of payment presumably because the harvest was poorer than expected.[76]

Thus we have an estate which belongs ultimately to Ptolemy but which has been given over in grant to Apollonius. The peasants of this estate must pay a share of their crops to Apollonius through Melas his agent and this payment the peasants consider too oppressive. Tscherikover concluded: "(This papyrus) furnishes a direct proof that the Ptolemies considered the land they conquered outside of Egypt also as fundamentally their own property."[77]

Is it possible that Beth Anath was part of that Ptolemaic movement to exploit the land of Palestine for wine production which the field towers described by Dar attest?[78] That possibility is even stronger if in fact Beth Anath was in the vicinity where the towers were concentrated. Alt, Freyne, and F. M. Abel[79] place Beth Anath in Galilee, but Avi-Yonah[80] identified it with Beth Yanai of T. Sheb 7:14 and modern Anin which was 15 miles east of Caesarea. Whether or not this identification is accepted, the date of the papyri certainly corresponds to the date of the beginning of the towers and thus argues that Beth Anath was part of that process. Certainly the Ptolemies are likely to have developed Galilee agriculturally as well as Samaria.[81]

c.) The King's Mountain Country. The Talmud speaks fairly frequently of (הר המלך) or the King's Mountain Country. Alexander Jannaeus (103-76 B.C.) is supposed to have owned 60 thousand myriads of cities in the Har Ha-melek each of which had a population equal to that of the Exodus, except for three cities each of which had double that number. Further, Jannaeus is said to have owned a city in the Har Ha-melek so large that he would have to supply 60 myriads of tuna fish each week to feed his fig-pickers. He received allegedly 40 seahs of grapes monthly from one vine in the Har.[82] Obvious exaggerations aside, if there is any truth at all that Jannaeus owned a large number of villages whose agricultural workers he had to supply with food and which produced not only figs, but a large amount of grapes, then Jannaeus controlled large stretches of land in what was called the King's Mountain Country.

It is quite likely that the name Alexander Jannaeus represents the Hasmoneans in general. As a matter of fact John Hyrcanus (135/4-104 B.C.) conquered Samaria (*A* 13.280f) where probably at least part of the estates of the Har were. Jannaeus is substituted for Hyrcanus one other place in the Talmud (b. Kidd 66a, cf. *A* 13.288-298) where he is alleged to have broken relations with the Pharisees.

From where did the name Har Ha-melek come? A. Büchler[83] argued that the "king" was Agrippa I. He was undoubtedly a Jewish king since the rabbis did not use the epithet king for the Caesars and only Agrippa I was called king by the rabbis. This conclusion however, makes the references to Jannaeus anachronistic since the area in such case would not already have been designated King's Mountain Country in his time. There is another passage in the Talmud (b. Men 109b) which would also be anachronistic. This passage describes Onias (presumably Onias IV, see *A* 12. 387) fleeing first to the Har Ha-melek and next to Egypt during the reign of Antiochus Epiphanes (187-164 B.C.).

Of course anachronisms abound in the Talmud,[83a] but one should attempt to explain it first apart from pleading anachronism. S. Klein[84] argued that the tract of land known to the rabbis as the Har Ha-melek began as a Ptolemaic estate, passed to the Seleucids and later became Hasmonean domain. The "King's Mountain Country" then, would refer to the Egyptian kings and would be an old designation. Klein's explanation avoids the anachronism and harmonizes well with what we have already seen was a pattern of estate ownership beginning in the Ptolemaic era or earlier. Of course it is also possible that the Hasmoneans began the estates.[85] If, however, Büchler is correct that the "king" refers to Agrippa, the result is that the Herod's still owned much of the Har Ha-melek in the mid-first century A.D. We would naturally expect that Agrippa inherited these lands ultimately from Herod the Great.

Further evidence that this area was royal domain can be seen in the fact that several of the Talmudic sages (Simon, Hiyya, Assi and Ammi)[86] owned land in the Har Ha-melek which they apparently rented out. One sage in particular, the Priest Eleazar ben Harsom, whose adult life mainly extended between the two great Jewish wars of A.D. 66 and 132,[87] is said to have owned large tracts of land in the King's Mountain Country and to have been extremely wealthy. He supposedly owned a High Priest's robe worth 20,000 minas, 1000 cities, 1000 ships, and so many servants that he had never set eyes on many of them.[88] The Jerusalem Talmud and Midrash Rabbah on Lamentations[89] attest that there were 10,000 cities in the Har and that Eleazer ben Harsom owned 1000. Again, these figures are obviously exaggerations, but the affirmation that Eleazar was a wealthy man with vast holdings of land in the Har Ha-melek must be seen as historical since there is no reason to attribute such wealth otherwise to a relatively unknown sage. We have no way of knowing how Eleazar's family acquired the lands from the Hasmoneans, but Applebaum's suggestion is plausible. He suggests that the Hasmoneans had made grants to Jewish notables among whom were Eleazar's High Priestly ancestors.[90]

Thus once again if Klein is correct, the pattern emerges of the Hasmoneans inheriting large private domains from the Seleucids (and Ptolemies) and maintaining them as such, passing them on to the Herod's and other notables at least until the first Jewish rebellion. In this case, the lands remained in Jewish hands even after the war. As to why and how a Jew could have kept his lands after the war when all of Judea became the private domain of Vespasian, Büchler's explanation is surely correct. He maintained that Eleazar (or possibly his father?) was one of those wealthy priests who remained loyal to Rome and so received back his land after the war of A.D. 66 (*B* 6.115).[91]

Where was the Har Ha-melek? S. Klein, based on t. Shab 7:10, argued that it was in the mountains of western Samaria and north-western Judea, or the area just north of Jerusalem, drawing a diagonal line from Bethel to the mountains east of Caesarea Maritima.[92] On this basis Dar believes the field towers discovered scattered throughout Samaria mark off the boundaries of the Har.[93] Other scholars, however, have argued that the term Har Ha-melek referred to the mountains around Jerusalem and corresponded to the *Orine* in Pliny and (ἡ ὀρεινὴ Ἰουδαία) in Josephus, the New Testament and the Septuagint.[94] The Mishnah seems to equate the Har with the hills of Judea (Sheb 9:2). Furthermore, Büchler pointed out that three of the villages often listed as being in the King's Mountain Country

(Kefar Bish, Kefar Shihlaya, and Kefar Dikraya) were actually in northern Idumea.[95] Thus one is compelled to admit that the exact location of the Har Ha-melek is now difficult to define. It seems to refer to royal estates scattered in the mountains of Judea, Samaria, and northern Idumea and perhaps concentrated around Jerusalem. The identification of the Har with the area represented by the field towers, therefore, is problematic since the royal estates were scattered more widely. The towers may represent a part of the Har Ha-melek, however.[96]

d.) Qawarat Bene Hassan.[97] Approximately 14 miles southwest of Shechem (see map 3) Dar's survey team found evidence of a very large estate and that other large estates were in the same vicinity. The ancient village had, according to Dar, from 175-200 family holdings.[98] Nearby are farm plots (see plan 1), marked off by stones, of which over half were devoted to grains, about one fourth to olives and just under one fourth to vines. The size of the vineyards (i.e. those with towers, most of which are from one to four acres) indicated to Dar that they were worked by individual families. The total area covered by the plots was 2000 acres with another 500 acres or so of pasture land.

Map 3

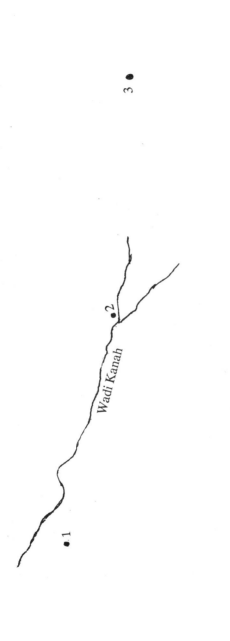

Wadi Kanah

1. Hirbet Berenike
2. Hirbet Basatin
3. Qarawat bene Hassan
4. Haris (Arus)

Scale of miles

Conder and Kitchener, *Palestine Exploration Fund Map*

40

Plan 1

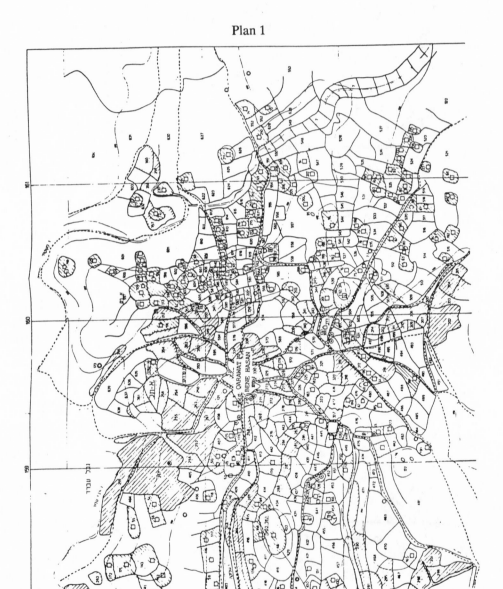

Dar. Figure 130. Qarawat bene Hassan – Distribution map of the agricultural
units.

North of the village and the adjoining farm plots is a building of massive stone blocks of the Herodian style which is called by the Arabs Qal'at Firdus, "Citadel of Herod." Dar reasons that this palace served the owners of this large domain. Also nearby is the Deir a-Darob, a large ornamental tomb built in the style of the Second Temple period which Dar dates to the late Hasmonean and Herodian periods. This was probably, then, concludes Dar, the tomb of those living in the palace and owning these lands.

On a hill overlooking the village is Hirbet Firdusi ("the Ruin of Herod") which had storage buildings, strong towers, cisterns and a residential area. Dar suggested that this was a fortified grainery such as Masada. He dates the building of the fortification to the Hasmonean era, but it continued in use through the Herodian period.[99] Dar suggests that the peasants of the village came to this fortified grainery to pay their taxes (rents) in kind.

The date for this entire complex is Hasmonean through Herodian. First, the pottery throughout the area though it begins with Iron II, is especially numerous for the Hasmonean and Herodian periods. Pottery declines sharply after the Herodian period. Second, a number of sites, not only those connected to Qawarat Bene-Hassan but also others just east of Arus (Haris) bear the Arabic name for Herod (Firdis), for example, Sejerat el-Firdis or Sheikh Ahmed el-Firdis. Third, near Qawarat Bene-Hassan is the village of Haris which has been for sometime identified with the Arus of Josephus (*A* 18.289, *B* 2.69) the domain of Herod's minister Ptolemy of Rhodes (see below). Thus it appears that Herod inherited these estates from the Hasmoneans and allotted some of them to his supporters. But the estates seem to encompass a much larger area than just Qawarat Bene-Hassan (no small area itself) as the many localities named "Firdis" attest.

Dar and Applebaum[100] believe this estate was inhabited by Jews until the Bar Cochba war since the estate ended at that time and it is unlikely, they assume, that Samaritan peasants took part in the revolt. Dar further surmised that because of the family-sized farm plots the cultivators were originally owners of these plots and later became tenants to the wealthy persons living in the nearby palace.

Thus we have indicated by the geographic relationships of these structures a large estate system complete with its own village, well-marked family farm plots, and its own grain storage site. Although these building structures may represent the Hasmonean-Herodian period, we must bear in mind that the field towers here (Dar counted 175) represent the larger tower system begun in the Ptolemaic age and thus the region must have been royal domain long before the Hasmonean era. This estate complex is important because it probably represents the typical features of a large estate in Palestine: a peasant village, farm area connected to the village, an administrative building or group of buildings. The palace is probably not the permanent residence of the landlord since most evidence shows that the wealthy landowners lived in the cities as absentee landlords. If Herod the Great himself owned this farm, as the Arabic name of the palace indicates, then this is only another of his many residences.

e.) Arus. One of the members of Herod's inner circle of government, Ptolemy of Rhodes (B 1.473, 667, 2. 14-16, 24, 64) owned a village (κώμη πτολεμαίου κτῆμα) called (Ἀρούς), which evidently lay south of Sebaste (A 17.289, B 2.69).[101] This village the Arabs burned after the death of Herod the Great because of their hatred both for Herod and his friends (A 17.290). This site was identified by F. M. Abel as the locality known in Arabic as Haris (see map 3). Abel argued both on philological and geographical grounds for this identification.[102]

Since Haris lies just east of Qawarat Bene-Hassan and thus in the region that must have been largely given over to the royal domains of Herod, Dar and Applebaum[103] are probably correct, that this village was a grant from Herod to his government minister, Ptolemy.

Dar dates the ruins of an ancient fort which stands near the village to the Hellenistic period. He concludes that Herod had inherited this fort and the lands around Haris from the Hasmoneans just as he also must have inherited Qawarat Bene-Hassan. Adjoining the village and extending throughout a broad valley are "several thousand dunams" (4 dunams = 1 acre) of land which perhaps, suggests Dar, were the estate of Ptolemy of Rhodes, with the fort as his estate center.[104]

f.) Lands around Sebaste. As Herod did at Gaba in the Great Plain, so also he settled military veterans in Samaria and built for them the city of Sebaste. Josephus records (*B* 1.403, *A* 15.296) that Herod gave highly productive lands in this area to 6000 veterans. If we estimate the average farm plot per veteran at 6 acres,[105] which seems to have been average for small freeholders, we need 36,000 acres of land available to supply all the veterans, (assuming Josephus' figure of 6000 men is not an exaggeration). Since Samaria has a total land area of around 350,000 acres,[106] this tract of land given to the veterans amounts to over ten per cent of the total area of Samaria.

g.) Hirbet Basatin. This locality which lies west of Qawarat Bene-Hassan near the Wadi Kana (see map 3), represents a modest-sized olive and grain plantation of perhaps only 100 acres. The farm would have required a work force of "several dozen hands."[107] Pottery finds indicate a Roman through Byzantine occupation. The interesting feature of this farm is the association of lands in this area with "Berenike." Hirbet Berenike ("Ruins of Berenice") recorded by the survey team of C. R. Conder and H. H. Kitchener in 1882,[108] lies approximately four miles west of Hirbet Basatin. Alt and Applebaum[109] suggest that this ruin was a village owned by Berenice the sister of Agrippa II, who also owned territory in the Great Plain (see above). Applebaum notes that the Fellahin apply the name Berenike "to lands all along Wadi Qana eastward as far as Shechem." This appellation would indicate, then, that Berenice owned a large tract of land in Samaria.

Thus the territory of western Samaria seems to have been to a great extent given over to royal domains under the Ptolemies, as the field towers attest. Certainly by the time of Herod large stretches of land were his personal estates and the estates of his friends. The many localities which have preserved the name of Herod and his descendent Berenice, plus the archaeological evidence and the literary evidence from Josephus all attest to this. Western Samaria, just as the Great Plain and the region around Jericho, was a major royal domain from the Ptolemaic era through the Herodian.

Batanea, Gaulanitis and Trachonitis.

Alt maintained that the entire region between Mt. Hermon and the southern shore of the See of Galilee including Batanea was the private domain of Ptolemy since there were no city-states existing in this area. This reasoning was based on the principle that whatever land did not belong to a polis was the private domain of Ptolemy. Nevertheless, while this reasoning may appear correct in principle such an argument is nonetheless gratuitous. As we have already seen it was only the best land that became royal estates even though all the land was legally considered the king's own property. E. Turner has voiced this same criticism recently of Rostovtzeff's reconstruction of Egyptian society under the Ptolemies. Turner maintains that private ownership of land always existed in Ptolemaic Egypt so that the land's being the personal possession of the king was only true in principle. In practice the king expropriated, to be sure, enormous tracts of land for himself, but not necessarily all the land. Therefore, we shall only claim as large estates those lands for which there is explicit evidence.[110]

a.) Batanea. When Herod determined to plant a colony in Batanea in order to protect his kingdom from attack from Trachonitis, he settled 500 Jewish mounted archers and their relatives on tax free land (*A* 17. 23-25). Such an action, argues Freyne, shows that Herod possessed the land he gave them and that he did not merely administer it.[111] Using the figure here employed above for the average allotment for veterans around Sebaste (six acres), Herod must have owned at least 3000 acres in Batanea.

We also read in the rabbinic sources that Rabbi Juda Ha-Nasi in the second century A.D. had an estate in (כותנייך) (jMaaser Sheni 4.1). S. Klein[112] argued that the context of the passage shows this place was not in Galilee and on the basis of the editio princeps of the Jerusalem Talmud changed the (כ) to (ב) and so (בותנייך) or Batanea. If he is correct then Judah the Patriarch had an estate in Batanea. This suggestion, however, while certainly possible is by no means proven. Yet if Herod owned estates in Batanea, we should expect the post-70 patriarchs of the house of Hillel, who became the heirs to the ethnarchs and kings of Palestine politically, also to be given their lands.[113] Thus the lands that Judah the Patriarch owned were probably originally Herodian. Though we cannot say with assurance that he owned lands in Batanea, Klein's hypothesis should be taken seriously.

b.) Gaulanitis. Josephus notes that a certain Philip, son of Jacimus, an official in the service of Agrippa II had control of villages (τῶν ἑαυτοῦ κώμων,) (V 47) near Gamala. Whether he controlled these villages as Ptolemy the official of Herod possessed Arus or only administered them we cannot determine assuredly, though the description of the villages as (ἑαυτοῦ) would lead us to believe that he owned them. If he owned the villages then we find here the same pattern as under Herod. Agrippa II has parceled out some of his royal land to a trusted advisor and official. This parcelling of land argues that Agrippa had large holdings around Gamala just as Herod did near Arus.

c.) Trachonitis. Herod settled 3000 Idumeans in Trachonitis in order to restrain the brigands in the area (A 16.285). This action would have required minimally 18,000 acres. We also read in the Vita (V 112) that nobles, subjects of Agrippa II, fled to Josephus from Trachonitis for protection during the Jewish war. We would naturally assume that these nobles were large estate owners. Thus, it appears Herod owned large tracts of land in Trachonitis which Agrippa II inherited, and some of which he parceled out to his friends, in the same manner we have already encountered for Herod.[114]

We should include this area (i.e. Batanea, Gaulanitis, and Trachonitis) in the list of territories where Herod owned crown lands. The huge tracts necessary for the settlements in Batanea and especially Trachonitis support this conclusion. Second, the pattern of inheriting these lands by succeeding monarchs, which we have seen for the lands in Jericho, the Great Plain, and Western Samaria, appears also in the villages which were probably owned by Philip and in the story of the noble subjects of Agrippa II. The same pattern might also be found in the estate of R. Judah the Patriarch if indeed Klein's hypothesis is correct. Therefore, Applebaum's assertion that Herod treated the "major part" of the Golan and Trachonitis as his crown domains is probably correct.[114a]

We should also conclude (pace Alt) that these domains were not formerly Ptolemaic (then Hasmonean) estates, but rather developed later than the three large estates described above. These lands were evidently first developed by Herod himself. In the first place, we cannot trace the history of the domains here as we have with the three great estates above. We can find no early mention of royal estates in this region. Second, an archaeological survey has found that pottery for the early Hellenistic period (third century B.C.) is non-existent in this region.[115] Another study has found very few settlements from any time in the Hellenistic period.[115a] Thus this area was "sparsely settled" in the early Hellenistic period when the other three large estates were being founded or expanded by the Ptolemies.

The Coastal Region

a.) Lydda. According to 1 Macc. 11:34, Demetrius I ceded Lydda to Jonathan. The Roman senate later confirmed this territory as belonging to the Hasmoneans in the same way that the Great Plain belonged to them (A 14.204). Thus it appears that the lands around Lyddawere a Hasmonean estate. We hear nothing about its state under the Herods, but after the Jewish war Gamaliel II, one of the Hillelite patriarchs, possessed an estate growing olives and vines and had tenants in the region of Lydda. Again, as we observed above, since the patriarches became the successors of the kings and ethnarchs of Palestine, Gamaliel probably was given royal land.[116] We also read of a Boethos ben Zonen, who was a wealthy Jewish landowner living in Lydda after the war.[117]

b.) Lands around Gezer. Eleven bilingual boundary inscriptions have been found – some of them as early as in the nineteenth century – near Gezer which probably indicate a large royal estate. The inscriptions read in Aramaic (תחם גזר) "boundary of Gezer." The Greek inscription on most of the stones reads "of Alkios," but one stone reads "of Alexas" and one "of Archelaus." The inscriptions seem to have indicated where the boundaries of a large estate met the boundaries of Gezer. B. Z. Rosenfeld has probably correctly explained the history of this large estate based on a comparison of the inscriptions with Josephus. The persons whose names are inscribed on the boundary markers were probably the Alexas who was married to Salome, Herod's sister (B 1.566), his son Helkias (A 18.138, 273,) and grandson Archelaus who married the daughter of Agrippa I (A 19.355, 20.140). These boundary markers, then, mark off the large estate of this family. Rosenfeld surmises that Herod bestowed these lands around Gezer to Alexas when he married Salome. If Rosenfeld is correct, the three generations of estate owners are a noble, wealthy family tied to the Herod's by marriage.[118] Rosenfeld's conclusions have been challenged, however. R. Reich and J. Schwartz[118a] conclude that the date of the inscriptions is the Hasmonean period, about a century earlier than Rosenfeld maintained. They further suggest that the occurrence of these three names in Josephus is pure coincidence.

Reich and Schwartz are certainly correct in demanding that Rosenfeld prove the inscriptions are first century instead of assuming that that they are. Yet the conclusion that they are Hasmonean does not appear firm either since stratigraphically, the inscriptions have no relationship with Tel Gezer. Furthermore, the suggestion that these names could occur in such a way in Josephus only coincidentally is difficult to accept.

We conclude, tentatively, that Rosenfeld's historical construction is the best so far, though it still has problems to be resolved. Schwartz also allowed that "Rosenfeld may be proved correct in some of his basic assumptions about the Gezer inscription."[118b]

c.) Azotus and Jamnia. Herod bequeathed to Salome the cities of Jamnia and Azotus (*A* 17.321) in his will. Since these cities can be inherited as private possessions they must include tracts of land which belonged to Herod. This was certainly the case with the third city which Herod left to Salome, Phasaelis (see above), which had a lucrative palm grove. Salome bequeathed Jamnia to empress Livia, wife of Augustus (*A* 18.31). It may have subsequently become the property of emperor Tiberius upon Livia's death (*A* 18.158).[119]

We would expect the rich lands of the coastal plain to have been owned by the Herods. The evidence we have for Azotus and Jamnia (and probably also Lydda and Gezer) indicates that much of it was. The land tenure patterns, however, changed often for this area. The plain did not belong to Judaea until the Hasmoneans conquered it. Later Pompey liberated it from the Jews and finally the plain was returned to Herod. Thus a long history of large estates cannot be established for the coastal plain.[120]

Never-the-less we should add the lands around these three towns to the Herodian domains.

Idumea

We can also be certain that the Herods owned large tracts of land in their native Idumea which were probably inherited from Antipater. We know that Herod rented out lands to the Nabataeans (*A* 16.291) and also that Costobar, his brother-in-law, owned estates in Idumea (*A* 15.264, (οἰκεῖα χωρία). Schalit[120] supposed that these lands were near Marissa since there is evidence that a number of wealthy families resided there.

Perea

Herod probably also had private lands in Perea. Upon his death one of his slaves, Simon, led an uprising with a group of fellow Pereans (*A* 273-77; *B* 2.57-59). Presumably, Simon and his band of rebels were slaves and perhaps tenants working Herod's estates.

That Herod possessed private lands in Perea is confirmed by the reference of Josephus (*V* 33) to Crispus the former prefect of Agrippa I. Crispus is said to be in Perea living on his estates (ἐν ταῖς ἰδίαις κτήσεσιν). One can conjecture that the Herodian family inherited lands from Herod the Great and that his grandson, Agrippa I gave an estate to his prefect, a pattern we have seen several times before in our investigation.

We have seen in our survey thus far that the royal estate, were widespread, existing most likely in every part of the kingdom of Herod and his successors except perhaps Galilee and the hill country of Judea. Many of these estates probably began as Ptolemaic domains, but since Herod is known to have confiscated the property of his political enemies (*A* 15.5-7, 17.305, 307), we should conclude that the number and size of these lands increased under his rule.[121]

But what about the lands owned by the other members of the aristocracy, the High Priestly and lay wealthy class? Most of these estates probably lay in Judaea and Galilee. At least the evidence which has survived indicates that is so.

Estates Of The Jewish Aristrocracy

Judaea

As we noted above, it is probable that part of the Har Ha-melek lay scattered in the western Judaean hills, but we cannot pinpoint definite villages or areas.

Goodman[123] argues that much of the Har Ha-melek belonged in the Herodian period to the Jerusalem aristocracy instead of being royal land as it was under the Hasmoneans. As Goodman points out we have no references in Josephus to royal lands belonging to Herod around Jerusalem. Nor do we read of any Roman imperial estates in this area. Therefore, Herod must have already parcelled these lands out to his friends, especially the High Priestly families which he appointed. We must bear in mind, however, that Dar has apparently found evidence of a complex of large estates in western Samaria (see above) which were also previously unknown from literary sources. It is, therefore, possible that the Herod family still also owned estates in Judaea. Yet until new evidence is presented we should tentatively accept Goodman's supposition that the large estates in Judaea were no longer royal estates, but now belonged to the non-Herodian aristocrats.

Applebaum has recently published a report on a number of villas found in northern Judaea and western Samaria. Some of these villas were reported on by Dar (see above on Qawarat bene-Hassan and below Qasr el Lejah). But many lie in northern Judaea. Applebaum reports that forty-two sites have been identified as having remains which possibly were Roman-type villas (i.e. medium-sized to large estates). Where the remains were datable Roman and Roman to Byzantine pottery was found. Some or most of these villas could represent the Har Ha-melek. Applebaum refers also to a fortified farmhouse which was discovered near Hebron. This building dates to the first century A.D. and represents presumably a medium-sized estate.[124]

We have beyond this evidence testimony that wealthy families lived in Jerusalem before the first Jewish war. The sources do not always indicate that these families and individuals derived their wealth from land, but we should usually assume that they did. It is axiomatic that wealth in the Roman empire as an agrarian society, was based on land.[125] Palestine was if anything even more agriculturally based, economically, with an even smaller merchant class than the other areas of the empire (*Apion* 1.12).[126] Thus references to wealth among citizens in Jerusalem probably are evidence also of owners of estates larger than the average small freeholder would have owned.

First, the New Testament furnishes us with the names of several landowners living around Jerusalem, such as Simon of Cyrene (Mk. 15:21), Barnabas (Acts 4:36f) and Ananias the husband of Sapphira (Acts 5:1). We cannot be sure that the "fields" alluded to in these instances are larger than the ordinary freeholder's, but the sale of property in the cases of Barnabas and especially Ananias seem to have involved a not inconsiderable sum of money. Therefore, we would suggest that the latter two landowners owned medium-sized estates.[127]

The rabbinic sources tell of three wealthy men, Naqdimon ben Gorion, Ben Kalba Shabua, and Ben Tzitzit, who lived in Jerusalem before and during the first Jewish war. They were allegedly, capable of supplying Jerusalem for twenty-one years. One of them could supply wheat and barley, one oil and wine, and the third, wood. These men were probably large estate owners whose estates produced these crops. Even allowing for obvious exaggerations, the three must have possessed great wealth (i.e. lands).[128]

The rabbinic sources also allude to other wealthy landowners who resided in or near Jerusalem during this time. Hyrcanus, father of Eleazar the famous student of Yohannan ben Zakkai, was a wealthy man who owned lands near Jerusalem.[129] Elisha ben Abuya was descended from a wealthy landowner who lived in Jerusalem before A.D. 66.[130] Rabbi Dosa ben Harkinas was an elderly and wealthy scholar during the time of the school of Jamnia (A.D. 70-125). Büchler argued that he must have, therefore, lived in Jerusalem before the war (along with the other sages?) and that he had been able to maintain his wealth even in the aftermath of the destruction of Jerusalem.[131]

Probably the most significant class of wealthy landowners was the class of aristocratic priests and especially the High Priestly families. M. Stern[132] suggests that the statement of Hecataeus (Diodorus Siculus 40.3.7., see the quotation above in chapter 1) that Moses gave the priests a larger share of land than other Israelites reflects the social situation in Palestine in the Second Temple period. Certainly Hecataeus did not base this observation on the Old Testament since, according to the Law, (Dt. 10:9, 12:12, 18:1, Num. 18:24) the priests and Levites did not own land. As Stern also notes, it is doubtful that the priests could have become wealthy from the tithes alone since the Mishnah indicates that many peasants did not always pay them.

At any rate a number of priestly families were quite wealthy. The most obvious example is the family of Josephus. He states that he has come from a wealthy and influential priestly family of the Hasmonean line (*V* 1f; *A* 16.187) and that he owned lands near Jerusalem (probably just west of the city) before the war (*V* 422). Since, according to his autobiography, he is never seen residing on his farm, we can assume that he had a bailiff to oversee his tenants or slaves and that he lived for the most part in Jerusalem.

Other priests, especially the High Priests, were also wealthy. Ananias son of Nebedaeus (High Priest in A.D. 48) was wealthy enough to pay bribes to Albinus the Procurator and the current High Priest, Jesus son of Damascus, so that he could continue a campaign of fraud and oppression against both the peasants and the poorer priests (*A* 20. 205-207) to extract forcibly the tithes for himself and his servants.[133]

Wealth was especially prominent in the main High Priestly families, that is the houses of Boethus, Hanan, Phiabi, and Kathros (Kadros).[134] The oft quoted Talmudic passage about these families is also appropriate in connection with our purposes:

> Woe is me because of the house of Boethus, woe is me because of their staves!
> Woe is me because of the house of Hanin, woe is me because of their whisperings!
> Woe is me because of the house of Kathros, woe is me because of their pens!
> Woe is me because of the house of Ishmail the son of Phabi, woe is me because of their fists.

For they are High Priests and their sons are (Temple) treasurers and their sons-in-law are trustees and their servants beat the people with staves.[135]

That these priestly houses were wealthy can hardly be doubted. The wealth of the house of Boethus, for example, was legendary (b.Pes 57a) as was that of the house of Phabi (b.Yoma 35b). Annas and Caiaphas of the house of Hanan apparently owned large mansions.[136] That some of this wealth was gained through extortion and violence is also likely. But such practices could not produce sustained wealth. They must have owned lands in Judaea and perhaps elsewhere which brought them such large fortunes.[137]

The rabbinic sources also refer to several priests who lived between the two Jewish rebellions who were wealthy. That priests should have maintained their wealth even after the war is not surprising. As Bchler maintained, Josephus indicates that many priests quickly capitulated to the Romans and so were allowed to keep their lands (B 6.115).[138] The most celebrated of these wealthy priests was Eleazar ben Harsom, who was discussed above. His fabulous wealth was based on his "1000 villages" which lay in the Har Ha-melek.[139] Mentioned alongside ben Harsom is Eleazar ben Azariah, also of priestly descent, who possessed extraordinary wealth.[140] Also to be included in this list is Rabbi Tarfon, a wealthy sage who as a young man had participated as a priest in the temple ritual. R. Tarfon owned an estate in Galilee and may also have owned land near Joppa.[141]

Thus the literary evidence indicates that a wealthy, aristocratic class lived in Jerusalem in the Herodian period, many of whom, but not all, were from one of the influential priestly families. In this context we must add the testimony of Josephus that we already cited in chapter 1. He writes of a significant group of wealthy citizens living in Jerusalem at the outbreak of the war who became the targets of the Sicarii and other revolutionary factions (B 2.428, 2.652, 4.140f). Surely many of these were wealthy landowners whose lands lay around Jerusalem.

The archaeological excavations of the Jewish quarter of Jerusalem confirm the impression we get from the literary sources that a significant wealthy class resided in Jerusalem before the war. The excavation team of N. Avigad[142] discovered large mansions owned obviously by very rich people. The "Herodian house" from the first century B.C., the "Palatial Mansion" from the first century A.D., and the "Burnt House"[143] from the first century A.D. are architectural testimony of this class. Perhaps more important for our purposes, however, are not the huge mansions but the rows of slightly more modest houses which still, according to Avigad "belonged to upper class families."[144] These houses are not only distinguished by their size from other houses of the same period, but by their furnishings and decorations. The costly pottery, the wine imported from Italy, the elaborate frescoes and floor mosaics, and the many water installations, among other items, point to the wealth of the occupants. That these people were Jewish is evident from the mikvaoth found in many of the houses. This evidence, then, fits hand-in-glove with the literary evidence.

It may be helpful at this point to compare the situation in Jerusalem with that of another city in the empire where archaeology has revealed considerable information about land tenure: Pompeii in southern Italy. It is clear that a substantial wealthy class lived in Pompeii in the first century B.C.. and the first century A.D. and that their wealth was derived from the land, that is from vineyards. Large, lavishly decorated houses in the city indicate the affluence of the ancient inhabitants. Corresponding to these structures in the city are the *villae rusticae* outside the city associated with landed estates. These villas were lived in part of the year when the wealthy owner was not living in the city. Also in the environs of the city were "agricultural factories" which the owner would only have visited periodically but would not have lived in. All of these estates were worked by slaves and day laborers, while the owners for the most part lived in Pompeii as absentee landlords. J. Day was able to identify over eighty landowners of this type from inscriptions and wine amphorae. A study of these names shows that the villa owners were members of the most prestigious and prominent families in Pompeii. Most of the estates, where the size could be identified, were in the medium range with 100 iugera (63 acres) apparently standard, but evidence indicates that some landowners owned more than one estate.[145] We have then a class of affluent absentee landowners, whose wealth is clearly derived from land, who are the most influential families in Pompeii, and who live most of the time in the city. This must have been similar to the life style of the elite of Jerusalem.

We get a glimpse in the rabbinic literature of how wealthy landowners living in Jerusalem "added field to field" to enlarge their estates. The Midrash Rabbah on Lamentations (2.5) describes how small freeholders from a village called Bethar, which was near Jerusalem, would often be cheated out of their fields or vineyards by fraudulent contracts drawn up by "councilmen" (בולורטיר) members of the Sanhedrin?)[146] of Jerusalem. Though some elements of this account may be late, Applebaum[147] argues that the main features are pre-A.D.70 and we would concur with his conclusion. Since this passage is explaining why Bethar was destroyed (b. Gitt 57a, j. Taa 4.5) during the Bar Cochba war – because its inhabitants rejoiced at the destruction of Jerusalem in A.D. 70 – it is quite likely that this account of fraud was only attributed to this village after it was destroyed. But that such fraud did take place in Jerusalem in this way is high probable. First, such fraudulent actions were typical in the Greco-Roman world as Macmullen has shown.[148] Second, there is no reason to question that this landstealing took place before A.D. 70 in such a way. Such an account accords well with the fact that a large population of landowners of medium to large estates lived in Jerusalem before the first Jewish rebellion. Although wealthy Jews may have still lived in Judea after the war, these conditions would probably be less typical after A.D. 70 than before. Thus, some of the wealthy class living in Jerusalem before the war expanded their estates by stealing small freeholder's plots.

The literary evidence pictures wealthy landowners who lived in Jerusalem and the environs before the war. Josephus and the archaeological findings indicate also the presence of a wealthy class in the city. We cannot locate in Judea large royal domains such as we have found at Jericho, in the Great Plain, in Western Samaria, in the Golan and on the Coastal Plain however. These estates in Judea seem more modest in size. The wealthy class living in Jerusalem probably owned medium-sized estates – the wealthiest of them owned several medium-sized estates – which were in Judea, although we cannot rule out that many owned lands also outside Judea. As P. A. Brunt has observed, most large landowners in Italy, owned several medium estates scattered all over Italy or even beyond.[149] We should conclude then, that the lands in Judea, in addition to those still owned by small freeholders, were not primarily owned by the Herods and their friends, but by those who had "added field to field," that is aristocratic entrepreneurs.

Galilee

a.) Upper Galilee. John of Gischala requested of Josephus in preparation for the Jewish war that he be able to seize the imperial grain stored in the "villages of Upper Galilee" (*V* 71). Alt maintained that these imperial graineries are indications that there were royal lands in Upper Galilee. We must, however, caution that it is also possible that these graineries held the land taxes which Rome, as the direct administrator of Galilee since A.D. 44 collected of all freeholding peasants.[150]

b.) Lower Galilee. As Freyne suggests, the area around Sepphoris must have contained several large estates belonging to wealthy nobles such as Joseph ben Illem, the High Priest, who came from that city (*A* 17.66).[151] One village nearby, in the Beth Netofa valley, named Asochis (Shichin) was after A.D. 70 the property of the wealthy landowner, Eleazar ben Harsom, the High Priest who also owned villages in the Har Ha-melek.[152]

c.) Around the Sea of Galilee. Josephus records that during the civil war between Herod and Antigonas (40-37 B.C.) the Galileans rebelled against certain "nobles" (δύνατοι) and drowned Herod's followers in the Sea of Galilee (*A* 14.450). Kippenberg and Freyne[153] suggest, plausibly, that these nobles were wealthy landowners who lived near the sea.

d.) Allusions in the Synoptic Gospels to large estates in Galilee. Several scholars, beginning with J. Herz,[156] have noted that the Synoptic Gospels reflect a society and economy in which large estates are common. Since the Gospels reflect mostly the social conditions of Galilee, we may use this evidence to indicate the extent of large estates in that region.

First of all, the parables of Jesus are replete with allusions to land tenure in Palestine. Hengel[155] has demonstrated that the parable in Mk. 12:1-12 portrays the actual social conditions of Palestine in the Herodian period. Hengel drew parallels both from the Zenon papyri (the Beth Anath estate) and from the rabbinic literature to demonstrate both that the animosity existing between tenants and landlord in the parable are typical and that the existence of large estates as a common phenomenon is assumed by the parable. This parable furnishes us with an amazingly clear example of how the estates worked. The owner is an absentee landlord (vs 1), hires tenants (vs 1), and has a bailiff (vs 2) who oversees the estate and collects the rent.

In addition to the clear example above, we have other hints that large estates as a common phenomenon were assumed in the Synoptic Gospels. Lk. 16:1-12 speaks of debts of 100 measures of oil and 100 measures of wheat which would have required at least a medium sized estate to produce, according to J. Herz.[156] Of course the figures may be only scenery in the parable, but the fact that they can be used in a story otherwise quite believable and ordinary shows that they are not out of line with experience, argues Herz. The same kind of argument can be made with the parable of the talents (Mt. 25:14-30=Lk. 19:11-27), the Parable of the Debtors (Lk. 7:41-43=Mt. 18:23-34) and the Parable of the Unforgiving Servant (Mt. 18:21-35). These parables speak of large sums of money which imply great wealth.[157] It is true of course that one could become wealthy as a merchant, but overwhelmingly, as we stated above, wealth in antiquity was obtained through land. Thus great wealth implies large estates.

Still other parables depict scenes on a large estate. The Parable of the Rich Fool (Lk. 12:16-21) for instance describes an estate owner hoarding grain in a manner reminiscent of V 119, the grainery of Queen Berenice. Lk. 17:7 refers to a man's servant ploughing his field for him. Mt. 20:1-15 is a parable about a large landowner who has so much land he must hire day laborers to work it. Lk. 12:42f alludes to a wealthy man who has a bailiff (οἰκονόμος) (cf. Mt. 24:45-51) to run his estate.[158] Mt. 13:24-30 describes a farm which requires several slaves to work it. Finally, Lk. 15:11-32 pictures an estate with day laborers and slaves.

To the evidence from the parables we may add the story of the Rich Young Ruler (Mk. 10:17-22) who had great possessions (κτήματα πολλά). We should understand by (κτῆμα) landed property,[159] and thus picture the young man as a land baron with tenants or slaves and farm overseers.

Based on the above evidence what was the extent of large-estate ownership in Galilee? Freyne[160] is correct to caution us against overly generalizing from the parables alone. But when the parables – presumably describing the conditions, in the main, of Galilee – harmonize well with what we have already learned about the rest of Palestine, their value as sources describing social conditions is increased. Freyne suggests that the Synoptics also commonly picture small freeholders. But of the three examples he offers (Lk. 15:11-31; Mk. 1:20; and Mt. 21:28-32) the first one describes a large estate (with day laborers and slaves) and the second one refers to fishermen. Freyne further argues that the "Galileans" during the Jewish war appear to be small freeholders since they are "in charge of their own agricultural affairs" (i.e. they can provision themselves with food for a military campaign). Yet he fails to explain why a tenant farmer could not do the same. At Gischala, he continues, the people were not interested in war because it was time for sowing crops. But tenants too depended on their own harvest. Finally, Freyne offers that most Galileans were not tenants (or day laborers or slaves) because they had to pay taxes as the account in A 18.274 (B 2.200) shows. In this story thousands of people from Tiberias declared that if Caius erected a statue in the temple they would neglect their fields (A 18.270, 272). Consequently, Aristobulus, Agrippa I's brother, feared that there would be a harvest of banditry when the tribute could not be paid. Yet this argument still fails to prove which type of agricultural worker was in the majority. All we see from this story is that there were still many small freeholders. Furthermore, we cannot be certain that the lands around Tiberias are typical for all of Galilee.

The evidence is simply not available to argue effectively either way regarding the dominance of freeholders or laborers on large estates. But at least we can say that large estates must have been common in Galilee at the time of Jesus. As in the case of Judea, moreover, we find no evidence for royal domains in Galilee. The estate owners were evidently land entrepreneurs.

Further Evidence of Large Estates

Finally, we shall list and briefly comment upon evidence of large estates in Palestine which describes conditions later than the period of time we are investigating, in our opinion falls short of being entirely convincing, or for some other reason falls into the category of miscellaneous. Late evidence should not be quickly disregarded since an estate may have been in the family for generations and thus could very well have been in existence during the Herodian era. Most of these estates discussed below would probably be medium-sized private estates although some of the evidence may point toward royal domains.

Klein suggested that the villages (כפר עריס)(which he read אריס) and (כפר סגנא) in the Beth Netofa valley near Sepphoris were part of a large estate. He saw the evidence for this in the names "village of tenancy" (if one accepts his emendation) and "village of the administrator."[161]

Krauss believed that the village (יבלונה) which belonged to Judah the Patriarch (j. Sheb 6.1) lay also in the Beth Netofah valley.[162]

Applebaum refers to archaeological remains of estates in Western Galilee. The findings were not published at the time his work was written.[163]

J. Kaplan describes a "villa" near Jaffa which possibly represents a large estate. The villa was destroyed during the Jewish war of 66-74 A.D.[164]

One wonders if some of the "fortresses" listed by M. Kochavi in his archaeological survey of Judea were not actually fortified farms.[165]

Klein attempted to demonstrate that there was a Ptolemaic estate called Arethusa near Bethlehem. His conclusions were challenged by Tscherikover.[166]

The archaeological survey of Y. Hirschfeld has found several farm sites from the Roman period just south of Herodium. The building remains appear to have been too small to represent more than a small freeholder, however. The largest farm house measured 11.5 x 12 meters.[167]

A. Raban in the survey north of Beth Shearim has located a "patrician house" connected to a cultivated field. This house which dates from the late Roman period is also near a village settlement which dates from the early Roman period. The patrician house then could represent a large landlord whom the villagers served as tenants. Did this relationship also exist in the early Roman period?[168]

A third century A.D. inscription on a synagogue column in Capernaum gives credit to "Herod son of Monimos and Justus his son with their children" for erecting the column. Is this family descended from Herod the Great and do they still own some of the Herodian lands in the area, from whose income they can participate in building the synagogue?[169]

An inscription from Scythopolis from A.D. 305/311 refers to the emperor's (δεσποτικαί χῶραι). Isaac and Roll conclude from this that the old royal lands of the Seleucids have become an imperial estate by the fourth century. But who owned the lands in the meantime?[170]

An inscription from Trachonitis from the third century credits a (Μασάλεμος Ἰάββος) with having built a building from his "own agricultural labor" (ἐξ ἰδίων κόπων γεωργικῶν). Is the name (Ἰάββος) Jewish? The Septuagint translates (ישׁבד) as (Ἰάβας) (1Chron. 4:3). "From his own agricultural labor" must mean from his agricultural income.[171]

Josephus mentions that Jonathan and John of Gischala once retired to the house of Jesus (*V* 246), evidently the same Jesus who was magistrate of Tiberias (*V* 278). The house is called (βᾶρις μεγάλη) "a great tower" and (οὐδὲν ἀκροπόλεως ἀποδέουσα) "equal to an acropolis". This castle must have been out in the country since Josephus camped just opposite it "in the plain" (εἰς τὸ πεδίον) (*V* 249) with his men "the Galileans." Could this castle have been a fortified large estate such as Qawarat Bene Hassan? T. R. S. Broughton has noted that such estates were common in Asia Minor and referred to as (τύρσις) "tower" or (πύργος) "fort."[172]

We list two estates described by Dar, in western Samaria. The first estate, which he calls the Qasr e Lejah Farm, lies 2.4 miles southeast of Um Rihan in Samaria and consists of an enclosed farmyard with several buildings (see chapter 4). Dar identifies the buildings as follows: the residence of the owner, the manager's house, five rooms for farm workers which could have housed twenty to thirty people, storehouses, a cistern, and an olive press. The pottery dates from the early Hellenistic period to the Roman period. Dar therefore, suggests that the estate was established in the third or second century B.C. and existed to the first century A.D. This is a farm belonging to a "medium or well to do landowner."[173]

The second estate, Hirbet Deir Sami'n lies approximately one mile east of Deir Balut also in Samaria. The buildings in the enclosed farmyard are not well preserved and thus Dar cannot ascertain what their function was. The five field towers nearby and the large winepress indicate that the vine was the main crop. Pottery indicates the farm was occupied from the Roman through the Byzantine periods. Dar estimates that the farm was established in the second or third century A.D. The terrain on which this farm lies would have required an "immense investment of labor" to begin production.[174]

Conclusions

The evidence surveyed above, incomplete as it is, indicates that large and medium-sized estates, that is estates large enough that one does not work them himself, but either hires day laborers, contracts tenants, or owns slaves (or a combination of these), were widespread. Such estates must have equalled anything from about 50 acres to the very large farm at Qawarat Bene-Hassan of 2500 acres. The Herods must have owned tens of thousands of acres in all.

Was most of the land in Palestine still owned by small freeholders, however? Did most peasants live on their own small plots, according to the Old Testament ideal? Scholars have disagreed on this question, but most have concluded that the majority of peasants in Palestine in the Herodian period were still freeholders.[175] We can see no way to settle the issue. Nevertheless, we would argue that even if the total of lands under control of the Herods and their friends and under the control of entrepreneurs was in the minority, it was still a sizable minority, affecting profoundly the economic and social structures of Judaism in the Herodian period.

END NOTES

1.   See de Vaux, 1961, pp. 124f; 1Chron 27:25-31; Neh 5:4; and M. Lurje, *Studien zur Geschichte der Wirtschaftlichen und Sozialen Verhältnisse im israelitische-jüdischen Reiche* (Giessen: Töpelmann, 1927) p. 16.

2.   J. Offord, "Archeological Notes on Jewish Antiquities" *PEQ* 50 (1918) 37.

3.   M. Hengel, *Judaism and Hellenism*, trans. J. Bowden (Philadelphia: Fortress 1974) p. 19; Tcherikover, 1975, p. 13; S. Klein, "Leqorot Haarisit Hagedolah Beeretz Israel" *Bulletin of the Jewish Palestine Exploration Society* I,3 (1933) 3; H. I.Bell, *Egypt from Alexander the Great to the Arab Conquest* (Oxford: Clarendon, 1948) p. 44.

4.   Tcherikover, 1975, p. 13; W. W. Tarn, *Hellenistic Civilization* (London: Methuen, 1952) p. 187; Rostovtzeff, 1941, pp. 276f; F. Preisigke, *Antikes Leben nach den ägyptischen Papyri* (Leipzig: Teubner, 1916) pp. 22f.

5.   M. Rostovzeff, *A Large Estate in Egypt in the Third Century B.C.* (Madison, Wis: University of Wisconsin, 1922) p. 66.

6.   Rostovzeff, *Social and Economic History of the Hellenistic World* (Oxford: Clarendon, 1941) p. 465.

7.   Hengel, 1974, p 20.

8.   See Tcherikover and A. Fuks, *Corpus Papyrorum Judaicarum* (Cambridge: Harvard University, 1957) vol. I, no. 6; Hengel, 1974, p 21; an Rostovzeff, 1922, p. 80 for the names of some of these adminstrators.

9.   See Rostovzeff, 1922, p. 26 and passim and Hengel, 1974, p. 19, Tarn, 1952, p. 196.

10   Hengel, 1974, p. 35.

11.   Tarn, 1952, p. 199.

12.'   S. Freyne, *Galilee from Alexander to Hadrian* (Wilmington, Delaware: Michael Glazier, 1980) p. 171.

13.   Kreissig, 1969, p. 231, *cf.* A. Applebaum, "Judaea as a Roman Province: the Countryside as a Political and Economic Factor," *ANRW* II.8 (1977) 360.

14.   See below on this. Also 1 Macc 16:11, *A* 14.207. See Also A Schalit, *Herodes* (Berlin: de Gruyter, 1969) pp. 171f.

15. S. W. Baron, *A Social and Religious History of the Jews* (New York: Columbia University, 1952) vol. I, p. 263. See Strabo 16.2.46 and *A* 16.154-156, 17.305-308, and Hengel *Die Zeloten* (Leiden: Brill, 1961) p. 329 "Auf diese Weise scheint Herodes einen großen Teil des Landes in seinen persönlichen Besitz gebracht zu haben, den er teilweise wieder an seine Günstlinge verschenkt." *Cf.* Kreissig, 1969, p. 235.

16. Hengel, 1974, pp. 18f; Rostovzeff, 1922, p. 127.

17. R. MacMullen, *Roman Social Relations* (New Haven, Conn.: Yale University, 1974) p. 38; *cf.* Finley, 1973, p. 102; K. D. White, "Latifundia" *Bulletin of the Institute of Classical Studies* 14(1967) 62-79; M. Rostovtzeff, 1957, p. 344; de Ste. Croix, passim; and F. M. Heichelheim "Latifundia" *OCD*.

18. See Cicero, *de leg. agr.* 3.14; Pliny, *Ep.* 3.19; Petronicus *Sat* 48, 77; Seneca *Ep.* 90.39, *de benef.* 7.10; Dio Chrysostom, *Or.* 7.11; all cited in MacMullen, 1974, p.6.

19. See P. A. Brunt, *Social Conflicts in the Roman Republic* (New York: Norton, 1971) p. 34 who cites Caesar, *Civil Wars* I.17.

20. Pliny, *N.H.* 33.135 cited by Brunt, 1971, p. 34.

21. Pliny, *N.H.* 18.35; see MacMullen, 1974, p. 6. Compare Cicero, *de leg. agr.* 3.8 who speaks of one man owning an entire region. Cited in Brunt, 1971, p. 34.

22. Finley, 1973, p. 99.

23. *Ibid.*, p. 100. See the evaluation of properties listed here, especially of Herodes Atticus (second century A.D.) whose father could leave 100 million sesterces to the city of Athens in spite of the fact that his grandfather had had an equal amount confiscated by Domitian. White estimates the size of some estates based on the "gross value." E. g. Pliny's estate (*Ep.* 3.19) must have been over 3000 acres. See White, 1967, p. 77. See also the extensive list of estates in Asia Minor in Broughton, 1938, pp. 664-676.

24. E.g. the estate of Asonius in the fourth century A. D. in Gaul cited by Finley, 1973, p. 104 and compare the estates connected with Pompeii cited by White, 1967, pp. 72f, where owners of estates this size were absentee, employing bailiffs as overseers. See also the example of Horace's estate described in Rostovtzeff, 1957, pp. 59-61.

25. Dohr, *Die italischen Guthöfe nach den Schriften Catos und Varros* (Köln: Ph.D., 1965) cited in K. D. White, *Roman Farming* (London: Thames and Hudson, 1970) pp. 385-87.

25a. The terms for bailiff in Latin and Greek were *vilicus* and (οἰκονόμος) respectively. See A. H. M. Jones "Colonus" in *OCD* and LSJM. In Hebrew the term was (איקרנומוס), clearly a loanword, and (סנטר). See Jastrow.

26.　See Finley, 1973, p. 104; K. D. White, *Country Life in Classical Times* (Ithaca, N.Y.: Cornell University, 1977) pp. 36-39, who quotes Xenophon, *Oeconomicus* XI and Cato, *On Farming* II as examples of absentee landlords; MacMullen, 1974, p. 5; and Rostovtzeff, 1957, pp. 18, 33, 35, 69, 179, 203, etc. For absentee landlords in Palestine see Mk. 12:1-8 and Lk. 22:42-46.

27.　A. Schalit, 1969, p. 259, n. 390. *Cf.* A. Alt, *Kleine Schriften* (München: Beck, 1959) II, p. 390; and Bell, 1948, p. 44.

28.　Nothing like a comprehensive list of these estates has yet been attempted. Applebaum gives the most complete list (1976, pp. 657-59).

29.　Pliny, *N.H.* 13.9.44; Pausanias 9.19.8; Horace, *Epist.* 2.184; Dioscorides 1.19.1. For Engedi see *A* 9.7.

30.　*Historia Plantarum* 9.6.1-4.

31.　Rostovtzeff, 1941, pp. 179, 444, 465, 503, 589, 1195; Hengel, 1974, p. 44.

32.　Pliny, *N.H.* 12. 111-124

33.　Hengel, 1974, p. 45.

34.　Strabo 16.2.41; Pompeius Trogus in Justinus, *Historiae Philippicae*, Epitome 3.2 See SVM, I, pp. 298-300.

35.　Strabo 16.2.41; Dioscorides, *De Materia Medica* 1.19.1; Diodorus Siculus 2.48.

36.　*A* 15.96; *B* 1-361.

37.　E. Nitzer, "The Hasmonean and Herodian Winter Palances at Jericho" *IEJ* 25 (1975) 89-100.

38.　*B* 1.361f, *A* 15.96.

39.　*A* 17.340. This village and its plantation passed to Salome who bequeathed it to empress Livia (*A* 18.31).

40,　*A* 16.145; *B* 1.418, 2.167. According to the Madaba Map from the Byzantine era palms still grew in Phasaelis in the sixth century. See M. Avi-Yona, *The Madaba Mosaic Map* (Jerusalem: Israel Exploration Society, 1954) p. 36. This plantation also was passed on to Salome (*A* 17.189, 321) and then to empress Livia (*A* 18.31).

41.　See *A* 18.2 and M. Stern, "The Provice of Judea" in *Compendia* I.l, p. 334.　For other lands in Palestine belonging to the emperor see O. Hirschfeld, *Kleine Schriften* (Berlin: Weidmannsche, 1913) pp. 516-575; and in general D. J. Thompson, "Imperial Estates" in J. Wacher, *The Roman*

World (London: Routledge and Kegan Paul, 1987) pp. 555-567. Also Broughton, 1938, pp. 643-663.

42.   *N.H.* 12.113. Translation by H. Rackham in LCL.

43.   *A* 17.273-77; *B* 2.57-59.

44.   Pliny, *N.H.* 12.118.

45.   Alt, 1959, pp. 384-95.

46.   *A* 14.207. τὰς τε κώμας τὰς ἐν τῷ μεγάλῳ πεδίῳ ἃς Ὑρκανὸς καὶ οἱ πρόγονοι πρότερον αὐτοῦ διακατέσχον, ἀρέσκει τῇ συγκλήτῳ ταῦτα Ὑρκανὸν καὶ Ἰουδαίους ἔχειν ἐπὶ τοῖς δικαίοις οἷς καὶ πρότερον εἶχον.
Text and translation by R. Marcus in LCL. The Great Plain is obviously the Plain of Esdraelon or Plain of Jezreel. Cf *A* 12.348.

47.   See LSJM. Polybius used the term for "hold in possession" (70.3). In an inscription (OGI 441.108) (διακατέχειν ἐπαρχείαν) is equal to the Latin expression *obtinere provinciam*.

48.   For a description of the stele and a text, translation, and commentary on the inscription see Y.H. Landau "A Greek Inscription Found Near Hefzibah" *IEJ* 16(1966) 54-70. A corrected text can be found in J. Robert and L. Robert, *Bulletin épigraphie* (1970) which is also in J. E. Taylor, *Seleucid Rule in Palestine* (Duke University, Ph.D., 1979) along with his translation.

49.   (ὑπομνήματα). See Taylor, p. 108.

50.   I am following Taylor's designations here. Landau designates this document IIIa.

51.   Translation and text in Taylor, pp. 109-113.

52.   LSJM.

53.   Landau, 1966, p. 66.

54.   Taylor, p. 131.

54a.   See the examples of owning villages given in Broughton, 1938, pp. 630f. Inscriptions speak of selling not only lands and manor houses but villages and the people in them. See also Harper, 1928, pp. 160f. For a later period see the list of inscriptions and other sources in MacMullen, 1974, pp. 159f, n. 4.

55.   T.R.S. Broughton, 1938, p. 629 maintained that peasants on royal estates in Asia Minor were "serfs." Rostovtzeff, 1941, p. 508, said the peasants were bound to the soil. Applebaum, 1976, p. 633 and Taylor, 1979,

pp. 135f, agree. See also C. B. Wells, *Royal Correspondence in the Hellenistic Period* (New Haven: Yale University, 1934) p. 18, lines 11-13, cited by Taylor. E. Bickerman, *Institutions des Seleucides* (Paris: Librairie Orientaliste Paul Geuthner, 1938) pp. 177f, followed by Freyne, 1980, p. 161, denies there was actually a serf status to the (λαοι). Freyne does emphasize that economic conditions usually made them the equivalent of slaves.

56.   See M. Avi-Yonah, "Scythopolis" *IEJ* 12(1962) 125-134. Avi-Yonah suggested that the lands south of the Sea of Galilee were royal estates as far back as the Davidic monarchy. On the history of Scythopolis see also SVM II, pp. 142-45.

57.   Ptolemy Philadelphus granted his dioiketes, Apollonius, two large tracts of land in Egypt and the estate in Beth Anath in Palestine. See Rostovtzeff, 1922; and below on Beth Anath. See also the example cited by Taylor, p. 129, of Aristodicides of Assus.

58.   Mt. Tabor divides the territory of the Great Plain from the territory of Scythopolis. See F. M. Abel, *Geographie de la Palestine* (Paris: Le Coffre, 1967) I, p. 412.

58a.   Isaac and Roll, 1982, p. 88.

59.   Avi-Yonah, 1962; SVM II, pp. 142-45.

60.   *A* 15.294; *B* 3.36. See Rostovtzeff, 1941, p. 465. For the location of Gaba see Avi-Yonah, *The Holy Land* (Grand Rapids, Michigan: Baker, 1977) p. 103; who follows B. Maisler "Beth Shearim, Gaba, and Harosheth of the Peoples," *HUCA* 24(1952) 80. Freyne, 1980, p. 163, thinks the settlement of Gaba was in the same region as the estates of Berenice described below.

61.   *V* 119. See Maisler, 1952, p. 76.

62.   Besara is a corruption of Beth Shearim according to Maisler, 1952, p. 76. Excavation of Beth Shearim has indicated that the earliest building remains are Herodian. See N. Avigad, *Beth Shearim III* (Jerusalem: Massada, 1976) p. 1.

62a.   For village graineries in Egypt see *CPJ* I. 33,44; and II. 472.

63.   Avi-Yonah, 1977, p. 201.

64.   Alt, 1959, p. 389.

65.   See the comments of H. St. J. Thackeray on the *V* in LCL.

66.   For historical references to the camp of Legio (the Mishnaic Kefar Otnay, Gittin 2:5, 7.7) see Avi-Yonah, *Gazetter of Roman Palestine* (Jerusalem: Hebrew University, 1976) pp. 74f. Also see W. M. Ramsay, "Colonia Caesarea (Pisidian Antioch) in the Augustan Age" *Journal of Roman Studies* 6 (1916) 129-131. E. M. Smallwood, *The Jews Under Roman*

Rule (Leiden: Brill, 1976) p. 436, maintains that the garrison was already stationed on the Plain by A.D. 130. For the Plain of Legio see Avi-Yonah, 1977, pp. 141f. Map on p. 134. The boundaries for the territory of Legio can be found in Eusebius, *Onomasticon* (ed. E. Klostermann, *Eusebius, Das Onomastikon der biblische Ortsnamen* (Hildesheim: Georg Olms, 1966). Eusebius usually describes villages in the Plain according to their relationship in distance from Legio. E. g. Klosterman, pp. 14.26, 28.26, 98.12, 100.10. For analysis of the *Onomasticon* see C. U. Wolf, "Eusebius of Caesarea and the Onomasticon" *BA* 27 (1964) 66-96.

67.   Alt, 1959, pp. 388f, Avi-Yonah, 1977, pp. 141f.

68.   B. Isaac and I. Roll, *Roman Roads in Judea: The Legio-Scythopolis Road* (Oxford: BAR, 1982) pp. 104f.

69.   S. Dar. *Landscape and Pattern* (Oxford: BAR, 1986).

70.   *Ibid.*, pp. 88-107. Mintzker cited in Dar, p. 95. An earlier description of the towers can be found in Applebaum, 1977, pp. 363f. Applebaum in the Appendix to Dar, 1986 ("The Settlement Pattern of Western Samaria from Hellenistic to Byzantine Times: A Historical Commentary," pp. 257-69) says that at least 1200 towers have been identified.

71.   Dar, pp. 120, 95.

72.   Applebaum, 1977, p. 363.

73.   Dar, pp. 110f. Applebaum (in Dar, p. 258) accepted Dar's conclusions on the towers being used for wine production.

74.   See. V. Tcherikover, "Palestine under the Ptolemies" *Mizraim* 4/5 (1937) 1-82 and the following papyri: P. Zen. 59011, 59004 (in C. C. Edgar, *Zenon Papyri* (Hildesheim: Georg Olms, 1971) Vol. I; and P.S.I. 594 (in *Papiri Greci e Latini: Pubblicazioni Della Societa Italiana* (Florence: Enrico Ariani, 1917) vol. 6.

75.   P. Lond. 1948 quoted in Hengel, "Das Gleichnis von den Weingärtnern Mc 12:1-12 im Lichte der Zenonpapyri und der rabbinischen Gleichnisse" *ZNW* 59(1968) 1-39, esp. 13.

76.   P.S.I. 554. This papyrus does not mention Beth Anath but Tcherikover argued strongly that it was referring to that estate. Tscherikover, 1937, pp. 45f.

77.   See Tcherikover, 1937, pp. 46f; and Hengel, 1968, pp. 14f. But compare the criticism of Tscherikover by Rostovtzeff, 1941, 1403, who believed that Apollonius purchased the village.

78.   Tscherikover, 1937, p. 47.

79.   Alt, 1959, p. 395; Freyne, 1980, p. 158; Abel, 1967, vol. II, p. 65. Abel maintained that Beth Anath was the modern el-Ba'ne. Klein, 1933, p. 4, placed Beth Anath northeast of the sea of Galilee.

80.   Avi-Yonah, 1977, pp. 141, 143f.

81.   Alt argued that the entire area of the former Assyrian province of Megiddo (Galilee, the Great Plain, the Plain of Acco, the area round the Huleh basin) was in the beginning of the Hellenistic period royal land. See Alt, 1959, p. 395.

82.   See b. Gittin 57a and b. Beracoth 44a.

83.   Büchler, "Die Schauplätze des Bar-Kochbakrieges" *JQR* 16(1904) 184.

83a.   If Jeremias is correct (1962, p. 98) we have exactly this same anachronism in b.Yeb 61a where Jannaeus is substituted for Agrippa.

84.   Klein, *Eretz Yehudah* (Tel Aviv: Debir, 1939) pp. 41f.

85.   As Applebaum in Dar, 1986, p. 259, maintains.

86.   J. Aboda Zara 1.9 and 5.4; j. Demai 6.1.

87.   See A. Schlatter, *Die Tage Trajans and Hadrians* (Gütersloh: Bertelsmann, 1897) pp. 55-56. Büchler, 1904, p. 191, makes him contemporaneous with the war of A.D. 66.

88.   B. Yoma 35b. The description of a wealthy person owning one thousand villages and ships was a standard one. See b.Erubin 86a where the same thing is said of Bonyis.

89.   J. Taanith 4.5, Midrash Rabbah Lamentations II.

90.   Applebaum, 1976, p. 636.

91.   Büchler, 1904, p. 191.

92.   Klein, 1939, pp. 42, 242f.

93.   Dar, 1986, p. 120.

94.   Pliny, *N.H.* 5.14.70; *A* 12.7; Luke 1.39,65; see for the LXX especially Judith 1:6, 2:22, 4:7, 5:3, 10:3, 11.2. See SVM II, p. 191 for these and other references and D. Correns, *Schebiit* (Berlin: Töpelmnn, 1960) p. 141. *Cf.* Sheb 9:2 and t. Sheb 7:10.

95.   Büchler, 1904, p. 185.

96.   Applebaum too, though he initially supported the idea that the towers were the remains of estates in the Har Ha-melek, later changed his mind,

and suggested instead that the estates were actually begun by Alexander Jannaeus and not before. See the Appendix in Dar, 1986, 259. A. Schalit notes in reflecting on Klein's research on the Har Ha-melek: "Seine Schlüsse sind allerdings nicht durchweg überzeugend." See Schalit, 1969, p. 260, n. 394.

97.   See Dar, 1986, pp. 230-245 and figures 115, 124, 130.

98.   The Israel Ministry of Agriculture (cited by Dar on p. 247) estimated that 145 families lived in the village.

99.   A similar fortified farm, built in the Hellenistic period and destroyed in the early Hasmonen period, was discovered near Modin in Judea. See Z. Yeivin and G. Edelstein, "Excavations at Tirat Yehuda" *Atiqot* N.S. 6(1970) 56-67, English summmry, p. 6.

100.   Applebaum in Dar, p. 262. Applebaum cites j. Demai 6.1 and j. Yebamoth 8.4 as evidence there was "a considerable Jewish element" in this region until Hadrian's time. An inscription found 1.8 miles south of Sebaste confirms that Jews lived there. The inhabitants of a tomb have Jewish names. See *CIJ* II. 1169.

101.   The village appears to have been south of Samaria because of the direction of Varus' march. See *A* 17.288f.

102.   Abel, "Sappho et Arous" *Journal of the Palestine Oriental Society* 7(1927) 89-94. *Cf.* H. G. May, ed., *Oxford Bible Atlas* (London: Oxford University, 1974) pp. 86f.

103.   See Dar, 1986, p. 236; Applebaum in Dar, p. 161.

104.   Dar, 1986, p. 221f.

105.   See Dar, 1986, pp. 74f where the average combined plots were 6 acres; B. Golomb and Y. Kedar, "Ancient Agriculture in the Galilee Mountains" *IEJ* 21(1971) 136-140 where the average acreage of an enclosed field in Galilee was 4 acres; and M. I. Finley, 1973, p. 106 where the average plot in Italy was 5 acres. Applebaum, 1977, pp. 364f, affirms that the average plot was just over 6 acres.

106.   See A. Ben-David, *Talmudische Ökonomie* (Hildesheim: Georg Olms, 1974) pp. 26-28, and n. 20.

107.   See Dar, 1986, pp. 24-26 and Figure 23. Dar says there are no natural or man-made boundaries around this farm, but estimates the farm was "several hundred dunams." (1 acre = 4 dunams). Cato (*de Agri Cultura* X) said an olive plantation of 160 acres needed a work force of thirteen people. See J. M. Frayne, *Subsistence Farming in Roman Italy* (London: Centaur, 1979) p. 93.

108. Conder and Kitchener, *The Survey of Western Palestine* (London: Committee of the Palestine Exploration Fund, 1882) vol. II p. 329; and map 3.

109. Alt, 1959, p. 386, n.3; Applebaum in Dar, 1986 p. 261.

110. Alt, 1959, pp. 385-95.

111. Freyne, 1980, p. 164.

112. Klein, "The Estates of R. Judah Ha-Nasi" *JQR* N.S. 2(1912) 545-556. See also Applebaum, 1976, p. 658.

113. Hengel, 1968, p. 21; M. Avi-Yonah, *Geschichte der Juden im Zeitalter des Talmuds* (Berlin: de Gruyter, 1962) p. 57; Klein, 1933, p. 8.

114. See F. M. Heichelheim, "Roman Syria" in T. Frank, ed. *Economic Survey of Ancient Rome* (Baltimore: Johns Hopkins, 1938) vol. IV, p.146.

114a. Applebaum, 1976, p. 657.

115. E. M. Meyers, J. F. Strange, and D. E. Groh, "The Meiron Excavation Project: Archeological Survey in Galilee and Golan, 1976" *BASOR* 230 (1978) p. 18.

115a. D. Urman, *The Golan* (Oxford: BAR, 1985) Appendix A.

116. See S. Klein, "A Great Estate near Lydda" *Sefer Ha-Jubel For Samuel Krauss* (Jerusalem: Reuben Mass, 1936) pp. 69-79 (Heb) for references to Lydda in rabbinic literature; also Avi-Yonah, 1962, p. 57; Hengel, 1968, p. 21.

117. Büchler, 1912, p. 39.

118. B. Z. Rosenfeld, "The 'Boundary of Gezer' Inscriptions" *IEJ* 38 (1988) 235-245. For earlier attempts to explain the boundary stones see D. Lance, "Gezer in Land and History" *BA* 30 (1967) 34-47; and W. R. Taylor, "New Gezer Boundary Stone" *BASOR* 41 (1931) 28f.

118a. Reich "The 'Boundary of Gezer' Inscriptions Again" *IEJ* 40 (1990) 44-46: Schwartz "Once More on the I Boundary of Gezer' Inscriptions and the History of Gezer and Lydda at the End of the Second Temple Period" *IEJ* 40 (1990) 47-57.

119b. Schwartz, *ibid.*, p. 57.

118. SVM I, p. 110.

119. See SVM I, pp. 227, 240, 289.

120. Schalit, 1969, p. 257f and n. 382.

121. *Ibid*

122. See Schalit, 1969, p. 258; Freyne, 1980, p. 163; Applebaum, 1976, p. 657.

123. Goodman, 1987, pp. 58-60.

124. Applebaum, 1976, p. 366; idem. "The Problem of the Roman Villa in Eretz Israel" *Eretz Israel* 19(1987) 1-5 (Heb).

125. Finley, 1973, p. 97; A. H. M. Jones, *The Creek City from Alexander to Justinian* (Oxford: Clarendon, 1940) p. 265; P.A. Brunt, *Italian Man Power* (Oxford: Clarendon, 1971) p. 87; D. J. Thompson, "Imperial Estates" in Wacher, 1987, p. 555; Rostovtzeff, 1957, p. 343; de Ste. Croix, 1981, p. 10.

126. Goodman, 1987, 55; Ben-David, 1974, p. 49; J. Klausner, "The Economy of Judea in the Period of the Second Temple" in M. Avi-Yonah, ed., *The Herodian Period*, (London: Allen, 1975) *WHJP* VII, p. 179; Schalit, 1969, p. 322; L. Finkelstein, "The Pharisees: Their Origin and their Philosophy" *HTR* 22 (1929) p. 189. Note the agricultural orientation of the Mishnah. Compare also Aristeas 112, *B* 3.42-53, T Issachar 5:3, 6:2.

127. Kreissig, 1969, p. 233, argues that these men owned large estates. Applebaum, 1976, p. 259 urges caution in assuming too much from these examples. Jeremias, *Jerusalem in the Time of Jesus* (Philadelphia: Fortress, 1962) p. 96, maintained that Joseph of Arimathea (Mk. 15:42) was a large landowner. But where was Arimathea? See on this K. W. Clark, "Arimathea" *IDB..*

128. B. Gittin 56a and Midrash Rabbah on Lamentations I.31. The latter source gives the names of four men. See Applebaum, 1976, p. 659. Jeremias assumed that these men were merchants. But if they could supply Jerusalem they must have produced the goods. See Jeremias, 1962, pp. 95f, 226. See also ARN Rec A 6, ARN Rec B 13, Eccl. R. 7:12 and Gen. R. 42.1 for the same three men called here the "great ones of Israel." *Cf.* Kreissig, 1969, p. 234.

129. ARN Rec A 6; Gen R. 42.1; Pirke R. Eliezer I; and S. Mendelsohn, "Eliezer ben Hyrcanus" in *JE*; Büchler, 1912, p. 40.

130. J. Hagigah 2.1; Eccl. R. 7:18. See Büchler, 1912, p. 14; and Jeremias, 1969, p. 92.

131. B. Yebamoth 16a for R. Dosa and Büchler, 1912, p. 40.

132. Stern, "Aspects of Jewish Society: The Priesthood and other Classes" *Compendia* I.2, pp. 586f.

133. *Cf.* Stern, *ibid*. and E. M. Smallwood, "High Priests and Politics in Roman Palestine" *Journal of Theological Studies* 13(1962) p. 27.

134.   See Stern, 1976, pp. 605-609; Smallwood, 1962, pp. 14-34. Stern wants to add the house of Kimchi to these other four families. Jeremias, 1969, p. 194, maintained that the fourth great High Priestly house was Kamaith instead of Kathros, and that Kathros was a branch of Boethus.

135.   B.Pes 57a. Translation in Epstein BT. See the notes on this passage also in *BT*. The whisperings represent secret meetings to devise oppressive measures. The pens write evil decrees. See the list of Appendix A of Smallwood, 1962, pp. 31f, of the High Priests in the Herodian period and the families to which they belonged. See the very important corrective of Smallwood's article by R. A. Horsley, "High Priests and the Politics of Roman Palestine" *Journal for the Study of Judaism* 17(1986) 23-55. This same lament appears in t.Men 13:21.

136.   Jeremias, 1962, p. 96. See Jn 18:15, 18:18, Mk 14:53.

137.   See Jeremias, 1962, p. 108 and Stern, 1976, pp. 586f. Goodman 1983, p. 33, also doubts that priests could have grown wealthy on even unearned tithes.

138.   Büchler, 1904, p. 191.

139.   See above for Eleazar ben Harsom. B. Yoma 35b; b. Kidd 49b; b.Shab 54b; b.Bezah 23a.

140.   See b.Kidd 49b; b.Shab 54b; b.Bezah 23a. He traced his lineage back to Ezra, b.Ber 27b and j.Yeb 1.3. See "Eleazar ben Azariah" in *JE* by S. Mendelsohn.

141.   J.Sheb 4.2; b.Ned 62a; Eccles. R. 3.11; b.Kidd 71a; j.Yoma 3.7; t.Hag 3.36. See S. Oscher "Tarfon" in *JE*; and Finkelstein, 1929, 190. For lands near Joppa see the tomb inscription of Tarfon's son in *CIJ* II.892.

142.   Avigad, *Discovering Jerusalem* (Oxford: Basil Blackwell, 1980) pp. 83-137; and idem. "How the Wealthy Lived in Herodian Jerusalem" *BAR* 2(1976) 22-35.

143.   The Burnt House apparently, from an inscription found in it, belonged to a member of the house of Kathros, the priestly family listed above. See Avigad, "The Burnt House Captures a Moment in Time" *BAR* 9(1983) 66-72.

144.   Avigad, 1980, p. 95.

145.   See J. Day, "Agriculture in the Life of Pompeii" *Yale Classical Studies* 3(1932) 167-208; and White, 167, pp. 72f.

146.   This Hebrew word is a loanword from the Greek which probably means a member of the Sanhedrin. See Mk 15:43, Lk 23.50, *B* 2.405 and BAG. For the term as loanword see S. Krauss, *Lehnwörter* (Hildesheim: Georg Olms, 1964) II, p. 140 and Jastrow. The text is found in Applebaum 1977, p. 371. The same word is used in a Greek inscription from the third or

fourth century A.D. found near Tiberias describing an evidently wealthy man buried in a large ornamental sarcophagus. See *CIJ* II.985.

147. Applebaum, 1977, p. 371.

148. *Cf.* the examples MacMullen gives, 1974, pp. 7-11, of land being taken by fraud or force in Asia Minor and Egypt.

149. Brunt, 1971a, pp. 331, 352.

150. Alt, 1959, p. 395. Rostovtzeff, 1957, p. 664, n. 32, also maintained that this grainery belonged to an imperial estate.

151. Freyne, 1980, p 165. See also t.Kippurim 1:4; b.Yoma 12b; and b.Meg 9b.

152. See Avi-Yonah, 1966, p. 67; S. Klein, *Neue Beiträge zur Geschichte und Geographie Galiläas* (Vienna: Menorah, 1923) pp. 10f; Lam R. 2.

153. Freyne, 1980, p. 164; H. G. Kippenberg, *Religion und Klassenbildung im antiken Judäa* (Göttingen: Vandenhoeck and Ruprecht, 1978) p. 118.

154. Herz, 1928; see also A. N. Sherwin-White, *Roman Society and Roman Law in the New Testament* (Oxford: Clarendon, 1963) pp. 127-143; Hengel, 1968; Derrett, 1963; and Freyne, 1980, p. 165.

155. Hengel, 1968, pp. 1-39. See also J. D. M. Derrett "Fresh Light on the Parable of the Wicket Winedressers" *Revue internationale des droits de l'antiquité* 10 (1963) 11-41.

156. Herz, "Großgrundbesitz in Palästina im Zeitalter Jesu" *Palästina Jahrbuch* 24(1928) 100. Herz claimed one needed 160 olive trees and 40 acres of wheat to lend such a sum.

157. See Herz, *ibid.* pp. 101.

158. See Herz, 1928, pp. 98-101; Freyne, 1980, pp. 165f, 170; Applebaum, 1976, p. 658; Hengel, 1968, p.23. With Mt. 20:1-15 *cf.* James 5:4 where again landowners need day laborers. We cannot be certain, however, of what geographical locality James attests.

159. See LSJM; J. H. Moulton and G. Milligan, *The Vocabulary of the Greek Testament* (London: Hodder and Stoughton, 1930).

160.Freyne, 1980, p. 165f.

161. Klein, 1933, p. 9.

162. Krauss, *Antoninus und Rabbi* (Vienna: 1910) p. 18, cited in Klein, 1912, p. 546.

163.   Applebaum, 1976, p. 643.

164.   Kaplan, *Two Groups of Pottery of the First Century A.D. from Jaffa and its Vicinity* (Tel Aviv/Jaffa: Museum of Antiquities, 1969). See generally J. Percival "The Villa in Italy and the Provinces" in J. Wacher, ed. *The Roman World* (London: Routledge and Kegan Paul, 1987) vol. 2, p. 527. Most villas were also farms.

165.   Kochavi, *Judea, Samaria, and the Golan: Archaeological Survey* (Jerusalem: Carta, 1972) (in Hebrew).   See especially numbers 13, 26, and 79.

166.   Klein, "Leqorot Haarisit Hagedolah Beeretz Israel" *Bulletin of the Jewish Palestine Exploration Society* 3/4 (1936) 109-116. Tscherikover, 1975, p. 104.

167.   Hirschfeld, *Archaeological Survey of Israel: Map of Herodium* (Jerusalem: Department of Antiquities, 1985).   See numbers 53, 58, 70, and 120.

168.   Raban, *Archaeological Survey of Israel: Nahalal Map* (Jerusalem: Archaeological Survey, 1982) number 48.

169.   *CIJ* II, 983. Another descendent of Herod's may have been buried in Beth Shearim. See *ibid*. II, 1004.

170.   See *Supplementum Epigraphicum Graecum* XX. 455 and Isaac and Roll, 1982, pp. 104f.

171.   *Corpus Inscriptionum Graecarum* III, 4659.

172.   Broughton, 1938, p. 629.

173.   Dar, 1986, pp. 10-12.

174.   *Ibid.*, pp. 26-30.

175.   Klausner, 1975, p. 190; Freyne, 1980, p. 165; Applebaum, 1977, p. 360; Tscherikover, 1975, p. 123; Baron,, 1952, I, p. 277, said that most Jews remained smll freeholders. *Cf.* Kreissig, 1969, p. 231. Schalit, 1969, pp. 260 and 280 said most Jews lived on Herod's estates. Cf. Hengel, 1961, p. 329.

CHAPTER 3

LABORERS IN THE SERVICE OF THE ELITE

The agrarian economy described in the last chapter demands a pool of laborers. There must have been workers for the large estates who farmed the lands of the wealthy and surrendered part of the produce to them. The workers must have sold their labor cheap – as tenants, day laborers, or agricultural slaves – for the landowners were often very wealthy even though the surplus the average worker could produce in antiquity was small.

Tenant farmers are well known in the Greco-Roman sources. They usually had no (or very little) land of their own and thus were compelled to enter into a contract with a landowner to farm his land, paying him rent for its use. The sources attest to tenants who paid a fixed amount of rent (in kind or in money), to those who paid a share or percentage of the crop, and to those who paid in labor (working special fields for the landlord, in addition to their own rented fields all of the harvest from which went to the lord).[1]

Tenants could be under contract for a definite period of time (one year, five years), for an indefinite time (thus they could be ejected at any time from the land), or could even be obligated to remain tenants for life. Even in the first case where one had a contract for a specific number of years, the tenant would often remain on one piece of property for life and be succeeded by his son.[2] This was especially true in the later imperial period. Most tenants because they were forever in arrears in their rent payments may have been de facto bondsmen.[3]

The amount of rent paid varied. De Ste. Croix maintains for the sharecropper that "half and half was common, but the landlord's share (often depending on the nature of the crop) might be as much as two-thirds and was hardly ever less than one-third."[4] As far as the other types of payment, we have very little means of knowing what the numbers mean. A tenant must pay so many measures of wheat, but what per cent of the crop does that represent? In a bad year it may represent far too large a percentage. Here we can only tell from the reactions of the tenants what the rent figures meant to them.

De Ste. Croix summarizes several examples of peasant protest in the empire: one from North Africa (A.D. 181), one from Phrygia in western Asia Minor (A.D. 244-247), one from Thrace (A.D. 238), and one from Lydia in Asia Minor (C. A.D. 200). The tenants in several cases claim that they are being forced to pay more rent than they were supposed to and have been beaten and tortured for filing a complaint. They threaten to leave their ancestral lands and go elsewhere to work.[5] Although de Ste. Croix's inscriptions are all later than our period under consideration, they harmonize well with earlier accounts of tenant protests in Egypt (third century B.C. and later) which we read about in the papyri. There peasants go on strike, threaten to move to another locality, are beaten and coerced, and file complaints to a higher official.[6] The pattern tended to remain the same throughout antiquity.

The tenant-landlord relationship then was one in which the landlord exercised "an effective superior power...over the cultivator" (tenant) which required the tenant to produce a fund of rent. There is a power imbalance – an "asymmetrical" power relationship – which results in the tenant having to furnish the landowner with not only his nutritional needs but his wealth.[7] Even when this requirement threatens the tenant"s own survival, he will often be compelled by violence to comply.

In addition to tenants as laborers on the large estates, day laborers and slaves were used. The former were perhaps more seasonal laborers, being used mainly at harvest time,[8] while the latter were especially found on the latifundia of Italy and Sicily.[9] Perhaps the day laborers were the most oppressed class of rural workers since they had neither land of their own nor a legal contract with a landowner. Even slaves were cared for more than day laborers. While the employer felt no responsibility for day laborers, he was solicitous of his slaves since they were his property. Therefore, the most unhealthy work was given to the day laborer since his plight was of little concern to the landowner. Further, the day laborer had no job security. Paid daily only if he worked and unable to work when the weather was bad, when he was sick or when the work season was over, the day laborer was at the mercy of the weather, the landlord and the strength of his own constitution.[10]

Landless Peasants

It is evident that landlessness (when peasants own very little or no land) was on the increase in Palestine in the Herodian period. First, the survey of large estates in the previous chapter has shown that at least a sizable minority of the acreage during that time was the property of large-estate owners. Such a landownership pattern meant that there was less and less land to go around for the small freeholders and we would naturally expect the number of landless peasants to have increased. This assumption is confirmed first of all by references in the Synoptic Gospels to landless agricultural workers (Mk. 12:1-8, Mt. 9:37f, 10:10, 20:1-8, Lk. 13:27, 15:17) and to the numerous references in Josephus to bandits. The latter phenomenon often overlooked or misunderstood, was surely the result, at least in part, of social and economic conditions, as Hengel and, more recently, R. Horsley and J. S. Hanson have maintained.[11]

What are the causes of the loss of land by so many freeholding peasants?

1) Applebaum and Schalit[12] argue that Pompey's expropriation of the coastal plain and transjordan in 63 B.C. (*A* 14.75f) greatly increased the number of landless peasants. But it is not clear that Pompey's actions cost so many Jews their lands. Josephus merely says these cities were returned to their original inhabitants. That Jews were driven out of those lands – or had even settled in those lands in great numbers in the first place – is speculation.

2) Klausner[13] suggested that landless peasants increased when the family farm plot was too small to divide among a man's sons so that only the oldest son inherited land. But this must always have been a problem in Israel. Why was there an increase in landlessness in the Herodian period? Applebaum[14] attempts to answer this question when he suggests that there was a population explosion during this period as the movement into the diaspora and an archaeological survey of Judea demonstrate. This suggestion may have some validity, but the survey which Applebaum cites did unfortunately not include the occupied West Bank and so is incomplete.

3) Applebaum[15] argues that Herod's confiscations (A 16. 154-156, 17. 305, 307;) by which he enlarged his landholdings contributed to peasant landlessness. These passages indicate, however, that Herod confiscated lands from the wealthy. We might expect that he also took lands from the poor, but we have no direct evidence of such action. Since Herod would only have wanted the best land, it was perhaps doubtful if land belonging to a poor peasant would have interested him. It seems possible, however, that Herod's allotments to his veterans involved some displacement of peasants.

4) Probably the best explanation for the loss of peasant plots is the entrepreneurial investment in land by the aristocracy in Judea and Galilee. We must recall that most of the bandits in Josephus seem to have been in Galilee and secondly that the evidence from the Synoptic Gospels cited above probably also mainly refers to Galilee.

How were the wealthy aristocrats able to wrench the lands away from the peasants? Oakman and Goodman[16] propose that much of the land was gained by foreclosure on a farm when a debt could not be repaid. Both scholars maintain that Palestine was rife with indebtedness during the Herodian period. We know from classical sources that wealthy people often loaned some of their money out. Finley[16a] informs us that they saw only two proper investments for their riches: buying more land or lending it out. Pliny's letters (Ep. 9.37.2-3) and the example of the Circumcellions in fourth-century North Africa show us the extent to which peasants could become indebted to aristocrats, argues Oakman. Goodman suggests that most wealthy aristocrats could have had only one motive for lending money to peasants: foreclosure when they could not repay. The returns on their loans, he argues, would have been in themselves too small to motivate lending.

Certainly there is evidence for indebtedness in Palestine in the Herodian period. Not only does the New Testament indicate that indebtedness was a problem (Mt. 18:23-34), but also the passage in Josephus (*B* 2.427) already cited in Chapter 1, in which the Sicarii burned the debt records in Jerusalem, would indicate this condition. As Goodman writes concerning this incident in Josephus, "for every borrower there must be a lender, and the expected enthusiasm at the destruction of the archives makes it clear that no social ties existed between debtor and creditor."[16b] Goodman's point seems to be that the debtors regarded the creditors as exploitative. We would add, further, that in the second century A.D. peasants were certainly losing their farm plots due to indebtedness (BM 5:3). Presumably the social relationship between debtor and creditor and the end result of many loan transactions (i.e., loss of one's plot) were no different in the second century than the first.

We must not forget the other methods the elites had to acquire land which were less legal but no less effective. First of all a larger estate could encroach upon a neighboring smaller one, especially if the estate were owned by a widow or other helpless individual.[17] Encroachment by illegally moving the boundary stones has a long history in Palestine.[18] Secondly, one could simply use threats and even violence to force the small farmer into selling or abandoning his land. Such action happened so frequently in the Greco-Roman world that it was almost common place.[19] The many texts which condemn violent wrenching of land from the small landowner attest to the fact that Palestine was no exception to this practice.[20] Finally, we must recall the midrash referred to in the last chapter which indicated that many aristocrats in Jerusalem robbed the peasants by drawing up fraudulent contracts. We would argue then that the major cause of landlessness in Palestine (which may have been especially pronounced in Galilee and Judea) was the movement everywhere in the Roman empire to concentrate more and more land into the hands of the few.

Tenant Farmers in Palestine

Tenant farmers in Palestine are known at least as far back as the Ptolemaic estate at Beth Anath in the third century B.C. There the tenants, as in Egypt in the same period[21] seem to have paid a fixed rent. The peasants petitioned in one papyrus for a reduction in the amount of produce they had to pay, but the agent (κωμομισθωτής), Melas, demanded they pay in full even if they had to use produce from their private gardens.[22] This estate was owned by Apollonius the finance minister of the king. Apollonius lived in Egypt and probably had never seen his farm.

Our knowledge about tenants in Palestine between the period of the Zenon papyri and the New Testament is non-existent. We would expect, however, that conditions that prevailed at Beth Anath, which are similar to conditions for tenants in Egypt at that time and later in the rest of the Greco-Roman world, remained.

The New Testament offers the Parable of the Wicked Tenants (Mk. 12:1-8) as evidence for the legal and social conditions of tenants in Palestine in the Herodian period. J. D. Derrett,[23] by comparing this parable with tenant contracts from Egypt roughly contemporaneous with the New Testament suggested that a typical contract in Palestine in the Herodian period would contain eight points. Among the points were that the landlord would accept less rent (only one-tenth, surmises Derrett) for the first four years, but collect one-half of the produce thereafter and that the landlord would reimburse the tenants for all capital expenditures. Although Derrett's speculations are plausible and based on contemporaneous documents from Egypt, they do little more than reveal the real lack of evidence about tenants in Palestine until the second century A.D.

The best sources for understanding tenant farmers in Palestine are the rabbinic sources supplemented with the newly found documents from Wadi Murabaat and Nahal Hever. The problems with using the rabbinic literature to describe the first century A.D. have been made abundantly clear to us in the past two decades. One must certainly proceed with caution in such an endeavor. Yet we would point out the following concerning the use of the rabbinic materials to describe our period: First, we are not attempting to understand the theological ideas of the New Testament by using the rabbinic literature, but the social and economic environment. Second, many social customs have so persisted in Palestine that one can often find similarities between traditional Arabs living in modern Israel and the customs reflected in the New Testament.[24] Third, the social relationship between the great landowners and the workers tended to remain the same in the eastern half of the Mediterranean world from the Hellenistic to the Byzantine period, as we suggested above. Fourth, much of the detail of the Mishnah and Tosephta is confirmed by the New Testament or Josephus, albeit in briefer and more summary form. Thus we shall turn to the rabbinic sources in the following pages for help in understanding how the socio-economic relationships worked.

From the Mishnaic and Talmudic evidence one can see that tenants in Palestine from the second to the fifth century lived under about the same conditions as tenants elsewhere in the Roman empire. The sources refer mainly to three kinds of tenants.[25] The (חוכר) and (שוכר) paid a set rent, the former in kind and the latter in money. The (אריס) paid a percentage of the crop.[26] The (חוכר) corresponded, according to Heichelheim, to the Greek (μισθωτής) and the Latin *conductor*. The (אריס) was roughly equivalent to (μέτοχος) and *patriarius*.[27]

For the (אריס) who paid a percentage of his harvest, the amount of the percentage probably depended on the type of crop he raised. The figures one-half, one-third, and one-fourth as the standard percentages appear frequently in the rabbinic literature.[28] But the landlord could, however, demand two-thirds of the crop as rent.[29]

Tenants appear to have had usually a written contract (BB 10:4). The only example of a contract for an (אריס) which we possess indicates that one-half of the produce went to the landowner:

> T. BM 9:13: I shall plough, sow, weed, cut, and make a pile (of grain) before you, and you will then come and take half of the grain and straw. And for my work and expenses I shall take half.[30]

We have no documents from the Herodian period itself which indicate the percentage normally paid in rent, but there is no reason to assume conditions were much different. Paying up to one half of one's harvest seems especially onerous and two-thirds, impossible. Even if the harvest is normal this payment requires a certain sized plot for the farmer to subsist, but if a peasant has a smaller harvest than usual the remaining percentage might not be enough to feed his family. Still, at least the landlord shared the risk with the tenant. If the harvest was poor, the landlord's portion would decrease as well.

With the (חוכר) the risk was entirely born by the peasant, since he had to pay a definite sum in kind regardless of the harvest.[31] A typical tenant contract from Murabaat has been reconstructed from parallel fragments by Wacholder:

> ...I of my free will have [re]nted from you today the land which is my rental in Ir Nahash which I hold as a te[n]ant (שחכרת) from Shimeon, the Prince of Israel. This land I have rented from you from today until the end of the eve of Shemitah, which are years full, [fi]scal years, five, of tenancy (חחכיר); that I will deliver to you in [Her]odium: wheat, [of good and pure quality,] th[ree kors] and a lethekh...[32]

The documents from Murabaat give specific amounts of crops – for example, 3 Kors and 1 Lethekh (=1/2 Kor) of wheat as above[33] – but we cannot judge the difficulty of paying this amount without knowing the size of the field rented. The Mishnah (BM 9:7) refers to a rent price of 10 Kors which Ben David[34] estimates would require 10 hectares (24.7 acres) of land to pay.

We also find rental price for the (שוכר) in the Mishnah, for example 700 denarii for seven years rent (BM 9:10). Again, as Ben-David[35] concluded, paying 100 denarii per year, or 116 denarii for six years if the tenant observed the sabbatical year law, would require a rather large tract of land. A contract from Nahal Hever made during the time of Bar Cochba, stipulates the figure of 650 zuzim (=denarii) for a year and another one demands 39 denarii.[36] In the former case the area farmed must have required either a very large tract of land or perhaps part of the lucrative balsam and date palm plantations around Jericho, Engedi, Archalais, and Phasaelis, as Ben-David suggested.[37] Perhaps then, the (חוכר) and (שוכר) were more small entrepreneurs than mere subsistence farmers. But as with the (חוכר) the risk for the (שוכר) is entirely the tenant's.

The length of the tenant contracts varied. All of the Murabaat contracts stipulate five years as the length of tenancy where the words are legible,[38] but the rabbinic literature also knew of a seven years term (BM 9:10). Four or five years seem to have been normal in the Greco-Roman world.[39] Probably some tenants remained on their rented land their entire lives, however, renewing their contracts repeatedly (BM 5:8). Nevertheless, one could also rent a vineyard or orchard or even one tree for the harvest season (t. Demai 6:6) in which case the tenant became much like the day laborer except that the tenant would receive a share of the crop.

When the crop was harvested and still on the threshing floor then descended on the tenant all those who had claims upon his labor. T. BM 9:14 informs us after the tenant "harvests the crop, makes it into sheaves, and winnows" then come "the measurers, the diggers, the bailiffs and the town clerks" to collect their fees.[40] The landlord collects his share of the crop through the bailiff. But that is not all the landlord collects. He also collects whatever debts are owed to him, that is grain he has loaned to use as seed, or even to eat, and other loans (BM 5:8, t. Demai 6.5, t. BM 6:9). Although the Mishnah forbade lending the tenant grain for food (BM 5:8) – evidently to prevent him from piling up debts – the mere appearance of such a prohibition indicates that it was done. So after everyone had first taken their share, while the crop was still on the threshing floor, the tenant could now size up his year's income, the results of his labor.

What sort of relationship existed between the tenant and the landlord? There were from time to time enlightened landlords such as Rabbi Gamaliel II who would allow his tenants to pay back loans with produce worth less than they had borrowed (BM 5:8). He often suffered a loss himself to ease the burden of his tenants. But such landlords were undoubtedly the exception. The parable in Mk. 12:1-8 pictures a landlord who demanded immediate and full payment. The relationship between landlord and tenants in this parable is certainly mirrored in the examples given us earlier by de Ste. Croix of tenants being beaten and threatened unless they paid all that was due the lord. Thus a relationship of hostility and distrust seems to have been usual. This condition may have been exacerbated often by the go-betweens who were employed to oversee the landlord's affairs. The example of Melas above who seems to have been in charge of Beth Anath was probably typical, as the papyri attest.[41]

But combined with those feelings were the tenants' feelings of dependence on the landlord. Not only did he need his land to make his living he also often needed to borrow seeds, tools, draft animals, and even his daily bread from the landlord. This resulted of course in only further indebtedness and dependency. The description in the Midrash Rabbah on Lamentations (5.8)[42] of a tenant trying to flatter the landlord so he will lend him ten denarii was probably all too typical. And if the tenant succeeded in convincing the landlord to lend him the money or grain, he only increased the burden of his rent for next harvest, perhaps making it necessary to borrow still more later.

The dependence on the landlord left the tenant often at the landlord's mercy because the landlord could demand more and more rent. Rent contracts were probably at times entirely at the discretion of the lord. BB 10:4 states "...they may not write deeds of tenancy save with the consent of both parties."[43] Thus the landlord at times must have tried to force a deed on the tenant that he had not agreed to.

What was the actual standard of living for the tenant? The (חוכר) and (שוכר) may have farmed larger plots, if Ben-David's observations above are correct. Yet since they took all the risks their economic status must have been very tenuous. In good years, however, perhaps they lived comfortably at the upper limits for a tenant.

The (אריס) seems to have been in general quite poor. Peah 5:5 speaks of two poor men leasing a field (אריסות) on sharing terms which would allow each to give the other his Poorman's Tithe. In addition if an (אריס) works a field in order to receive only one-third of the produce he may take Gleanings (לקט), the Forgotten Sheaf (שכחה) and Peah (פאה). He may, then, receive what is designated for the poor.[44]

Klausner's conclusions about the tenants in Herodian Palestine are accurate.[45] Tenants in general and the (אריסים) in particular were "a class of serfs," if not legally, at least economically (see Chapter 2). In many cases, such as at Qawarat Bene Hassan, an entire village contained tenants all working for the same landlord. In other cases a few tenants worked a smaller estate either living in a village with other tenants, small freeholders, and day laborers, or perhaps living in huts on the estate.[46]

Day Laborers

Day laborers (called פועלים in the Mishnah and ἐργάται in the New Testament) and hirelings (שכירים and μίσθιοι or μισθωτοί) were numerous in the Herodian period.[47] There were of course landless inhabitants in Palestine even before the exile who hired themselves out especially at harvest time (Ruth 2:3).[48] But the growing tendency toward larger estates in Palestine in the Herodian period, must have increased their number. As more and more people lost their land they would have become either tenants or day laborers.

But not all paid laborers were landless. J. Klausner also has surmised that younger sons of an impoverished farmer would not have received enough land as inheritance to maintain them and thus resorted to working as a hired hand to supplement the income from his tiny farm plot.[49] Others were probably simply poor small freeholders whose families were too large to be supported by their plot of ground and thus were forced to supplement their income.

Once again the best sources for describing the condition of the laborers are the rabbinic sources. There were different types of paid laborers just as there were different types of tenants. The (פועל ירם) or (פועל)[50] was a poor worker who did not own any land and depended entirely on his daily wage to live. This worker "had neither the means nor the instrument of production, only his labor."[51] He lived only from day to day and had no other income.

The second type of worker, the (שכיר) owned a small piece of ground but found it necessary to supplement his income. They usually hired themselves out for a definite period of time (an hour, a day, a month, a year, three years, or seven years say the sources).[52]

The laborers could perform any number of jobs. Of course there were craftsmen and other skilled laborers who were in a better economic situation than the unskilled laborers. But these must have been a minority judging from the references in the rabbinic literature. One of the most common jobs was working seasonally in the field ploughing, weeding, harvesting, threshing, picking fruit and other agricultural work.[53] The laborer often worked as a burden bearer, called in the rabbinic literature (כתף) or (סבל). He might carry reeds, wood, harvested crops, people or other burdens.[54] One story tells of five men who were paid to carry a polished stone from Galilee to Jerusalem to be used in the temple.[55]

Another category of employment for the day laborer was as watchman. The worker might be paid to watch over animals, fields of crops, children, the sick, the dead, or the city gates.[56]

But laborers can be found doing also every imaginable task for their daily hire such as barbers, bath-house attendants, cooks, messengers, scribes, manure gatherers, thorn gatherers, or workers with building skills. Some of the jobs required skill and so would have produced more wages while others required no skill at all.[57]

The life of a daily paid laborer must have been physically hard. Pathological examination of some skeletal remains from the Herodian period has identified some examples of these workmen. For example the remains from the Qumran cemetery, dating prior to A.D. 68, contained the skeleton of a man who died at age 22, who had done hard physical labor with his hands from an early age, and who had walked barefoot all his life. Another example was the skeleton of a man who had died at age 65 who had been a "laborer." This laborer had carried heavy weights on his shoulder much of his life so that his bone structure was permanently deformed. Such cases along with the skeleton of the man also found at Qumran who had received a serious head wound which required several years to heal (at Qumran?) lead one to wonder if many did not join the Qumran community as much out of health or economic reasons as out of religious conviction.[58]

Most scholars agree that the average daily wage of the laborer was one denarius or one drachma based mainly on the parable in Mt. 20:2,9,13.[59] There are other indications that one denarius was the average wage,[60] but one must emphasize that this was only average, especially in light of the work done on prices and wages in ancient Palestine by D. Sperber. Sperber's work indicates a great variation in wages in the period he considered (second century B.C. to second century A.D.). The variation seems to have been based mainly on the type of task done rather than on inflation or recession. In general the economy of Palestine was stable, except for times of famine, until the third century A.D.[61] Hillel the scholar received, for example, one-half denarius as a woodcutter (b. Yoma 35b). Another source (Sheb 8:4) tells of a man offering a laborer 1/24 denarius to gather vegetables for him. There are also higher wages per day than one denarius (e.g. t. BM 6:15, b. BB 87a) especially during harvest time.

There is good evidence that the workers were defrauded at every opportunity. Some landowners tried to pay less than the seasonal value of the labor. The Tosephta and Babylonian Talmud give a legal ruling against an owner trying to pay harvesters the normal rate of one denarius when the labor is really at that particular time, worth a Selah (=four denarii; t. BM 6:15; b BB 87a). In addition to trying to underpay the worker, many employers tried to withhold the wages of the laborer until a later time or pay him in a different way than was agreed before hand.[62] Or if a laborer were pressed into a corveé before his job was finished the employer often refused to pay him for his labor up to that point.[63] Still other landowners would try to force a man's son to glean behind him during harvest, hoping evidently to gain a little more produce for the same daily wage.[64]

What was the standard of living for the day laborer? It depended on the skill needed for his job. The scribe or calligrapher, for example earned on average two denarii per day.[65] But most daily workers were unskilled and so earned on average only one denarius. Except in famine years one denarius could buy one seah of unground wheat (about 13 liters or three gallons).[66] How far that amount of grain would go depended on how large the man's family was and how much grain per person was normally consumed.

Ben-David[67] argued that each family contained six to nine people. He based his conclusions on Talmudic references to family tombs (usually with eight niches) and to village sizes (e.g. a village of fifty people with six houses). He also notes that the Fellahin of Palestine normally had families of six to nine people in the early twentieth century. We shall, therefore calculate our standard of living for the day laborer based on a six-member family.

How much grain per person was consumed?

Ben-David and Jeremias have based their estimate on the Mishnaic precept (Peah 8:7) that a poor man must be given no less than a *dupondion's* worth of bread (Ben-David says this equals 400 grams) and on the statement of Athenaeus (III.20) that a *Choinix* of wheat (about the same as a *dupondion's* worth) was the daily ration in Greece. P. Brunt based his estimate on "the evidence we have for soldiers' and slaves' rations." The figures of Brunt and Ben-David/Jeremias are similar.[68] The chart given in Table A gives the calculations of daily rations and the cost for a family of six, according to the Mishnah. Ben-David recognizes that the daily ration of bread was only the staple of the diet in Palestine which must have been supplemented by other sources such as fruits and olive oil.

TABLE A: COST OF CALORIC INTAKE

Ben-David/Jeremias

Ration Daily	400	gr.
Cost Daily	1/12 denarius	
Cost for six Persons for One Year	182 denarii	

Based then, on Ben-David/Jeremias' estimate of the daily average bread intake for a poor person, a day laborer with a family of six people would have to have earned 182 denarii per year to buy the daily bread. The other caloric needs either required extra income, a garden patch, gleaning the fields, or gathering wild fruits and vegetables (see below under Small Freeholders).

The next question is how much money could a laborer earn per year? Obviously not 365 denarii since we must allow for Sabbaths and festivals. Also we must reckon bad weather and illness into the amount of the wage. Ben-David has further argued, based on a report of the Land Office of Israel, that the average worker in Palestine can work only around 200 days.[69] Ben-David noted that 200 denarii seem to be the borderline for poverty in our period. When a man has below 200 denarii (a year?) he may collect the provisions offered to the poor: Gleanings, Forgotten Sheaf, and Poorman's Tithe (Peah 8:8). Thus he concludes that 200 denarii were the "subsistence minimum" in Palestine in the Mishnaic period.[70] Since the value of the denarius remained stable until the third century A. D. this would also be the subsistence minimum in the Herodian time.

Obviously, the 200 denarii would barely supply the minimum ration of daily bread for a family of six, leaving very little for clothing and supplemental caloric needs. Thus most day laborers must have supplemented their income and food intake beyond the 200 denarii per year. In the first place small garden patches may have been available. The Tosephta indicates (t. BM 8:2) that day laborers were often forced to work for themselves by night and hire themselves out by day. The rabbinic sources also inform us that most workers ate some of the produce they harvested (BM 7:2-5, t. BM 8:8).

We are probably forced to conclude nevertheless that the average day laborer lived in poverty and stood on the edge of hunger. His caloric intake was probably like the poorer third world countries of today (below 2000 calories).[71] As the Tosephta (t. BM 8:2) indicates workers often had to deprive themselves of food in order to give it to their children.

Life could be a daily struggle for the laborer just to subsist. As long as he was healthy, as long as he could find work, and as long as there were no famines, he survived. But take away any of those conditions and life must have been desperate for him. We would expect that these people along with the beggars were the first to succumb to famine.

Slaves

Ben-David lists three ways a Jew could become a slave in Herodian Palestine:

1) As punishment for thievery (Ex. 22:1f, *cf. A* 16.1f and Mt. 18:25).

2) As the last recourse for a peasant who because of bad harvest or debt had lost his land (Lev. 25:39f, Gitt 4:9).

3) As payment to a debtor (Isa. 50.1, Amos 2:6, 8:6, Neh. 5:4).

Probably only non-Jews became slaves as prisoners of war before A.D. 70. The Hebrew slave was a debt bondsman who theoretically would be liberated in the sabbatical year. The non-Hebrew slave or "Canaanite" slave was a slave for life.[72]

The extent of slavery in Palestine during the second temple period is debated. Krauss and Jeremias argued that agricultural slavery played a small role, and M. Stern has suggested that this was true especially for Hebrew slaves.[73] Grant, Klausner, Kreissig, Ben-David, and Urbach give more weight to the role of slaves during the Herodian period.[74] Klausner is probably correct in noting that slaves in Palestine were never as numerous as the slave classes of Greece and Rome.[75] Jeremias, however, is also correct to reject Krauss' contention (based on b. Arak 29a and parallels) that Hebrew slaves were not allowed in the second temple period since the Jubilee which would have liberated them was no longer in force. The Talmudic passages are not only "pure speculation" but *A* 16.1f and Mt. 18:25 indicate that Hebrews were being enslaved.[76]

One can find numerous references to slaves in general in Josephus and the New Testament but the references to agricultural slavery are less frequent. Josephus narrates the story of Simon, Herod's slave, who upon Herod's death put on a diadem and wandered around Perea burning and looting (*B* 2.57-59, *A* 17.273-277). Since he came from Perea one might assume he worked on Herod's estate in that region (see chapter 2) as an agricultural worker. Josephus also narrates the proclamation of emancipation given to slaves by Simon Bar-Giora during the Jewish war (*B* 4.508). Since Simon Bar-Giora was in the hill country of Judea (εἰς τὴν ὀρεινήν) when he made this proclamation and began soon after to take control of the villages (*B* 4.509) we can assume that these slaves who later joined his army (*B* 4.510) were dissatisfied agricultural workers.

The New Testament also alludes to slaves as agricultural workers. In Mt. 13:27 slaves report to the owner of an estate that weeds are growing in the fields. In Mk. 12:2 the landlord sends his slave to collect rent from the tenants. In Lk. 15:22 the landowner – who also employs day laborers, Lk. 15:19 – orders his slave to kill the fatted calf. Finally Lk. 17:7 refers to a slave who works in his master's field.

Thus agricultural slavery does seem to have been practiced, but as to what extent we have no clear evidence. Grant's[77] assertion that the great holdings of the wealthy were worked largely by slaves finds no strong support. We discover as much evidence if not more that tenants and day laborers worked these estates. One is led to conclude that although agricultural slavery was certainly employed in Palestine in the Herodian period (*pace* Krauss and Jeremias) it never reached the extent of the great *latifundia* of Italy and Sicily which were worked mainly by slaves.

The life of a Hebrew slave was, according to the Tannaitic sources, not as grim as for slaves elsewhere in the Greco-Roman world. One could own only his labor not his body. In addition he was not a slave in perpetuity, but a bondman. Yet, as Klausner warns, many of the rabbinic rules on slavery should be viewed as later than the Herodian period and thus not truly representative of conditions during that time. Klausner believed even Hebrew slaves endured a harsh life.[78] But we should on comparison with the plight of agricultural workers in general in the Greco-Roman world, assign to the slave conditions somewhat better than the day laborer. The slave was property and thus had to be properly cared for so that the landowner did not lose his investment.[79]

Were the Hebrew slaves set free in the Sabbatical year? We have no hard evidence that they were. Kreissig maintains that in light of the decreasingly observed Sabbatical year we should conclude that slaves were not released.[80] Since Simon Bar Giora freed all slaves during the Jewish war and these appear immediately to have joined the rebellion we might conclude that they were desperate people who were not to be released after six years. Yet these slaves may have been Canaanite instead of Hebrew slaves. We are forced to argue mostly from silence, but also from clear evidence that the Sabbatical year legislation was being more and more ignored and that probably Hebrew slaves were no longer released.

In contrast to the Hebrew slave, the non-Jewish slave was a slave in perpetuity and was owned as property. Stern believes that many slaves of this sort were prisoners of war (or their decendants) from the earlier Hasmonean campaigns and from Herod's Nabataean conquests.[81] But foreign slaves were probably bought on the open market as well. Jeremias believed that importing slaves, especially from Tyre, was an important economic feature in Herodian Jerusalem.[82] The rabbinic sources indicate that occasionally foreign slaves were circumcised and given the ritual baptism to become at least legally proselytes.[83] Though these slaves were theoretically different from Hebrew slaves, their lot may not have been significantly harsher. In the first place slaves in the Greco-Roman world did not always have a grim existence,[84] and second, there are examples in the Talmud of non-Hebrew slaves who were loved by their masters.[85]

Landed Peasants: Small Freeholders

We must also include small freeholders (בעלי הבית) , t. Peah 2:2) in this chapter on agricultural workers in the service of the elite. They served the elite mainly in that they paid taxes, probably the brunt of the taxes for Palestine under Herod and his successors.[86] Much of these revenues went to build cities such as Caesarea Maritima, Sebaste, and Phasaelis and palaces such as Masada and Herodium which did not benefit the peasants at all. Moreover, Herod made large gifts to neighboring Greek cities and political notables from his revenues.[87] The concept of taxation for the good of the nation as a whole is not an ancient one. Moreover, the average Jewish peasant supported an aristocratic priesthood (at least partially) through tithes. Thus the taxation-tithing relationship that existed between the elites and the peasants was just as much an "asymmetrical power relationship"[88] as that between landlord and tenant. Indeed there is very little difference between having to pay a percentage of one's crop in rent and having to pay a percentage in taxes.

The main difference between small freeholders and tenants was that the former was totally responsible for his harvest. As Finley has observed: "The freer the ancient peasant, in the political sense, the more precarious his position."[89] A tenant might receive assistance during a drought from a beneficent (or shrewd) landlord and perhaps a relaxation of rent payments. But the freeholder would pile up debts against his land during those times and probably wind up losing his land. "Debt was always the nightmare of the small freehold peasant...."[90]

Although there were probably some small freeholders who lived fairly comfortably, the peasant in the Greco-Roman world in general "was always at the margin of safety."[91] This condition was due to small farmplots, natural and man-made disasters, and taxation. Ben-David[92] (whose figures match those of Oakman) has calculated that a family of six to nine people would have needed seven hectares or around 16.8 acres (half of which would lie fallow each year) to subsist comfortably and pay taxes or rents. A study by Hopkins found that a family of 3.25 persons would require in Italy 7 to 8 iugera of land (=around 4.5 acres) to meet the minimum food requirements or 8 acres for a family of six people. But K. D. White argues that this acreage is too low and that a peasant holding such a small amount of land would have to hire out as a day laborer to supplement his income. Dar maintains that a peasant owning 5 to 6 acres could live comfortably meeting all his subsistence needs. Applebaum, however, has challenged Dar's estimate on the amount of land needed to feed a family especially since Dar failed to consider that virtually all ancients let half their land lie fallow every year to replenish it. Brunt's estimate as to how many iugera could feed one person in Italy results in the sum of 10.8 acres for six people.[93] Thus the suggestions of necessary acreage are as follows:

1.	Ben David	16.8 acres
2.	Oakman	16.5 acres
3.	Hopkins	8
4.	Dar	6
5.	Brunt	10.8
6.	White	(more than 8 acres)
7.	Applebaum	(more than 6 acres)

We must remember that half of this land would lie fallow every year, a standard practice in the ancient world.

Perhaps the simplest way to figure the crop yield for Palestine is to take the standard measurement of a Kor's space (i.e., the area which one Kor's measurement or 5 bushels seed could sow). A Kor's space was approximately 5.8 acres[94] and would yield normally five fold.[95] Thus one Kor's space (leaving half fallow) could feed a family of six, after taxes (see below) for about 110 days at the rate of 400 grams of wheat per day. A farm consisting of three Kor's spaces then (17.4 acres) could feed the family the basic grain staple for a year.

This calculation is purely hypothetical, however. In the first place most peasants, as Dar has shown, probably cultivated vines, olives, and grains. Perhaps the vines and olives yielded more equivalent calories than grains. Second peasants probably sowed grains in between the rows of olive trees thus utilizing every available inch of space.[95a] Thus our calculation above can only serve as a rough guideline in determining a peasant's income.

In spite of the fact that a family might need more land, evidence exists that many family plots were no larger than 6 acres. First of all we might point to the references to 7 iugera (=4.5 acres) farms as standard size in republican Rome.[96] Second are the references in the Latin sources to allotments made in the first century which according to literary allusions and other considerations must have been around 10 iugera (6.3 acres).[97] Many families in Palestine must have subsisted on similar plots. The reference in Eusebius (HE 3.20) to the two grandchildren of Jude the brother of Jesus indicates they possessed between them 39 plethra of land, which would be probably around 6 acres per family.[98] In addition, we have the archaeological evidence from Galilee that most farm plots in antiquity were 4 acres (though they vary commonly from 1 to 15 acres).[99] Finally there are the conclusions from Dar's survey of Hirbet Buraq in Samaria which is one and one half miles southeast of Qawarat Bene Hassan (see above Chapter 2). The team discovered an area of small marked-off plots around an ancient village ruin, evidently owned by small freeholders, since there was no evidence of a tenurial system here such as was found at Qawarat Bene-Hassan. The area totaled 445 acres which was divided by 70 households for an average of 6 acres per family.[100] Naturally some might have owned more or less land, but a combination (as existed at Qawarat Bene-Hassan for tenant farmers) of a vineyard, an olive orchard, and a field for grain probably in most cases was close to the average. Similar results have been found also in Judea.[100a] Thus, although we cannot say that most freeholders in Herodian Palestine only owned 6 acres of land (since our evidence is very incomplete), still some of them did. On the other hand we can find no evidence that indicates most peasants owned more land than this.

Obviously, then, if our figures are representative of at least a significant minority of peasant freeholders throughout Palestine, the many freeholders had to supplement their income. According to our calculations above this plot size (approximately equal to one Kor's space) would only feed a family of six people for one-third year. As E. Wolf[101] has observed there are only two strategies available for the peasant to adjust his income: He can increase production or he can curtail consumption. To increase production the farmer could put more labor into his plot of ground. But the returns are negligible in this strategy. A better strategy is to supplement the income of one's plot. Supplementing could be done in various ways. First, one could hire himself out as a day laborer doing seasonal agricultural work or working as a craftsman. Surely many small freeholders had to seek such labor. But one could not always be certain of finding agricultural work and at the very time work was available one needed to be free to labor on his own plot. Supplementing one's income as a craftsman or working for a craftsman was a better strategy. A second way to supplement one's income was to gather wild plants. J. M. Frayne has made a strong case that the typical Italian freeholder gathered wild roots, berries, nuts and other plants to increase his caloric intake. In addition one could hunt wild game and fish. The availability of wild game in Herodian Palestine may be questionable, but those living near the Sea of Galilee could certainly fish. In addition, the peasant, as Frayne has suggested, may have kept sheep on common village land and probably other small domesticated animals such as chickens.[102]

Thus the peasant had other options to maintain his subsistence in addition to his small plot. Still it is quite likely that the second strategy was also often employed. In other words, the average peasant probably consumed not much more food per day than the day laborer. We must also bear in mind that many small freeholders possessed only about an acre or even less as the rabbinic and papyrological sources show.[103] These peasants had to rely even more on supplementing their income. Peasants with such a small plot may more properly be called "hirelings" (see above under Day Laborers) than small freeholders.

We should not forget that there was actually a third alternative for poor peasants which Wolf did not mention. When one could not maintain one's subsistence on the small plot one could become a bandit. Precisely such a recourse was chosen by the inhabitants of Trachonitis when their harvest failed (A 16. 271f). Banditry was also the result predicted by the Jewish delegation to Petronius, the proconsul of Syria when Caligula attempted to erect a statue of himself in the temple. The Jews announced that the peasants had gone on strike, refusing to sow the land. The delegates feared that, since the tribute could not therefore be paid to Rome, there would be a "harvest of banditry" (A 18.274). That is to say, the peasants would have to turn to banditry in light of there being no harvest and, therefore, not only nothing to eat, but nothing with which to pay one's taxes. Under economic duress, then, banditry was the obvious last resort.[104]

What was the standard of living for the average peasant then? Did they go hungry much of the time or at least consume a poor diet? Oakman[104a] asserts that they must have been chronically undernourished, that is, below the 2500 calories per day for adults that he believes are required. A study by C. Clark and M. Haswell, however, should invite caution in drawing conclusions about such an issue without proper information. They note that many people living in third world countries consume fewer calories than that per day and show no signs of malnutrition.[104b] Oakman seems to assume that peasants must have been undernourished since they could not possibly have had much of their harvest left over after paying taxes or rents. We need, however, more positive evidence in order to decide the question.

The best evidence available so far is the pathological examination of skeletal remains from the Herodian period. The problem with this evidence, however, is that first of all, we cannot usually tell what sort of peasant (tenant, day laborers, slaves, or freeholder) the remains represent. Some of the remains are clearly from the tombs of the well-to-do. Second, the remains, coming from different localities may represent purely geographical distinctions. That is to say, perhaps peasants in one village were poorer because the soil or rainfall in their area were poorer. Finally, it may be difficult to know if the skeletal remains represent usual conditions or a disaster (e.g. famine).

One way to measure the abundance of nutrition in antiquity is by examining the ratio of children to adults in tombs (the mortality rate for children) and the pathology of the remains of children, since they usually succumb to malnourishment the easiest. R. Hachlili and P. Smith[104c] have given a chart of various sites in Palestine ranging from the first century B.C. to fourth century A.D. They also offer a comparison with the average figures from Greece in antiquity. Of the four tombs from Palestine studied (two from Jerusalem, one from Meiron, and one from Jericho) three reported a lower child mortality rate than in Greece.[104d] The tomb complex with the highest rate of child mortality, Meiron, whose child mortality rate was similar to that in Greece, does show evidence of poor nutrition in the skeletal remains. P. Smith, E. Bornemann, and J. Zias suggest (based on an analysis of the children's skulls found at Meiron) that most suffered from an iron and protein deficiency and that this deficiency was due to either "socio-economic conditions" or disease.[104e] Further, it seems clear that people of well-to-do means have been buried in the tombs in Jerusalem (Givat Ha-mivtar and Mt. Scopus) and Jericho.[104f] There were three cases of children buried in the Givat Ha-mivtar tombs who evidently starved to death, but the starvation seems to be connected to the siege during the first Jewish rebellion.[104g]

98

It appears from the evidence above that those of poorer socio-economic conditions could be malnourished. But our problem is that we have so far only one published example of a pathological examination of the skeletal remains of village residents. We need a broader base of evidence than this to be conclusive. At least, however, this evidence is suggestive that the average peasant suffered chronic malnutrition in Palestine in the Roman period. The same conditions would seem to have been existent in ancient Greece and probably then throughout the Mediterranean world.

The second problem the freeholder had in maintaining his subsistence, in addition to too small a farm plot, was natural and man-made disaster. We know from Josephus and other sources, for example, that Palestine suffered at least two severe famines (from drought) in the Herodian period, one in 29 B.C. and one during the reign of Claudius (A.D. 41-54).[105] In addition the farmer was always subject to locusts and other pests[106] and destructive winds.[107] During such natural disasters the price of grain could multiply sixteen times.[108] P. A. Brunt and de Ste. Croix have demonstrated from the records of famines around Antioch of Syria in the fourth century A.D. that the small cultivators suffered as much as the urban poor. While the large landowners would hoard the grain to drive prices even higher, the peasants were forced to flee into the city to plead for food.[109]

We also know from Josephus and from archaeological evidence that Palestine endured seven earthquakes during this period of time. Josephus says the earthquake of 31 B.C. killed 10,000 people "and many cattle" (A 15.121, B 1.370). Later quakes in 24 B.C., A.D. 19, 30, 33, 37 and 48 ranged from slight to moderate in intensity. More recent examples of earthquakes in Palestine have demonstrated not only the potential for loss of life in this region but the economic devastation as well.[110]

In addition to the disasters which arose from nature the peasant had to contend with threats to his subsistence which stemmed from war, the bivouacking of troops and bandits. The wars during this period (the disturbances when Herod died, A 17. 271-298, and the great rebellion) must have also taken a heavy toll on the peasantry. Not only might one be killed from either side in the conflict (A 17.282)[111] but one's crops would often be confiscated to feed troops who were quartering in the neighborhood (A

14.411f, 414) or one might have to pay tribute to an invading army (*A* 14.271-276). W. Stenger describes, from Tacitus (*Agricola* 19) the harsh demands Roman soldiers could make on the peasantry who if they did not have enough grain for a troop of infantry, were often compelled to buy more elsewhere.[112]

Complaints about peasants having to supply bivouacking soldiers in peacetime are found in Palestine from the Hefzibah inscription in 200 B.C. to the second century A.D. As we saw in the last chapter, Ptolemy the Strategos complained because soldiers quartering near Scythopolis were evicting peasants from their homes and confiscating their grain.[113] Virtually the same complaint appears in another inscription from Trachonitis as well as in Talmud Jerushalmi over four hundred years later. Villagers had to billet soldiers who often forcibly threw them out of their houses.[114]

Finally, the peasant always had to worry about bandits who not only "robbed the rich" but plundered the poor (*B* 2.253; 2.581f; 4.135; 406; *A* 14.159; 17. 285; 20. 185; 256; *V* 77f; Peah 2:7f; LK 10:30).[115]

The third burden which made life hard for the small freeholder was taxation. The main direct tax for Palestine as indeed for all the Roman empire was the *tributum soli* or tax on the soil.[116] The rate of this tax had been under the Seleucids one third of the grain and one half of the fruit crop (1 Macc 10:30) though this extremely high rate may have been levied as a punishment for the Maccabean revolt. Taylor maintains that the common rate under the Seleucids was one tenth.[117]

The Hasmoneans may have relaxed the rate of this tax or cancelled it altogether since we hear nothing about it during this period. But Julius Caesar reinstated this tax collecting one fourth of the produce which was sown (*A* 14.203). Josephus adds in his description of this tax the puzzling words "in the second year." Does this phrase mean that the Jews paid the tax every two years in which case they would pay 12 1/2% of their crops to Ceasar?[118] Or should one emend the text and substitute "month" for "year" in which case the Jews had to pay 25% every year in the second month of the year?[119] Or should one interpret the phrase as referring to the year after the sabbatical fallow-year so that the Jews paid 25% every year except the Sabbatical year?[120] The lowest figure would be more in line not only with the Seleucid monarchy, as Taylor pointed out, but with the Ptolemaic. S. L. Wallace[121] observes that the average land tax in Egypt was one artaba of wheat per arura (.68 acre). Since an arura could produce from five to ten artaba,[122] taking the mean as eight artaba, the tax was approximately 12 1/2%.

We have no explicit record that Herod had such a tax, but as Schalit[123] has argued, since the Seleucids and Caesar employed this tax, it is highly likely that Herod inherited it from them. Taxes on the soil were common in antiquity[124] and Herod certainly needed (and collected) large sums of revenue.[125] We would assume that Herod's successors Archelaus, Antipas, and Philip as well as later Agrippa I and Agrippa II maintained his tax system.

After A.D. 6 Judea, Idumea and Samaria came under direct Roman rule, and after A.D. 44 Galilee and Perea likewise. Certainly the Romans would have maintained the *tributum soli*. They customarily levied a tax in money on the *usus fructus* or use of the land plus a percentage of the harvest paid in kind.[126] The amount of the tax varied according to the quality of the soil and the amount of rainfall. Tax assessors would examine the land, estimate its produce and determine the tax.[127] After the harvest the yearly tax would be paid in kind to the village grainery and the peasant's name would be recorded.[128] We would presume that the rate of 10 to 12% was still average. If Egypt can serve as our model of tax collection in Palestine, the large and medium-sized estates of the family and friends of Herod paid either no land tax or a reduced rate.[129] Josephus's own experience would indicate that this practice prevailed in Palestine. His land, which he received after the war from Vespasian, was at first taxed but under Domitian the tax was remitted, "a mark of the highest honour to the privileged individual" (*V* 429).[130]

The second direct tax which the Palestinian cultivator paid was the *tributum capitis* or poll-tax. This tax was levied in Syria on every male between the ages of 14 and 65 years old and on females between 12 and 65. In Egypt both men and women paid the tax from the age of 14 to 60.[131] In order to compile a list for this tax a periodic census was required. In Egypt, for example, a householder had to provide the tax authorities with a list of the residents of his house every fourteen years.

The rate of the tax varied from locality to locality. Even within Egypt the amount varied markedly from nome to nome. Payments could range from 40 drachmas per person for peasants and 20 for the privileged classes to 16 drachmas for peasants and 12 for privileged classes. There seems usually to have been a distinction especially in lower Egypt, in the amount paid, with the upper classes receiving a tax break. Some officials of Egypt did not pay the tax at all.[132]

For the well-to-do the *tributum capitis* was a tax on movable property according to Stenger. Thus the tax would vary from person to person. The citizens of Syria and Cilicia paid a yearly tax of 1% of their worth (i.e., movable property such as animals, ships, slaves). Everyone had to give an accurate account of his possessions under threat of heavy fines.[133]

For the poor, however, who possessed little or nothing of any value in movable property the tax was on his (σῶμα), his body. Just as all land was considered as belonging ultimately to the Roman empire, and thus, subject to taxation as a kind of rent, so also did one's body belong to Rome. As Stenger writes, "The poll-tax is none other than the payment for (one's body)."[134] Therefore, the poor had to give an accurate account of the members of their household.[135]

The average amount paid for the *tributum capitis* by the poor agriculturalist in Palestine may have been one denarius per person per year. At least this is commonly assumed by scholars, based on the story of Mk. 12:13-17.[136] Since Josephus explicitly states that the poll-tax after the Jewish war was two denarii (*B* 7.218), and this may be viewed as a punishment, the figure of one denarius per year is a reasonable conjecture. As Schalit[137] observed, it is unlikely that this tax was as high in Palestine as in Egypt, where generally speaking the peasantry endured harsher conditions. In addition, the Egyptian drachma had less value than the Tyrian or Attic.[138]

We do not know if the Jews paid a poll-tax to Herod and his successors, though Schalit speculates they did since he believes Herod would have imitated the Egyptian tax system.[139] Certainly Idumea, Judea, and

Samaria paid this tax to Rome, however, after A.D. 6 (*A* 17.355, 18. 2f) and presumably Galilee and Perea after A.D. 44.

The details of the tax system under Agrippa I are also unknown. He was declared king in A.D. 37 by Emperor Caligula and given the tetrarchies of Philip and Lysanias, followed by that of Antipas in A.D. 39 or 40 and finally by Judea and Samaria in A.D. 41. Nevertheless, since Agrippa received yearly income not unlike Herod the Great's (1200 talents)[140] we must assume that he left the system intact.

There were also indirect taxes levied on Palestine but one cannot determine the effect these would have had on the peasantry. These were tolls, crown taxes, salt taxes, trade taxes, and for residents of Jerusalem a house tax, and perhaps also a corve.[141] Except for the last tax, it is unlikely that these taxes affected peasant life very much.

The taxes were collected by the (τελῶναι), probably small tax farmers, who could bid on the collection for a toparchy, a city or perhaps even a village. The geographical tax divisions as well as the system of using small tax farmers probably derived from the Ptolemaic organization of Palestine in the third century B.C.[142]

But the freeholding peasant had other obligations which could also be termed a tax. These were the religious dues or tithes. F. C. Grant[143] in his 1926 monograph on the economic life of first century Palestine, listed no less than twelve different religious obligations which a landowner in Palestine would have had. Scholars have since that time, however, concluded that most of these tithes and offerings were not paid by the ordinary Jewish peasant.[144]

We must be careful how we understand the expression (עַם הָאָרֶץ) "people of the land" which was actually in the rabbinic era a religious term (and not a sociological one) distinguishing everyone else from the (הברים) "associates."[145] Still, we would have to agree that the am ha-aretz included most peasants in Palestine in the first century (though some wealthy people were also am ha-aretz). The am ha-aretz probably seldom paid tithes. The rabbinic sources agree that they paid the "wave offerings" which were an unspecified percentage of the crops given to the priests to be eaten in ritual purity (Num. 18:5, 18:11f, 21-32, Dt. 18:4, Lev. 22:10-14, Maaseroth 1:1).[146]

The rabbinical schools specified the amount as 1/40 or 1/30 of the harvest (1/50 if one were not generous and 1/60 if one were especially stingy) but the old Testament left the amount unspecified.[147] Beyond this offering it is difficult to say what the peasants contributed in religious taxes. Surely some gave at least the "first tithe" to the priests and Levites when it was possible and perhaps this tithe was even sometimes ruthlessly exacted as *A* 20.206f indicates. Many Galileans during the Jewish war paid the first tithe (*V* 63). But obviously some did not pay the tithe since the Mishnah speaks about the suspicion (דמאי) which always accompanied the produce of the am ha-aretz.

Thus the peasant paid around 12% of his harvest in land taxes, one denarius for everyone in his household over 14 years old, and a wave offering perhaps equalling 1/40 of the harvest. We would estimate, then, that the freeholder paid out at least around 15% of his harvest each year. Since his land yielded usually five-fold, then he had to keep back also 20% of the crop for seed for next year. Thus the peasant fed his family on 65% of his yearly harvest. If he paid the first tithe, then he had only 55% left. This latter figure would be equal to the share the tenant received who sharecropped for two-thirds of the harvest (see above).[148]

Thus the cultivator paid a land tax, poll tax and at least a small religious tax. Were the taxes considered burdensome? Scholars have debated this issue. A. H. M. Jones, F. C. Grant and A. Momigliano[149] argued that taxes under Herod the Great at any rate were not a burden but actually probably stimulated the economy. Jeremias, Baron, Applebaum, and Schalit[150] on the other hand have concluded that the taxes under both the Herodians and Rome were a heavy burden. We do know of at least two references to the taxes being burdensome. The first is expressed by the Jewish delegation to Augustus after the death of Herod. The second is a statement in Tacitus that the people of Syria and Judea appealed to Tiberius for relief from taxes in A. D. 17.[151] We should take this evidence seriously and not attempt to dismiss the charges against Herod as merely trumped-up or to compare his supposed annual income of 1000 talents with that of Agrippa I fifty years later (1200 talents) to conclude that Herod was more lenient.[152] Conditions may have changed during that time that would account for the increased revenue and, moreover, these figures are only based on estimates anyway.[153] That taxation was generally a burden in the empire is clear enough. Stern cites the rebellion in Gaul in 21 B.C. as an example of dissatisfaction over taxes. Egypt also suffered under heavy taxation. Under Nero taxation generally in the empire was considered too heavy by the peasants.[154]

The last question we should ask is whether conditions were much the same in all of Palestine or whether the economic situation was better in some regions. Freyne[155] has argued that the standard of living in Galilee was better than in Judea. The inhabitants of Galilee suffered less than those in Judea at the hands of foreign overlords. Further, the Galileans were obviously not starving peasants because during the war they are able to provision themselves. These rebels are also able to pay their tithes without any complaints (V 63). Goodman[156] has also affirmed that socio-economic conditions were much worse in Judea than in Galilee.

Freyne's evidence for better economic conditions in Galilee needs scrutinizing, however. Freyne says the Galilean peasants were not starving, but we would deny that the Judean peasants were starving under normal conditions. Further, Josephus does not say that the peasants in Galilee paid their tithes without complaint (though he mentions none), nor does he even say that most peasants in Galilee paid the tithes at all.

On the other hand we have evidence that at least on occasion poor Galileans came to Judea to find employment. Archaeologists have found a tomb complex in Bethphage near Jerusalem which probably dates from the first century A.D. From the inscriptions on the chamber walls it seems probable that all of these families were engaged in the production of stone coffins and that they all came from Galilee. Evidently they had come to Judea to seek better economic conditions.[157]

Further, Jesus' teaching concerning care for the poor which is attested in all the Synoptic Gospels (Mt. 5:3 = Lk. 6:20; Mt. 11:5 = Lk. 7:22; Mt. 25:35f; Mk. 10:21; Lk. 4:18; 12:33) would indicate that economic hardship was also a reality in Galilee. The hatred of the Galileans for both of the urban centers in Galilee, Tiberias and Sepphoris (V 375), indicates that the aristocratic citizens of these cities exploited the peasants economically and thus argues as well that conditions in Galilee could be economically harsh.

Such evidence, though inconclusive, does at least urge us to be hesitant in accepting Freyne's and Goodman's hypothesis. We would suggest that socio-economic conditions were similar in most parts of Palestine in the Herodian period. Freyne suggests that peasant freeholders were able usually to earn their subsistence in Galilee but with no or little margin for error. We see no reason why that judgment cannot also apply to Judea.

Conclusions

We attempted to demonstrate in Chapters 1 and 2 that three notions concerning land tenure existed in Palestine in the Herodian period, that which saw the land as sacred and as belonging ultimately to God, that which saw the land as belonging to the monarch by right of conquest, and the entrepreneurial or latifundial concept which was spreading throughout the Greco-Roman world from the first century B.C. on. From these latter two ideas of land tenure developed an economic trend which gobbled up small freeholdings from the Ptolemaic era in Palestine on, leaving many peasants to become tenants and day laborers. Those who were able to cling to their land were burdened under taxation.

Life was undoubtedly hard for the peasants in Palestine. According to the rabbinic evidence, which describes conditions similar to other parts of the eastern Roman Empire, tenants paid rents up to fifty per cent, sometimes more. Day laborers may have had the harshest existence of all. If the slaves liberated by Simone bar Giora were agricultural slaves then this class of peasant worker must have felt exploited also. The small freeholder had to contend with the elements, with farm plots that were on average too small, and with high taxes.

END NOTES

1.   See de Ste. Croix, p. 214; White, 1970, pp 388f, 404, 407f, 410-412; Heichelheim, 1938, pp 147f; and Columella 1.7; *Legal Digest* XIX. 11.19.3. White says (p. 411) in Egypt fixed payment in kind was the norm; in Africa share-cropping prevailed; and in Italy it was money rents primarily.

2.   De Ste. Croix, p. 213; Heichelheim, 1938, p. 148.

3.   P. Garnsey "Non-Slave Labour in the Roman World" in Garnsey, ed. *Non-Slave Labour in the Greco-Roman World* (Cambridge: Cambridge Philological Society, 1980) p. 39.

4.   De Ste. Croix, p. 216; *cf.* Garnsey, 1980, p. 39.

5.   *Ibid.* pp. 215f. Texts and translations of most of these inscriptions can be found in T. Frank, *Economic Survey*, vol. 4, pp. 96-98, 656-661.

6.   See Rostovtzeff, 1922, pp. 76, 80, 85f and e.g., P.S.I. 502, P.Z. 35 (both from early third century B.C.); and Tcherikover and Fuks, Papyri 37 and 43 from the third and second century B.C. respectively. *Cf* also the sermons of John Chrysostom against abuse of peasants (fourth century A.D. Antioch), quoted in Jones, 1940, p. 296.

7. E. R. Wolf, *Peasants* (Englewood Cliffs, New Jersey: Prentice Hall, 1966) pp. 9f.

8.   De Ste. Croix, p. 217; White, 1970, p. 348.

9.   See White, 1970, p. 411; A. H. M. Jones, *The Later Roman Empire* (Oxford: Blackwell, 1964) vol. 2, p. 794; Garnsey 1980, p. 35.

10.   White, 1970, p. 348 and Cato 4,5, 144, 147; Barro I.17.3.

11.   Hengel, 1961, p. 34; Horseley and Hanson, 1985, pp. 48-87.

12   Applebaum, 1976, p. 66; and 1977, p. 367; Schalit, 1969, pp. 168f.

13.   Klausner, 1975, p. 189.

14.   Applebaum, 1976, p. 659; and 1977, p. 367.

15.   *Ibid.*

16.   Oakman, 1986, pp. 72-77; Goodman, 1987, pp. 56f; idem., 1982, pp. 417-427, But *cf.* Sherwin-White, 1963, p. 141, Finley, 1973, pp. 96-98.

16a.   Finley 1973, pp. 96-98.

16b.   Goodman, 1987, p. 57.

17.   See the example of encroachment in Egypt in A.D. 155 described by a woman's (a widow?) petition for justice in Husselman, 1971, number 526.

18.   Dt. 19:14, 27:17. Is the same action being alluded to in CD 5:20 (*cf.* recension B given by Vermes, 1975, p. 105 and by R. H. Charles, *Pseudepigrapha* (Oxford: Clarendon, 1913) on 9:13 and 9:49)? See A. Cronbach, "The Social Ideals of the Apocrypha and the Pseudepigrapha" *HUCA* 18(1944) 119-156.

19.   See the examples given in MacMullen, 1974, pp. 6-11.

20.   Test. Judah 21:7, Test. Dan 5:7, Test. Moses 7:6, Mk 12:40, 2Enoch 10:5, Jubilees 9:14. See Cronbach, 1944.

21.   Rostovtzeff, 1922, pp. 77f.

22.   P.S.I. 544 and Tscherikover, 1937, pp. 46f. See, however Rostovtzeff, 1941, vol 3, 1403, for another interpretation of this papyrus and indeed of the organization of the plantation at Beth Anath. Rostovtzeff suggests that Melas may have simply been a tax collector and not the bailiff.

23.   Derrett, 1963, 11-41, esp. p. 20. See P. Oxyr. 729 (A.D. 137) and P.B.M. 163 (A.D. 88). The latter papyrus, notes Derrett, says the lessor must pay the tenant two thirds of the produce.

24.   See Dalman, 1964; Stager, 1985.

25.   A large tenant or entrepreneur, (קבל) , rented large amounts as a business venture not as a subsistence income. See Krauss, 1966, vol. 2, p. 108. See *e.g.* Demai 6:1, 6:8, t.Demai 7:1. The large entrepreneur is to be distinguished from the (חוכר) or small entrepreneur, described below.

26.   Ben-David, 1974, p. 60; Krauss, 1966, pp. 109f. See for (חוכר) : Bikk 1:2, 2:3, t.Demai 3:5, t.Peah 3:1, t.Demai 6:2. For (שוכר) see: t.Demai 6:2, 7:6, BM 9:10. See for (אריס): Bikk 1:2, 2:3, BM 5:8, 9:10, t.Peah 3:1, t.Terumot 1:7. For the Hebrew texts of the Mishnah see Ch. Albeck, *The Six Orders of the Mishnah* (Jerusalem: Bialeck, 1952-1958). For the text of the Tosephta see S. Zuckermandel, *Tosephta* (Jerusalem: Gilead, 1963). There was also a tenant called (שטלא) which Ben-David, 1974, p. 659 claimed was only a Babylonian tenant. Applebaum, 1976, p. 659 claimed on the other hand that t.BM 9:17-18 suggests the (שטלא) existed earlier than Amoraic times.

27.   See Heichelheim, 1938, p. 147f; Krauss, 1966, II, p. 109 makes the (אריס) equal to the (γεωργός) and *colonus*. The term for tenants in Mk 12:1-8 is (γεωργός). The day laborer was also called (μισθωτός) in Greek. See BAG.

28.   Peah 5:5, t.BM 9:11, Pesikta de R. Kahana VI.8, j.Demai 6.1.

29.   Peah 5:5. *Cf.* a papyrus contract from Karanis in Egypt (A.D. 46) which demanded two thirds of the crop for the landlord. See E. M. Husselman, ed. *Papyri from Karanis* (London: Clowes, 1971) number 560.

30.   Translation by Neusner, *Tosephta*, vol. 4. A similar contract can be found in b. BM 105a.

31.   Krauss, 1966, pp. 109f.

32.   Wacholder, 1973, p. 177. For a French translation see *DJD* II, 24E.

33.   *DJD* II, 24E. See also a translation and discussion in Bardtke, 1962, pp. 88f of 24B; and the discussion in M. R. Lehman "Murabaat and Nahal Hever Documents" *Revue de Qumran* 13(1963) 72-81. *Cf.* 24D which demanded 6 Kors and 3 Seahs and 24B which stipulated 4 Kors and 8 Seahs.

34.   Ben-David, 1974, p. 63.

35.   *Ibid. Cf.* the tenancy contract from Egypt dating A.D. 121 which demanded 378 drachmas "clear of every risk" for 10 1/2 arurae (7 acres) of grass. See A. S. Hunt and C. C. Edgar, *Select Papyri* I, 42 (LCL).

36.   Y. Yadin, "Expedition D--The Cave of the Letters" *IEJ* 12(1962) 227-257. See documents 42 and 43.

37.   Ben-David, 1974, p. 63.

38.   DJD II, 24 A-E.

39.   See Cicero, *Verres* 3.13, 5.53 and Applebaum, 1976, pp. 559f; Heichelheim, 1938, p. 148.

40.   Translation in Neusner, *Tosephta*.

41.   See e.g., the Papyri in V. A. Tcherikover and A. Fuks, *Corpus Papyrorum Judaicarum* (Cambridge: Harvard University, 1957). Papyrus 37 (222B.C.) is a petition complaining about Demetrios (evidently the overseer) made by three tenant farmers. They were seeking it appears, a reduction in rent due to poor growing conditions. Papyrus 43 complains about the village scribe who has arbitrarily raised the amount of annual rent to be paid. *Cf.* the unjust raising of taxes by the village scribe in J. Hengstl, *Griechische Papyri aus Ägypten* (Munich: Heimeran, 1978) number 29.

42.   Cited by Krauss, 1966, p. 110.

43.   Translation in Danby.

44   See Ben-David, 1974, p.64; W. Bauer, 1915, p. 39.

45.   Klausner, 1975, p. 192.

46.   See Dar, 1986 p. 101 for an example of the latter.

47.   Mt. 9:37f=Lk 10:2; Mt. 10:10=Lk. 10:7; Mt. 20:1,2,8; Lk. 13:;27; James 5:4; Lk. 15:17,19,21; Mk. 1:20; Jn. 10:12. *Cf* Tcherikover and Fuks, papyrus 36 (γεωργοὶ μισθῶι) "peasants for pay."

48.   See L. Schottroff, "Human Solidarity and the Goodness of God. The Parable of the Workers in the Vineyard" in W. Schottroff and W. Stegemann, ed. *God of the Lowly*, trans. M. J. O'Connell (Maryknoll, N.Y.: Orbis, 1984) p. 132.

49.   Klausner, 1975, p. 190.

50.   Krauss indicated these workers were called (פועלא), (רוזגר), or (עמלא) in Aramaic (1966, p. 102. Ben-David, 1974, p. 65, maintains that the (פעל) was the equivalent of the Latin *operarius* and the Greek (μισθός). In the New Testament, however, the word(ἐργατής) would seem to be a literal translation of (פועל).

51.   Kreissig, 1969, p. 249.

52.   BM 9:11, t.Sheb 5:21, t.BM 8:1, 10:2, t.Shab 17:27. See Ben-David, 1974, p. 66; Krauss, 1966, p. 102. Ben-David lists two other types of laborers, but these appear in later non-Tannaitic sources and so are probably a later development (pp. 66f).

53.   T. Maaserot 2:13,15; t.BM 7:5,6; BM 7:5, 7:4, 7:7, 6:1, 8:8; Maaseroth 5:5; Peah 5:5. See Krauss, 1966, vol. 2, p. 105. Mekhilta de Ishmael 8 also gives a good summary of the laborer's tasks. See Goodman, 1983, p. 39.

54.   Krauss, 1966, vol. 2, p. 105. See t.BM 7:4; BM 6:1.

55.   Qoheleth Rabba 1.1. Ben-David, 1974, p. 294 suggests they hired donkeys to carry the stone.

56.   Krauss, 1966, vol. 2, p. 106. See BM 7:8,9; BK 8:1; Shebuoth 8:1; t.Shab 17:26; t.BM 8:1; t.BK 11:8.

57.   Krauss, 1966, vol. 2, p. 106; Kreissig, 1969, p. 236.

58.   See S. H. Steckoll "Excavation Report in the Qumran Cemetery" *Revue de Qumran* 6(1968) 323-336. Compare the skeletal remains from the cemetery at Giv'at ha-Mivtar just north of Jerusalm. These remains are evidently from a group of skilled craftsmen (e.g., Simon the temple builder, Johonathan the plotter) who possessed enough means to purchase a hewn tomb and ossuaries. See J. Naveh "The Ossuary Inscriptions from Giv'at ha-Mivtar" *IEJ* 20(1970) 33-37 and N. Haas "Anthropological Observations on the Skeletal Remains from Giv'at ha-Mivtar" *IEJ* 20(1970) 38-59.

59.　See Krauss, 1966, vol.2, p. 105; Ben-David, 1974, p. 66; Grant, 1926, p. 68; Jeremias, 1969, p. 111; Klausner, 1975, p. 191; Kreissig, 1969, p. 236. But see Applebaum, 1977, p. 374 who maintains that the wage of one denarius per day is post-seventy since Hillel (b. Yoma 35b) only earned one half that amount (latter first century B.C.)

60.　Tobit 5:14; j.Sheb 8:4; b.BB 87a; b.AZ 62a. See Ben-David, 1974, p. 66, and D. Sperber "Costs of Living in Roman Palestine I" *Journal of the Economic and Social History of the Orient* 8(1965) pp. 248-271.

61.　See Sperber, 1965, pp. 250f. For the third century see Sperber, "Costs of Living in Roman Palestine IV" *Journal of the Economic and Social History of the Orient* 13(1970) 1-15. Also see Ben-David, 1974, pp. 291f who notes that a stable silver coinage from Tyre kept prices stable in the Herodian period.

62.　See BM 7:1-7, 9:11f, 10:5; t.BM 10:2f,6; James 5:4; Tobit 4:14.

63.　T.BM 7:8. On (אנגריא) see Jastrow. The corve was a real possibility in the Herodian period as Mt 5:41 attests.

64.　Peah 5:6. See Kriessig, 1969, p. 249.

65.　See Sperber, 1965, p. 251, and Eccles. Rab. 2.17.

66.　See Jeremias, 1969, p. 122; Krauss, 1966, vol. 2, p. 378; and Peah 8:7; Erubin 8:2; Kelim 17:11; b.Taan. 19b; b.BB 86b. *Cf. A* 14.28 for the famine price. See also Sperber, 1965, p. 251.

67.　Ben-David, 1974, p. 45. See BB 6:8; b.BB 100b for the tomb sizes and Erub 5:6; j.Erub 5.5; b.Erub 59a, 60a for village sizes. *Cf.* Yeivin, 1971, p. XV and Dar, 1986, p. 85 who note that most peasant houses could hold five or six people.

68.　See Ben-David, 1974, p. 136; Jeremias, 1969, pp. 122f; and Brunt, 1971a, p. 126 and 1971b, p. 35. Brunt cites no text in support of his figure of daily food rations. For information about food rations in ancient Rome and on Roman farms see G. Hamel, *Poverty and Charity in Roman Palestine, First Three Centuries.* (University of California, Santa Cruz: Ph.D., 1983), pp. 122-126. Hamel maintains that the dupondion's ration of bread was around 550 grams (see p. 120).

69.　Ben-David, 1974, p. 293. The report was based on 1961 findings. He also cites a 1930 study of the Fellahin which resulted in about the same number. The Roman agriculturalist Columella (II.12.7-9) wrote that one could only work 250 days in a year in Italy. If we subtract from this figure a year of sabbaths we arrive at Ben-David's figure. See White, 1970, p. 345.

70.　Ben-David, 1974, pp. 292f. He also notes that 200 denarii are the divorce money given to a wife (Keth 1:2, *DJD* II, number 115).

71.   Wolf, 1966, p. 5.

72.   Ben-David, 1974, p.70. *Cf* Jeremias, 1969, pp. 312f on this same topic. Jeremias notes the practice of selling young girls (under age 12) into slavery. See Mekhilta on Ex 21:7, 21:20. For a contrary view on Jews as prisoners of war before A.D. 70 see R. Hachlili, "The Goliath Family in Jericho; Funerary Inscriptions from a First Century A.D. Jewish Monumental Tomb" *BASOR* 235 (1979) 31-66. Hachlili thinks Theodotus, mentioned in an ossuary inscription, might have been enslaved as a war captive.

73.   Krauss, 1966, vol. 2, p. 83; Jeremias, 1969, pp. 110f; Stern, 1976, pp. 628f.

74.   Grant, 1926, p. 66f; Klausner, 1975, pp. 193f, and idem. *Jesus of Nazareth*, trans. H. Danby (London: Allen and Unwin, 1925) p. 181; Kreissig, 1969, pp. 237-39; Ben-David, 1974, p. 69, E. E. Urbach "Laws Regarding Slavery as a Source for Social History of the Period of the Second Temple, the Mishnah and Talmud" *Papers of the Institute of Jewish Studies, University College London* 1(1964) 1-94,

75.   Klausner, 1975, p. 193.

76.   Jeremias, 1969, p. 110; Krauss, 1966, vol. 2, p. 83. See also b. Kidd 69a, b. Gitt 65a.

77.   Grant, 1926, p. 65.

78.   Klausner, 1975, p. 193.

79.   See White, 1970, p. 348 and L. Schottroff in W. Schottroff and W. Stegemann, 1984, p. 133.

80.   Kreissig, 1969, p. 237.

81.   Stern, 1976, p. 627.

82.   Jeremias, 1969, p. 36; see Sifra Lev 25:2; Sifre Dt 26 on 3:23; and Krauss, 1966, vol. 2, p. 362.

83.   See b. Shabb 137b; b.Yeb 48b; Mekhilta Ex 20:10; and Stern, 1976, p. 628; Jeremias, 1969, p. 111.

84.   See S. S. Bartchy, *First-Century Slavery and 1 Corinthians 7:21* (Missoula, Mont: Scholars Press, 1973) pp. 67-86.

85.   Klausner, 1975, p. 195. E.g., R. Gamaliel (A.D. 80-120) mourned the death of his slave Tabi, Ber 2:7.

86.   In general see de Ste. Croix, 1981, p. 13; Rostovtzeff, 1957, p. 661, n. 24; Lenski, 1966, p. 267. For Palestine see: A. H. M. Jones, *The Herods of Judea* (Oxford: Clarendon, 1938) p. 89; Applebaum, 1977, p. 373, "It is axiomatic that in ancient civilizations the main weight of contributions fell upon the cultivator." Also M. Stern, "The Reign of Herod" in M. Avi-Yonah, ed *The Herodian Period* (London: Allen, 1975) p. 97.

87.   See *A* 15.5, 132; 16. 146, 147, 149 for Herod's lavish gifts, Jeremias, 1969, p. 124. For Herod's building activities see *A* 15.274, 295, 318, 16. 136-141, 143.

88.   Wolf, 1969, p.9 uses this phrase to characterize peasant society.

89.   Finley, 1973, p. 108.

90.   De Ste. Croix, 1981, p. 214.

91.   Finley, 1973, p. 107.

92.   Ben-David, 1974, p. 44; Oakman, 1986, p. 64.

93.   White, 1970, p. 336f, cites the study by K. Hopkins. See also Applebaum, in Dar, 1985, p. 262. Also for fallowing in antiquity see White, 1970, p.47. See also Brunt, 1971b, p.35.

94.   Ben-David, 1974, p. 135, says a Kor's space is 25,520m^2 which is, I believe, an error. It should read 23,520m^2 which equals roughly 5.8 acres.

95.   So agree Heichelheim, 1938, p. 128f, Ben-David, 1974, p. 136; Oakman, 1986, p. 63. This figure is not only based on the average of figures found for Italy and Egypt but also the statement in the Talmud (b.Keth 112a) "A Seah of a field in Judea yielded five Seahs." Columella the Roman agriculturalist (*Ag* 2.9.1.: 3.3.4) indicated a four fold yield in Italy. Brunt, 1971b, p. 35, maintains, however, that this figure would only be valid for the large estates. The small peasant must have cultivated his plot more intensively. Hence Brunt argues for a five fold harvest as normal. Naturally the fertile lands of Egypt could yield more. See Johnson, 1959, p. 59. Hamel, 1983, p. 259, accepts the five fold yield for Palestine, but on a different basis.

95a.   Dar, 1986, p. 74.

96.   White, 1970, pp. 345f; Brunt, 1971b, p.35. References to two iugera farms in the monarchy period of Rome are probably to pastoralists' subsidiary land. As S. M. Frayne maintained (1979, p. 57), "a 2 iugera farm could not have fed a family."

97.   P. Brunt, *Italian Manpower* (Oxford: Clarendon, 1971) pp. 314f. One area comprised around 204,000 iugera granted to 20,000 families; thus 10 iugera a piece. See also Cicero, *Att*. 1.16.1; and Finley, 1973, pp. 105f. But Frayne, 1979, p.91 refers to an allotment made in 192 B.C. at Vibo Valentia of 15 iugera (= 10 acres) plots (Livy 34.53.1; Strabo 6.1.5).

98. See Oakman, 1986, p. 61, who notes that a plethron could equal twice this amount. Applebaum, 1977, p. 365, accepts the figure of 6 acres, as does Goodman, 1983, p. 35. See LSJM for the meaning of plethron.

99. Golomb and Kedar, 1971, p. 138.

100. Dar, 1986, pp. 60-76. See also p. 46 of Dar for farm plots of a similar size at Hirbet Karqush.

100a. S. Gibson "Jerusalem (North-east), Archaeological Survey" *IEJ* 32(1982) 156f, describes a farm from the Second Temple period consisting of six acres.

101. Wolf, 1966, p. 15.

102. Frayne, 1979, pp. 57-66. Harper, 1928, p. 151, has shown that many villages in Syria owned public land. See also Jones, 1940, pp. 272, 286.

103. See BB 1:6, b.Ketub 112a; *DJD* II, p. 145; and Dar, 1986 p. 75. *Cf.* also Frayne, 1979, p. 91, who reports that in 1961, 33% of the farms in Italy were only 2 1/2 acres or less.

104. See also Baron, I, p. 281 and t. Men 13:22.

104a. Oakman, 1986, pp. 58f says that people need 794 grams of wheat per day (=2500 calories). *Cf.* Wolf, 1966, p. 4.

104b. C. Clark and M. Haswell, *The Economics of Subsistence Agriculture* (New York: St. Martins, 1966) pp. 1-22.

104c. Hachlili and Smith "The Genealogy of the Goliath Family" *BASOR* 235 (1979) 67-71.

104d. The average percentage of children from 0-19 years old in Greek tombs was 49%. For the Jericho tomb (first century A.D.) the percentage was 39%. For Meiron in Galilee (first to fourth century) A.D.) the percentage was 47%. The two tombs in Jerusalem (from first century A.D.) averaged 43%. See Hachlili and Smith, 1979, p. 69.

104e. P. Smith, Bornemann, and Zias "The Skeletal Remains" in E. Meyers, J. F. Strange, and C. L. Meyers *Excavations at Ancient Meiron, Upper Galilee, Israel 1971-72, 1974-75, 1977* (Cambridge, Mass: ASOR, 1981) p. 118.

104f. P. Smith and J. Zias "Skeletal Remains from A Late Hellenistic French Hill Tomb" *IEJ* 30(1980) 115; Hachlili and Smith, 1979, p. 69.

104g. See N. Haas "Anthropological Observations on the Skeletal Remains from Giv'at Ha-Mivtar" *IEJ* 20(1970) 38-59. Other people buried in these graves died in the first century A.D. from an arrow wound, from a blow by a mace, by accidental death by fire, by execution by fire, and by crucifixion.

105.   See Acts 11:28; b.Yeb 15b; *A* 15.299f, 310; and *A* 20. 51, 101; *B* 320. See also Jeremias, 1969, pp. 141-143; and Schlatter, 1897, pp. 80f. The Talmud also refers to famines which happened after A. D. 70 (b.Taan 19b-20a, 24b; b. Ketub 97) which show that famine must have been a regular occurence in Palestine in antiquity. See Freyne, 1980, p. 178. For bad harvests see *A* 15.365. For famine in general in the Roman Empire see R. MacMullen, *Enemies of the Roman Order* (Cambridge: Harvard, 1966) pp. 249-254.

106.   Jeremias, 1969, p. 144. See b.Hull 65a.

107   *A* 14.28.

108.   Jeremias, 1969, p. 123 and *A* 14.28.

109.   Brunt, 1971b, pp. 703-706; de Ste. Croix, 1981, pp.219-221. De Ste Croix summarizes the account of Ambrose, *De offic. ministr.* III. 45-51, in which the city prefect of Rome ca. A.D. 376 argues that they must not allow the free peasants to die of starvation otherwise they will have to "buy cultivators," i.e., slaves, to replace them. It is in the context of such a mentality that one should understand Herod the Great's actions during the famine of 29 B.C. when he distributed grain to the starving (*A* 15.305-310).

110.   See D. H. Amiran, "A Revised Earthquake Catalogue of Palestine" *IEJ* 1(1950-51) 223-246; *Ibid.* "A Revised Earthquake Catalogue of Palestine II" *IEJ* 2(1952) 48-65. The earthquake of 1837 was of comparable intensity to the one of 31 B.C. The casualty figures from this quake are somewhat less than those given by Josephus. In this quake 2158 people died, seventeen villages around Tiberias were destroyed, many others in Galilee and Samaria were severely damaged. See U. Ben-Horin, "Official report on the Earthquake of 1837" *IEJ* 2(1952) 63-65.

111.   *Cf.* not only the behavior of the revolutionaries in A.D. 66 (*B* 2.264f) but also that of Bar Cochba who persecuted Christian Jews (Justin I *Apol.* 31.6) and threatened peasants in general if they did not obey him (see Fitzmyer and Harrington, 1978, documents 53,54, 59). Also see 1Macc. 2:44-46.

112.   Stenger, *Gebt Dem Kaiser was des Kaisers ist* (Frankfurt: Athenäum, 1988) pp. 35-37.

113.   See the text in Landau, 1966, p. 59.

114.   See S. Lieberman, "Eretz Israel in the Palestinian Talmud" in M. Davis, *Israel: Its Role in Civilization*, p. 86; and *Corpus Inscriptionum Graecarum*, III, 4551. Harper, 1928, p. 158 has other examples of military requisitions on villages in Syria.

115. The picture of bandits in E. J. Hobsbawm, *Primitive Rebels* (New York: Horton, 1965) followed by Horsley and Hanson, 1985, is at times too romanticized. Peasants suffered from bandits as well as did the wealthy. A more balanced picture is in B. Isaac, "Bandits in Judea and Arabia" *Harvard Studies in Classical Philology* 88(1984) 172-203.

116. Schalit, 1969, p. 278; G. H. Stevenson, "The Imperial Administration" *CAH*, vol. 10, p. 196.

117. Taylor, 1979, p. 102.

118. See Heichelheim, 1938, p. 235; Applebaum, 1977, p. 373; Stern, "The Province of Judah" *Compendia* I.1, p. 331.

119. As Reinach did. See R. Marcus in LCL.

120. Grant, 1926, p. 90.

121. Wallace, *Taxation in Egypt* (Princeton: Princeton University. 1938) pp. 11-19.

122. A. C. Johnson, "Roman Egypt to the Reign of Diocletian" in *Economic Survey*, ed. T. Frank, 1936, vol 2, p. 59; *cf.* pp. 52-56.

123. Schalit, 1969, p. 278.

124. Taylor, 1979, p. 101.

125. See *A* 17.318-321, *B* 2.97f and Schalit, 1969, p. 263f. Herod's annual revenues were probably over 1000 talents or 10 million attic drachmas.

126. See Schalit, 1969, p. 280; Stenger, 1988, p. 23.

127. See Stenger, 1988, pp. 22f; and Ulpian, *Digest* L.15.4.

128. See Tcherikover and Fuks, 1957, papyri 33, 44, 45, 471, 472, 492. *Cf. V* 71. Also see R. S. Bagnall and M. Lewis, *Columbia Papyri VII* (Missoula, Montana: Scholars Press, 1979) number 136, 137.

129. Wallace, 1938, p. 12.

130. Translation by Thackeray in LCL.

131. See Heichelheim, 1938, p. 237; Stenger, 1988, p. 24; SVM I, p. 403; and Ulpian, *Digest* L.15.3.

132. Wallace, 1938, pp. 120-127; Schalit, 1969, p. 272; Stenger, 1988, p.24. Egyptian drachmas were worth less than Attic or Tyrian (Wallace, p. 492, n. 26).

133. Stenger, 1988, p. 24; SVM I, p. 402; and Apprian *Syr.* 50/253.

134.   Stenger, 1988, p. 25.

135.   See examples of these accounts in Husselman, 1971, number 537, and Hengstle, 1978, number 25, 26.

136.   Stern in Avi-Yonah, 1975, p. 167; Applebaum, 1977, p. 373; Schalit, 1969, p. 272.

137.   Schalit, 1969, p. 272.

138.   Wallace, 1938, pp. 492, n. 26.

139.   Schalit, 1969, p. 272.

140.   See *A* 19. 352. I assume with SVM II, p. 63 that Josephus valuates the tax revenue in Attic drachmas (10000= 1 talent).

141.   See Schalit, 1969, pp. 282-291; Taylor, 1979, pp. 87-102; Stenger, 1988, pp. 26-37; A. Mittwoch, "Tribute and Land Tax in Seleucid Judea" *Biblica* 36(1955) 352-361. I leave aside here the unresolvable question of whether Palestine also paid tribute to Rome under Herod's rule. See Applebaum, 1976, p. 661; SVM I, p. 317.

142.   See H. C. Youtie, "Publicans and Sinners" *Zeitschrift für Papyrologie und Epigraphik* 1(1967) 1-20; F. Herrenbrück, "Wer waren die 'Zöllner'" *ZNW* 72(1981) pp. 178-194; Schalit, "Domestic Politics and Political Institutions" in Schalit, ed. *The Hellenistic Age* (London: Allen, 1976) p. 266; Stern in Avi-Yonah, 1975, p. 93; J. R. Donahue, "Tax Collectors and Sinners" *CBQ* 33(1971) 39-61; O. Michel, "TELONES" in TDNT.

143.   Grant, 1926, pp. 93-97; *cf.* Moore, 1954 (originally published 1927) vol. 2, pp. 70-72.

144.   J. Neusner, "The Fellowship (חבורה) in the Second Jewish Commonwealth," *HTR* 53(1960) 125-142; S. Mandell, "Who Paid the Temple Tax When the Jews were Under Roman Rule?" *HTR* 77(1984) 223-232; G. Dalman, *Arbeit und Sitte in Palästina* (Hildesheim: Olms, 1964, 1933) III, p. 177; S. Safrai, "Religion in Everyday Life," *Compendia* II, p. 819; Kreissig, 1969, pp. 243f.

145.   See Oppenheimer, 1977, p. 21.

146.   See t.Sotah 13:13; b.Sotah 48a; and Safrai, 1976, p. 819.

147.   Terumot 4:3; t. Terumot 5:3 and Safrai, *ibid*; SVM II, pp. 262f.

148.   Subtract 20% for seed then subtract 33% from that sum and it leaves around 54% of the harvest.

149.   Jones, 1938, p. 87; Grant, 1926, p. 46; Momigliano "Herod of Judea" in *CAH*, vol. 10, p. 331.

150.   Baron, 1952, vol. I, p. 263; Applebaum, 1977, p. 374; Schalit, 1969, p. 280; Jeremias, 1969, pp. 124f.

151.   See *A* 17.307f=*B* 2.85 (*cf. A* 17.204f) for the criticism of Herod's heavy taxes. See Tacitus, *Annales*, 2.42 on the appeal to lighten taxes made by Judea and Syria in A.D. 17. Also see SVM I, p. 373 and Heichelheim, 1938, p. 234.

152.   As does Jones, 1938, p. 87.

153.   See M. Stern "Herod and the Herodian Dynasty" *Compendia* I.1, p. 260, who suggests the apparent increase under Agrippa I may have been due to additional agricultural areas in his kingdom, and Jeremias, 1969, p. 91, for the same argument. See also the comments of L. H. Feldman on *A* 19.352 (LCL). Some MSS indicate that the figure of 12 million drachmas was the amount "at the highest" of Agrippa's income. That is, his income fluctuated-- as one would naturally expect--but was usually lower than this.

154.   See Stern in *Compendia*, 1976, p. 332; and *WHJP*, vol. 7, p. 168; and Tacitus, *Annales* 15.45; Philo, *de Spec. leg.* 3.159-163; Rostovtzeff, 1957, p. 572, n. 6; Wallace, 1938, p. 340.

155.   Freyne, 1980, pp. 193f, 208.

156.   Goodman, 1983, p. 133 and 1987, pp. 419-421.

157.   See P. G. Orfali, "Un Hypogée Juif a Bethphagé" *Revue Biblique* 32 (1923) 253-260; E. L. Sukenik, "The Cave at Bethphage and its Inscriptions" *Tarbiz* 7(1935) 102-109; J. H. Heinemann, "The Status of the Labourer in Jewish Law and Society in the Tannaitic Period" *HUCA* 25(1954) 263-325, esp. p. 273.

CHAPTER 4

THE PEASANT HOUSEHOLD AND VILLAGE

In this chapter we investigate the social units within Palestinian peasantry and what effect the changing value of land and its corresponding socio-economic changes had on family and village life. Did the growth of large estates mean changes in family structure? What relationship did the village have to the city and how was this relationship affected by the concept of the land?

The smallest peasant social unit was the nuclear family which we have maintained, following Ben-David, consisted on average of six people. The nuclear family occupied normally one room of a courtyard house. The next unit was the courtyard neighborhood – nearly all houses in this period were attached to a courtyard – which may or may not have been an extended family. The next social unit consisted of those whose courtyards opened onto a common alley. Finally, the largest social unit was the village. We shall discuss each of these units below. To this picture of interconnected relational units within the peasant village however, we must also add the description of the individual isolated farm. Peasant dwellings, then, were of two types: individual farmhouses and village houses.[1]

The Isolated Farm

The archaeological period known as Iron II witnessed the emergence of the isolated farm. The survey team led by Dar found over sixty such farms in an area of around 20 square miles. All date from Iron II and continued to the Hellenistic period. They had farmyards measuring on average 20 x 20 meters surrounded by walls, and containing crude buildings. The farmyards were connected to plots of land that averaged around 30 acres. None of the farms demonstrated any evidence of wealth; all seemed to be about on the same economic level. Dar suggests that these farms represent ancestral land which was worked by the extended family, since each farmyard contained buildings that could house 20-30 persons.[2] Applebaum calls these extended-family groups the (בית אבות) which are referred to often in the Old Testament.[3] These farms are not only typical of Samaria. Hundreds of them have been found also in the Negev, and Z. Yeivin and G. Edelstein have excavated one in Judea.[4]

Why did these farms cease to exist in the Hellenistic period? Yeivin and Edelstein have suggested that they came into existence in the Iron II period because of improved security. But with the Hellenistic age and its disturbances such isolated farms were no longer viable.[5] It does seem feasible that the farm that they excavated in Judea (Tirat Yehuda), which lay near Modin and was destroyed in the second century B.C. by fire, met its end due to the Maccabean revolt.[6] Thus the conquest of Palestine under the Hellenistic kings and the later Maccabean revolt made such ancestral farms unsafe. We see then a shift in living arrangements in the Hellenistic period.

The major change was that peasants in the main ceased living on these isolated farms and seem to have lived almost exclusively in villages. Those peasants that did live in the isolated farmyards were now probably workers on large estates. One such estate was found by Dar's excavation team at Qasr e Lejah (2.4 miles southeast of Um Rihan). This estate was built in the third or second century B.C. according to the pottery indications and existed until the first century A.D. The buildings are in a farmyard 26.5 x

36 meters (see Plan 2) and consist of the owner's residence (1), the manager's house (5), rooms for the tenants, slaves or day-laborers who worked the estate (9,10), an olive press (11), storage and workshop rooms (12-15). Dar concludes that this is the estate of a "medium or well-to-do landowner."[7]

What is important about this estate is that the living quarters of the workers, if Dar is correct, have been found. Housing workers on the the estate itself was typical of Roman society as the examples from Pompeii indicate,[8] but few examples of this phenomenon have yet been found in Palestine. Obviously, however, large estates removed from a village must have had workers living nearby, perhaps in dwellings so poorly made that nothing is left of them today.[9]

The Hellenistic age, then, changed the living pattern for many Israelites who had formerly lived in extended-family arrangements on isolated farms, working communally to earn their subsistence. In the place of living with the beth-av or extended-family, most peasants now living away from villages lived on large estates as laborers perhaps only with the nuclear family.

Plan 2

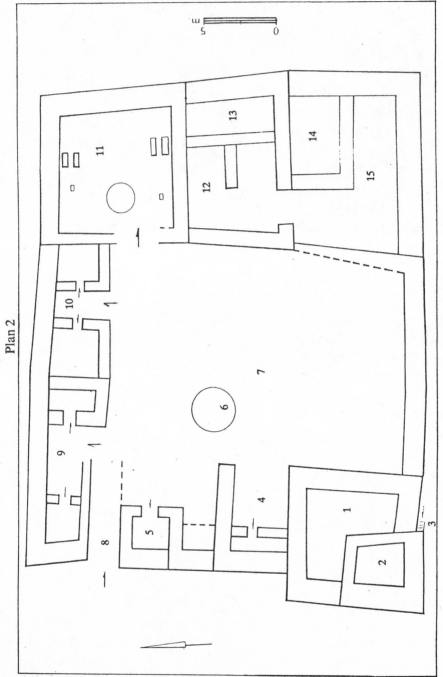

Dar. Figure 12. Um-Rihan – The Farm of Qasr e-Lijah.

The House

Peasants of course never completely left the villages empty, from Iron II to the Hellenistic age, to live on isolated farms.[10] Those who remained in villages probably experienced less trauma by the coming of the Hellenistic age since they were not necessarily forced to abandon their lands and houses. Yet they too experienced changes. Many of those who had before been small freeholders, living in villages and farming nearby lands now lost possession of their land and became tenants on their own ancestral plots. If Dar is correct, this is precisely what happened at Qawarat Bene-Hassan (see Chapter 2).[11] Other villages probably continued much as usual except that their taxes may have been higher under the Ptolemies than the Persians.

The village house, however, underwent a change from the typical four-room house of the Israelite period in which the extended family lived to the "courtyard house" of the Hellenistic and Roman periods.[12] The four-room house consisted of "a back room the width of the building, with three long rooms stemming from it.[13] The house style which succeeded the four-room house usually had an internal courtyard and probably developed due to foreign influence.[14]

Z. Yeivin, examining excavation and survey reports for Galilee and the Golan, places the courtyard houses into four categories:

1) Houses whose entrance is directly on the street and whose courtyard is usually in the back of the house.

2) Houses with exterior courts that open out into the street. (See t.BB 3:1).

3) Houses whose courtyards are inside the house. The rooms then are built around the court. This style is parallel to the buildings at Ostia, Pompeii and Herculaneum.

4) Non-symmetric buildings compiled from two squares or more.[15]

Dar suggests that the courtyard houses were built separate from each other at first but as the villages grew and space became scarce the buildings began to touch each other.[16] This suggestion might also help explain the appearance of insulae in several Palestinian villages and cities.

The development of insulae in Palestine, evidently due both to lack of space and to foreign influence is a peculiarly Roman period phenomenon. An insula consists of a "group of buildings standing together in a block or square isolated by streets on four sides."[17] Insulae have been discovered in Rome, Pompeii, Ostia and other Italian sites.[18] They appear in Palestine in the Roman period at sites such as Samaria,[19] Capernaum,[20] Meiron,[21] Arbel,[22] and in the Negev.[23] The excavations at Dura-Europos in Syria have also shown that insulae were common dwelling types in that region in the Roman period.[24]

A good example of an insula in Herodian Palestine is that at Capernaum described by V. Corbo. This insula, one of five identified by Corbo at Capernaum, was made famous by his claim that the house of Peter is preserved in it (see Plan 3). For our purpose, however, it is more important that the insula demonstrates the typical dwellings of poor villagers of the first century A.D. The houses (actually single rooms) were constructed of crude basalt stones which were undressed and without mortar. The walls are so weak that Corbo surmises they could never have held the kind of stone slab roof which the rabbinic sources often allude to (see below). Each nuclear family lived in a single room and shared the courtyard with other unrelated families or perhaps with other kinsmen. The largest house-room, the venerated room, measured 7 x 6.5 meters. It is important for our purposes to note that this simple architectural style was typical for all the insulae in first century Capernaum. All the other residences indicate similar economic and social conditions.[25]

Most houses were in Herodian Palestine made of stone, either the white limestone so abundant in much of Palestine or the black basalt found north of the Sea of Galilee. Sometimes the stone was hewn from a quarry and dressed, but poorer peasants constructed houses of Wadi stones. The exception was in the Sharon Plain where houses were built of mud brick.[26] A. C. Bouquet also suggested that very poor peasants even in the Hill Country must have had huts built entirely of perishable material (branches, straw, and mud) so that no trace of them has survived.[27] In extreme cases people may have had no houses at all, but merely wandered from place to place.[28]

Plan 3

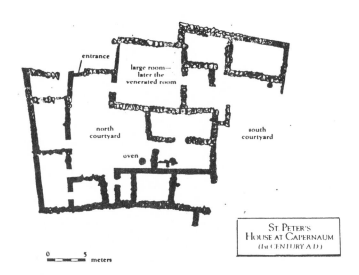

Plan in Strange and Shanks *BAR* VIII:6 (1982) 32, adapted from Corbo, Cafarnao I (1975).

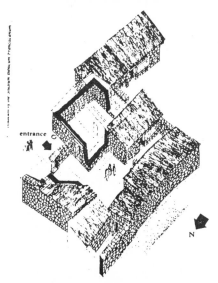

Reconstruction in Strange and Shanks *BAR* VIII:6 (1982) 31, from the Museum of the Studium Biblicum Franciscanum.

The roofs were often made of limestone slabs.[29] Nevertheless, the poorer houses such as those at Capernaum must have had roofs of tree branches covered with mud and straw (cf. Mk. 2:4) since the walls would have been too weak to support stone slabs.[30] The roofs were flat and very often, when the walls were made strong enough to support it, an upper room stood on the roof, either the full size of the room below or only as a partial second story.[31] Yeivin's survey found several ancient two-story houses still in use by Arabs.[32]

The individual house (בית) (actually only one room)[33] which held the nuclear family is the smallest social unit in the peasant village. Yeivin estimates that on average the typical peasant village room could house five people,[34] thus it is doubtful that anyone more than the nuclear family lived in a house under usual circumstances. Families with more than five people might be compelled to build a smaller upper room. Nevertheless, some evidence does exist that the extended families occasionally lived together in the same room (BB 9:8-10. Mk. 1:29).[35] Dar notes that the Mishnah describes a small house as 4:48 x 3.36 meters and a large house as 4.48 x 5.6 meters (BB 6:4). Dar found these same measurements commonly in his survey of Samaria and thus we would conclude they represent house sizes generally in Palestine in the Herodian period.[36]

Courtyard

The next social unit was the (חצר) or courtyard, the place of both domestic work and leisure; the place to find privacy from the street and to meet and talk to neighbors and kinsmen. Krauss described the courtyard as follows:

> The courtyard was occasionally dug up and planted with decorative trees and fruit trees or vines. One walked around at leisure, ate, did the wash, and took care of all business necessary in life in the courtyard.[37]

Most courtyards appear to have been walled around with a wall at least (BB 1:4) of two meters.[38] Courtyards, as the insula in Meiron,[39] may have had flagstone pavements, or simply packed dirt.

Some courtyards must have been quite small. The Mishnah (BB 1:6) rules the smallest one can make a courtyard by dividing it up was 4 cubits or 2 meters (2 X 2 meters).[40] But most courtyards were much larger. The Tosephta (t.Erub 7:9) refers to a courtyard of 10 cubits or 5 meters (i.e., 5 X 5 meters?) as "small." The courtyard in Meiron I was 7.5 X 5 meters.[41] A typical courtyard described by Dar for the village of Hirbet Buraq in Samaria was of similar size. The courtyard from the Insula I in Capernaum (see Plan 3) appears from the plan to have been around 10 X 7 meters.

Most courtyards appear, according to the Mishnah, to have had at least two houses. Arakin 9:6 describes a walled city as needing at least three courtyards with two houses in each.[42] Dar found in Samaria that most courtyards contained five or six living quarters or houses, but notes that the later courtyard houses (Roman-Byzantine) tended to become smaller.[43]

In addition to the living quarters which were attached to the courtyard one could find other buildings used for crafts, for animals (cattle barns), straw sheds, wood sheds, and storage houses for wine and oil.[44] Krauss maintained that the animals would have been kept in buildings behind the living quarters, or when there were two courtyards, in the second courtyard.[45] But L. E. Stager suggests that livestock was usually brought into a room close to the living quarters at night, either under the living quarters or in a room next to it. The practice was maintained in the Israelite period and is still done by Arabs today. He suggests that side rooms found at Capernaum with "fenestrated walls" actually contained not windows but storage niches for animals.[46] If Stager is correct then animals often slept on the ground floor or adjoining room to the living quarters.

Also in the courtyard were ovens, cisterns, millstones, gardens, ponds, and cellars. Krauss suggests that many of these things were the common property of all sharing the courtyard.[47]

The relationship of the social unit centered around the courtyard is a matter of some debate. Some scholars believe the *Beth Av* relationship which existed in the Old Testament period survived into the Herodian period. The *beth av* was "an extended family composed of two or more nuclear families united by consanguineous ties."[48] The *beth av* was a producing and consuming unit in ancient Israel which worked to ensure the subsistence of its component nuclear families. N. Gottwald believed a *beth av* might have consisted of all related patrilineally (i.e., parents, unmarried sons and daughters, married sons and wives) for five generations.[49] Not only do we have literary evidence for such kinship groupings[50] but archaeological evidence as well.[51]

Some scholars believe this kinship relationship continued into the Roman period, though some are uncertain how far into this period. Stager affirms that the extended family (beth av) continued to function in the Herodian era. He points out first of all that the Israelite practice is also found in modern Arab villages. Secondly, he affirms that the houses in Capernaum of Insula II comprised an extended-family compound. Finally, he points to references to "paternal houses" in Philo (*de Somniis* I.43, 256) and the Gospel of John (14:2).[52]

We must be cautious, however, in using modern Arab social customs to interpret the past. They may help us to understand customs we are sure existed in the past but cannot argue that they existed. We must also be cautious in using these two literary references to prove that the *beth av* still existed in the Herodian period. Both of the allusions to a "father's house" may be based on Old Testament language. Since Philo lived in Egypt his allusions are suspect for our purposes anyway.

Dar[53] believes the usual inhabitants of the courtyard in the Second Temple period were members of the extended family. He finds not only archaeological support for this thesis in his many courtyards containing on average five or six dwelling houses (or space for around 25 to 30 people), but also Mishnaic support. Erubin 6:7 states "brothers ate at their father's table but slept in their own houses..."[54] The Tosephta alludes to the same practice: "A father and his sons, wives, daughters-in-law, man servants and maid-servants, when no one else lives with them in the courtyard." (t.Erub 5:10).[55] Dar speculates that the *beth av* in Second Temple Judaism functioned as the extended family in Byzantine Greece where even after the death of the father the sons kept the entire farm together and worked it in common. Yet Dar also accepts that at some point the *beth av* began breaking up, as more and more families lost their land. He offers no suggestions however, as to when that was.

Dar's suggestion about the continuation of the *beth av* relationship even after the death of the pater familias is certainly reasonable if the *beth av* actually existed commonly in the Herodian period. Some New Testament passages, however, (Lk. 12:13, 15:12) where people are claiming their share of the inheritance of the father might call that suggestion into question.

Applebaum on the other hand doubts that the extended family as an economic unit survived the Hellenistic age. In particular he points to the many fermentation towers with their small connecting farm plots. These plots are clearly marked off to show ownership and yet are so small (from 1 to 4 acres) that they could not have supported an extended family. We must point out that the peasants also evidently had a small olive orchard and a small plot for raising grain. Still most of these taken together were not over around 6 acres, hardly enough acreage for an extended family (see Chapter 3). Applebaum concludes that at least in Samaria where most of the towers were found, the extended family had broken up into its constituent nuclear families by the Herodian period.[56]

N. Rubin has concluded that the patriarchal family began to disintegrate in the Second Temple period due to economic and social problems brought on mainly by the Roman conquest. He mainly relies on the regulations concerning mourning which in the age of the Amoraim apply only to the nuclear family. He suggests that perhaps as early as the Herodian period the confiscation of land and reducing many families to tenancy destroyed the economic (agricultural) basis of the courtyard as extended-family domain.[57] Yet his evidence is too late to argue effectively about Herodian Palestine.

M. Goodman argues against the extended family living together in courtyard houses in the Mishnaic period. He maintains (incorrectly) that the Mishnaic passage quoted above (Erub 6:7) is the only text suggesting that a young couple lived with the husband's parents. On the other hand there are no laws about women and their mothers-in-law, notes Goodman. Secondly, a man turns to his neighbors for help instead of his kinsmen (BM 5:10).[58]

More recently, Goodman[59] has argued that the extended family had broken up at least in Judea by the first century A.D. He points to the lack of endogamous marriages in the first century compared to the book of Tobit which comes, according to Goodman, from the fourth century B.C. Secondly, Goodman notes that tombs of this period in Judea are smaller in contrast to earlier periods and indicate that they were only for the nuclear family. As R. Hachlili and A. Killebrew observe in their work on Jewish funeral customs:

> It is noteworthy that First Temple rock-cut tombs served large numbers of people, probably an extended family,.... Second Temple period tombs served the immediate family.[60]

Goodman attributes the breakup of the extended family to two causes. First, the size of the family plots in this period became too small to support an extended family forcing many Jews to immigrate to the diaspora thus losing contact with relatives. Second, the larger kinship group, which Goodman calls the tribe, had already disappeared by this time and the breakup of this large family structure must have weakened also the smaller.[61]

In general the rabbinic evidence seems to refer to partners or neighbors living in the courtyard rather than kinsmen (BB 1:5f, Maaseroth 3:5, t.BQ 1:1, t.BB 1:4, t.Maaseroth 2:20, t.Erub 5:24, 6:1, 6:8). One text even refers to a man sharing the courtyard with a Gentile (Erub 6:11). Further, it appears that people often rented out their upper rooms to strangers (BM 8:6-9, b.Shabb 29b).[62] Also significant is the fact that the guarantee of one's subsistence no longer comes from extended family, the logical source in the Iron II period family units, but from donations within the village. Not only did the ancient law of *Peah* still apply, but there were also funds for the poor collected by village officials (Peah 8:7, t.Peah 4:9, 4:10, 4:15, t.Demai 3:16, t.BQ 11:3).[63] Thus almost certainly by the Mishnaic period (second century A.D.) the beth av seems to have disintegrated, though there may have been some isolated remnants of this picture as Dar's two quotations indicate.

We must of course be cautious in this case using rabbinic evidence to describe social conditions in the Herodian period. The two Jewish wars (A.D. 66 and 132) may have changed the family relationships far more than any economic factors prior to them so that the rabbinic texts only describe the particular situation of post-war Palestine. On the other hand, this evidence does support the archaeological evidence that Applebaum and Goodman point out, and such agreement argues that the disintegration of the family began even in the Hellenistic period. Certainly the process of transferring land into the hands of a few wealthy aristocrats, which we attempted to document in Chapter 2, would indicate that the family began well before the Roman period to break up, for the *beth av* could not have held together without its agro-economic base.

E. Wolf[64] lists four reasons why the nuclear family prevails in some peasant societies over the extended family. The first reason is that land is so plentiful in relation to the population that it offers opportunities to couples wishing to go it alone. This condition is usually only temporary, however, and probably not applicable to Herodian Palestine. The second condition is when land has grown "so scarce that a family can no longer use landed property as the base for further consolidation and must turn to other sources of income to make up the deficits." Thus when the agro-economic base is removed extended families tend to disintegrate. Wolf notes that in such circumstances the wealthy families tend to become both wealthier and larger, but the poorer families, poorer and smaller. The third reason nuclear families tend to emerge among peasants is when wage-labor is introduced. "...The worker is hired only for his labor and released when that labor is completed." The emphasis is on one's individual labor power not on the labor of the entire (extended) family. In other words the extended family no longer functions as a unit. Instead the unit is the individual worker. The fourth set of conditions bringing the rise of the nuclear family over the extended family are those under which a small amount of land can produce sufficient (and more) crops for a nuclear family. These conditions occur when nuclear families raise, for example, crops on a capitalistic basis for profit. These would be somewhat rare and expensive items such as famous wines. It is doubtful too that these conditions existed widely in Herodian Palestine.

The second and third conditions given by Wolf may have been at work in Herodian Palestine and indeed long before the Herodian period. The rise of large estates must have made land scarcer plus must have increased the number of day laborers working for a wage. We have seen that the farm plots in Samaria tended to be nuclear-family-sized and those surveyed in

Galilee are about the same.[65] Further, we have attempted to indicate in Chapter 3 that day laborers were numerous in the Herodian period. Thus the economic pressures in the Hellenistic period were against the *beth av*.

That some extended families among the small freeholders and other peasants did stay together well into the Roman period, however, is also quite likely. This family disintegration process would have been slow and not all regions would have felt its effects at the same time. Galilee, or perhaps only the area around Capernaum, for example shows evidence that the *beth av* was in some sense still intact in the first century A. D. Mk. 1:29 seems to indicate that both the families of Peter and Andrew shared the same house in Capernaum. Peter and Andrew also worked together to earn their living (Mk. 1:16). James and John worked with their father Zebedee (Mk. 1:19-20) in his fishing boat. As we reported above, Stager maintains that Insula II in Capernaum shows evidence of an extended family arrangement. Further, Jesus' mother and brothers came together to him in Mk. 3:31. This evidence though inconclusive, suggests that we should not assume a cataclysmic social change in the family during the Hellenistic and Roman periods, but a gradual change. The extended family was slowly breaking up.

Thus, slowly, more and more nuclear families must have begun to stand alone. The economic and social support of the beth av that enabled practically every nuclear family in the Israelite period to earn its subsistence entered a period of disintegration from the Hellenistic period on. There was now in some cases no one to guarantee one's subsistence. Of course, to say extended families had now nothing to do with each other would be a mistake. Kinship must always have played a role in ancient Judaism in guaranteeing subsistence, giving labor assistance or perhaps even loans. But without the pervasive agro-economic basis of the beth av, the ability of a kinsman to help, because he himself lived on the edge of subsistence, was greatly reduced and could no longer be considered automatic.

The Alley

The next social unit was the (מבוי) or alley which connected usually to several courtyard complexes. Five courtyards per alley are often alluded to in the rabbinic sources and so were perhaps average (e.g., t.Erub 6:8, Erub 5:24). Yeivin found abundant archaeological evidence for these village alleys in Galilee and the Golan (e.g., Korazin and Hirbet Amudin).[66] Dar also alludes to the residential alleys in Samaria.[67] Aside from the obvious social unit that neighbors living on a common alley might form, there could also be a religious partnership among them based on the (שתוף) which was similar to the (ערוב) . Members of the same courtyard could form an *Erub*, whereby they establish a fictional joint ownership of all property in the courtyard and become one family for the Sabbath, in order to move about freely in the courtyard.[68] In the same manner members of the same alley could form a *Shittuf* whereby they joined together for the Sabbath all the courtyards of the alley. Thus they could become cultically one family though they may actually be unrelated.[69] Such cultic relationships must have strengthened the normal ties between neighbors and may have helped alleviate to some extent the effect of the disintegration of the family.

The Village

The largest social unit of the peasant was the village. If the *beth av* seems to have been in a process of disintegration as a socio-economic institution in Herodian Palestine, the larger lineage components, the clan (משפחה) and tribe (שבט), had evidently already disappeared as socially effective units. True, some allusions to tribes can be found in the New Testament (Phil. 3:5, Lk. 2:36 and Acts 4:36) but these references seem to indicate no more than that one remembers from which tribe one has come. Tribal units and clan units no longer function except for priests and Levites.

The dearth of references especially to clans in the New Testament period is significant and contrasts with the Persian period and before. The *mishpahoth* were according to N. Gottwald groups of *beth avoth* all of whose members had mutual obligations to extend the assistance of their own *beth av* to any needy *beth av* within the *mishpahah*. If a *beth av* were for some reason "decimated" the *mishpahah* would take the surviving members into other *beth avoth*. In general, says Gottwald, the *mishpahah* "(sustained) the family in its vulnerable autonomy."[70]

Hopkins[71] also emphasized the subsistence guarantee function of the *mishpahah*. The *mishpahah* functioned in "risk spreading and labor optimization." If everyone in the *mishpahah* concerned himself for the subsistence of every other family then the agricultural risk was spread over the entire clan. One way this risk spreading may have been accomplished according to Hopkins was in communal land tenure, though we probably should not conclude that all peasants in Israel in the Old Testament period practiced communal farming.[72]

The *mishpahoth* apparently functioned as social units also after the exile. First of all we have the references to leaders ("elders" or "dignitaries") of the Jews in Ezra and Nehemiah who some claim were heads of clans.[73] Neh 4:13 (Heb. 4:7) states that people stood watch over the wall in Jerusalem by clans (למשפחרת). Finally, there is the evidence of the book of Ruth – "an explication in popular form of the function of the *mishpahah*"[74] – if we are indeed to date the book to the post-exilic period.[75]

Yet in the Hellenistic period and following we find almost no literary references to *mishpahoth*. The usual Septuagint translation of (משפחה) in the Old Testament ($\delta\hat{\eta}\mu o\varsigma$) means in the Apocrypha "people" not clan (e.g., 1Macc 8:29, 12:6). The same is true for Josephus and the New Testament (where the word is only found in Acts).[76] Only in the Qumran scrolls do we find *mishpahah* used in the same sense as the Old Testament. For example, 1QM 4:10 and 1QSa 1:15 clearly indicate that a *mishpahah* is a smaller unit within a tribe.[77] Yet this usage should be seen as an archaizing and idealizing tendency based on the Old Testament and probably not reflecting actual conditions. Thus, arguing from silence, we would conclude that the clans had ceased as viable social units by the late Second Temple period. With this cessation went also the "risk-spreading" means of guaranteeing one's subsistence.

Why the clans disintegrated we can only speculate. We should suspect they broke up for the same reasons that the *beth av* was in the process of breaking up in the Herodian period, namely, economic reasons. The organization of Palestine under the Ptolemies into toparchies for tax purposes put the emphasis on regional similarities instead of kinship. Second, the growth of large estates and the change to values of land as capital to be exploited must have weakened the communal function of the mishpahah.

The urbanization of Palestine may have contributed the most to the disintegration of the clans. The large cities such as Jerusalem, Sebaste, Tiberias, and Sepphoris in the Hill Country as well as the coastal cities and Caesarea Philippi captured the role of social, economic, cultural, and political leadership of the nation. The old power of the clan elders gave way to an urban aristocracy based especially on wealth. Since most of these urban aristocrats must have been absentee landlords, their concern was for the profit of their estate not in guaranteeing subsistence of distant kinsmen. The aristocrats must have considered themselves citizens of the city first and kinsmen last. This process seems to have been at work in the Golan area where inscriptions indicate that urbanization and Hellenization led to the dissolution of the nomadic tribes and in their place developed loyalty to one's village.[78]

We must not forget of course that many, perhaps most, of the inhabitants of a village would have been related by blood or marriage. This has been affirmed for village life in general in the ancient Mediterranean world[79] and common sense would tell us that children tended to stay in their ancestral villages when reaching adulthood. But whether kinship ties beyond the extended family were emphasized or utilized in "spreading the risk" in order to maintain subsistence is another question.

Thus, one's neighbors in the village formed the new socio-economic basis of relationships. The village was the largest social unit for the Palestinian peasant and consisted probably of both kinsmen and non-related neighbors.

Villages were almost always supported by agriculture. There were village craftsmen, but many of these may have been small farmers or day laborers who supplemented their income during the winter months. If Dar's findings in Samaria are typical, the individual farm plots (one for each nuclear family) were marked off in the fields surrounding the village. The farmer, then, did not reside on his farm plot, but walked out to it from the village to work it. A good example of this arrangement can be seen in the plan of Qawarat Bene-Hassan given in Chapter 2 (see Plan 1). Similar village farm plot systems were discovered by Dar's survey team in several other villages.[80]

In defining ancient Palestinian villages we must deal with the Greek and Hebrew terms for village and city. The two Greek terms which in the main are found in Josephus and the Gospels, (πόλις) and (κώμη) seem to have been used in a confusing way. Technically a (πόλις) had its own constitution, coinage, territory and (βουλή).[81] But these texts often seem to refer to villages as cities and cities as villages. Sherwin-White suggested that the solution to the problem was to consider the city (πόλις) in both Josephus and the Gospels as a capital of a toparchy, even if the place was not technically a city.[82]

The rabbinic terms for cities, towns and villages are: עיר , כרך , קריה , כפר , עירה . The middle three terms appear to have been roughly equivalent in size representing a median between (כרך) the large walled city and (כפר) the small unwalled village An (עיר) could also be a very small hamlet. Krauss followed by Dar affirmed that the (כרך) was the equivalent of the (πόλις) in the technical sense.[83] Applebaum affirmed that the (עיר) was not only a medium-sized town but also could mean an isolated farm (similar to a Roman villa).[84] This position has been accepted by S. Safrai and Dar, but received with skepticism by Goodman.[85] Applebaum further asserts that the terms (עירה) and (קריה) referred to settlements linked to large administrative centers, either in a tenurial relationship to the center of a vast estate or to an urban center.[86] So much of this seems speculative that we would have to agree with Goodman to be cautious in giving consent.

The simplest procedure is to refer to the three most common usages in the rabbinic literature: The (כרך), the (עיר) and the (כפר).[87] Of these three terms the most frequently used is (עיר).[88] Thus it could be concluded that most peasants lived in the Mishnaic period in a town or large village in population midway between the small village (כפר) and the city (כרך).

The number of inhabitants of a typical town and village is only now being determined by archaeologists. Yeivin[89] discussed ten towns in Galilee and the Golan falling mainly into the following categories: large towns (22 to 25 acres) and middle-sized towns (10 to 17 acres). He also listed one town with 2.5 acres. D. Urman's[90] survey of the Golan discovered one site over 175 acres, four sites from 30 to 50 acres, 14 sites with 10 to 30 acres, 28 sites which were 5 to 10 acres, 54 sites which were 2.5 to 5 acres and 33 sites with less than 2.5 acres. Those 87 sites of 5 acres or less were either small villages/hamlets or single farms. The distinction cannot without excavation be determined. E. Meyers[91] notes that most villages in Upper Galilee range from 7.5 to 12.5 acres with Meiron and Gischala being unusually large at 75 acres. Finally Dar[92] gives the measurement of certain villages in Samaria at 4 to 5 acres, 3.5 acres, 6 acres, 6 to 7.5 acres, 2.4 acres, and 10 acres. It appears from these findings that most peasants lived in towns or villages of 2.5 to 12.5 acres. The ten towns examined by Yeivin may not then be typical of Palestinian peasant life, at least for the Herodian period. We can only presume that the same conditions that prevailed in Galilee, the Golan and Samaria also existed in Judea.

The population of these towns and villages may be figured by counting the number of houses and multiplying by five, for five inhabitants on average to a room, then subtracting 25% to allow for rooms for storage and animals. Yeivin has in this manner estimated the population of several cities in Galilee and the Golan:

Juhadr	5250 persons
Mazraat Kuneitra	900
Hirbet Shema	1250
Arbel	5000
Usha	3000.[93]

Most of these towns appear to have flourished in the Mishnaic period and thus we must be cautious in affirming that they give us an appropriate sample in size of a typical Herodian peasant village or town.

Another method of determining population is to multiply the number of acres times the supposed number of people that on average lived on one acre in antiquity. The figure accepted by both M. Broshi and Y. Shiloh is 160 to 200 people per acre.[94] Thus, for the moment, using the higher number for convenience, most villages and towns in Upper Galilee ranged from 1500 to 2300 inhabitants according to the figures given by Meyers. Yeivin's towns ranged from 4400 to 5000 for large towns, 2000 to 3400 for medium-sized towns and the one village of 500 people. Likewise, according to Urman's figures, the Golan had one town with over 35,000 people (Caesarea Philippi), four towns with 6000 to 10,000 people, 14 towns with populations ranging from 2000 to 6000 people; 28 towns with populations of 1000 to 2000; 54 villages with populations of 500 to 1000; and 33 villages with populations less than 500 people. The four Samaritan villages had populations of 800-1000 people, 700 people, 1200 people, 1200-1500 people, 480 people, and 2000 people, respectively.[95]

The dates for most of the villages cited by Dar are Hasmonean through the Herodian (one through Byzantine) period. The towns in the Golan range from the early Roman to the Byzantine period. Meyers does not give dates for the towns he discusses but the one example of a town size he offers, Hirbet Shema, dates continuously from the Hellenistic period to the Byzantine.[96] Thus if we can draw any conclusions from this data, we would cautiously suggest that most peasants in the Roman period lived in towns or large villages of around 1000 inhabitants. But many peasants must have lived also in small villages (כפרים) of only a few hundred people.

Ben-David has attempted to define the Hebrew terms for town in the Mishnaic period assigning to each a population figure:

1. A hamlet (עיר) n–50 inhabitants
2. A village (כפר)–400 to 600 inhabitants
3. A country town (עיר)–600 to 7500 inhabitants
4. A large city (כְּרַךְ)–10,000 to 60,000 inhabitants.[97]

The upper limit of a country town population may be too high on average for the Herodian period, but apart from that his figures seem to harmonize well with what we have discussed above.

The average peasant then, lived in a village or town ranging from perhaps a few hundred people to one or two thousand.

TABLE B

Palestinian Villages

Size in Acres		*Population* (200 person/acre)
Yeivin	22-25	4,400-5,000
	10-17	2,000-3,400
	2.5	500
Urman	1 site 175	35,000
	4 sites 30-50	6,000-10,000
	14 sites 10-30	2,000-6,000
	28 sites 5-10	1,000-2000
	54 sites 2.5-5	500-1,000
	33 sites less than 2.5	less than 500
Meyers	most are 7.5-12.5	1,500-2,300
Dar	4-5	800-1000
	3.5	700
	6	1,200
	6-7.5	1,200-1,500
	2.4	480
	10	2,000

We shall describe a typical Palestinian small town or village by comparing the hypothetical "medium-sized town" in the Mishnaic period which Yeivin has constructed with an actual peasant village of the Herodian period described by Dar. Yeivin has put together a composite of an (עיר בנונית) or town of medium size based on the plans of Khorazin and Einan in Galilee, Nahef and Naaran in the Golan and Horvat Susia in Judea. Although these towns flourished in the late second century A.D., they do not seem to differ markedly from the Herodian village described by Dar.

Yeivin's composite town indicates no street planning. The streets were haphazardly determined often leaving open areas which became public domain. The city had no gates or fortified walls but the houses were often built touching each other so that they formed a kind of protective outer wall. Yeivin's hypothetical town has a synagogue. Nearby is the cemetery (בית הקברות).[98] According to Yeivin's previous estimates a "medium-sized town" would have an area of 10 to 17 acres and a population of 2000 to 3400 people.

The village in Samaria known as Hirbet Karqush will serve as our example of an actual village from the Hasmonean-Herodian period. Dar[99] was able to date the village from the tombs in the nearby cemetery. The village covers an area of 3.5 acres and thus would have had a population of from 560 to 700 people according to Broshi's method of computing population. Dar used Yeivin's method of determining the population and concluded that the village held around 600 people. Dar divides the village structures into two main blocks: Blocks A and B (see Plan 4). Block A which may be a later (Byzantine) section of the village contained several courtyard houses. Across the street from Block A were several more courtyard houses (numbers 6, 9, 16, 18 and probably also 12 and 13). Dar believes building 11 was a water reservoir. Building 10 had an unknown function and was built in the Hellenistic period. Numbers 20, 23 and 24 are parts of an oil press not *in situ*.

Dar believes buildings 7 and 8 were public buildings. He found several other examples of such buildings in Samaritan villages[100] and from other evidence we know that most villages in Syria, even small ones, had public buildings of some sort.[101] The buildings were not evidently financed from taxes but from donations of wealthy families, when such families lived in or near the village, and perhaps also from the revenues of village owned land.

The one public building we cannot be sure existed in ancient Palestinian villages was the synagogue. Certainly synagogues existed in the Herodian period, but that most villages had a separate building for them is unproven. Most of the remains of the oldest synagogues are from the end of the second century or beginning of the third century A.D.[102] Probably many of the towns also had commercial buildings.[103]

142

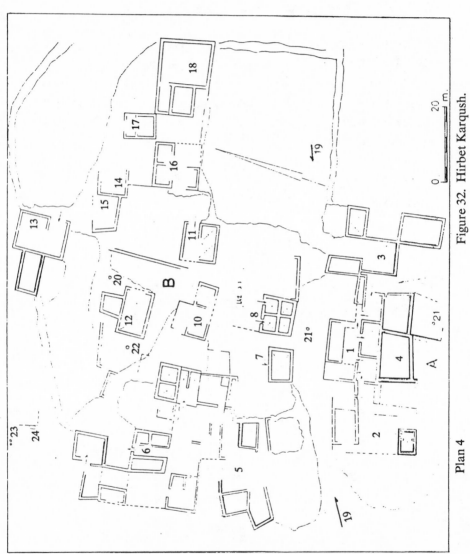

Figure 32. Hirbet Karqush.

Plan 4

Southeast of the village lay the cemetery with both Kukh type of burial and open cist graves. Dar found sixteen systems of Kokhim tombs and twenty dwelling units in the village. Thus he concludes that most families had a hypogeum. Evidently, however, the poorer families did not.

There was some evidence that one family was wealthier than the others. Dar found an ornamental tomb in the cemetery and a larger than usual courtyard house (building 18). Yet the difference in economic status must have been small argues Dar, so that this family is only *primus inter pares*. In other words, this family probably did not own the village.

Just north of building 11 was a large open square. One wonders if this area had a specific purpose such as a village market place, the center for exchange in ancient Palestine.[104] The Synoptic Gospels indicate that most small towns and villages had markets (Mk. 6:56, 7:4, 12:28, Mt. 11:16=Lk. 7:32, Mt. 20:3, Mt. 23:7=Lk. 11:43) in addition to the major market centers such as Jerusalem, Sepphoris, Shechem, Lydda, and Antipatris.[105] It is possible that such open areas served as temporary market places in villages on the market day.[106]

The hypothetical medium-sized town of Yeivin and this actual village in rural Samaria described by Dar indicate then common patterns. Most villages of any size had not only residences but public and commercial buildings, agricultural structures (oil or wine presses), cemeteries outside the village, and open spaces perhaps used on market days as temporary markets.

We are left with the final question of what the relationship was of the peasant village or town to the large urban centers. We should think here not only of Tiberias, Sepphoris, Caesarea, Philippi, Sebaste and Jerusalem, but also the main towns of toparchies (e.g., Jericho, Lydda),[107] The statement of Jones concerning the general relationship in the eastern Roman empire between urban centers and the rural peasant is a helpful starting point in answering this question:

> The cities were...economically parasitic on the countryside. Their incomes consisted in the main of the rents drawn by the urban aristocracy from the peasants...the growth of cities meant the concentration in towns of the larger (land) proprietors and converted them into absentee landlords....The wealth of the countryside – and it must be emphasized that the bulk of the wealth of the empire was derived from

agriculture–was drained into the towns. The peasants were thus reduced to a very low standard of life.[108]

The question is to what extent this description applies to Palestine in the Herodian period. Goodman affirms that it does not describe Galilee in the Mishnaic period, but affirms that Judea in the Herodian period does fit this description.[109] Applebaum, on the other hand argues for animosity between urban centers and the countryside in general and offers as evidence the passage described in Chapter 2 from Lam R (2.5) where the villages of Bethar are defrauded of their land by the Jerusalem aristocrats and thus rejoice when Jerusalem is destroyed in A.D. 70.[110]

Perhaps the most telling evidence for a rural-urban animosity in Herodian Palestine comes from Josephus' account of the Jewish war. This feature of the rebellion has been most convincingly demonstrated by Horsley and Hanson. The Zealots must actually be closely identified with rural peasants who fled to Jerusalem before the advancing Roman armies (*B* 4.135, 138, 419-39, 451). When these bands of fleeing peasants reached Jerusalem they "began attacking members of the ruling aristocracy, especially the Herodian nobles" (*B* 4.139-145, 315, 325-327, 335, 357f, 5.439-442, 527-532). Horsley and Hanson conclude: "The Zealots, no matter how much their struggle was against the alien Roman oppressors, were first fighting a class war against their own Jewish nobility."[111]

We should also bear in mind that the Sicarii not only executed wealthy Jewish nobles at the outbreak of the war but burned the debt records (*B* 2.426f). Cornfeld concludes on the basis of the behavior of the Sicarii that "the uprising started as a civil war...." Cornfeld also calls Simon ben Giora, who freed all slaves, led an army of the dispossessed (*B* 4.508-510), and opposed the wealthy (*B* 5.309), "the leader of the lower classes in Judaea, Peraea, and Idumaea."[112]

P. Brunt has pointed out the same sort of animosity ($\mu\hat{\iota}\sigma o\varsigma$ or $\dot{\alpha}\pi\epsilon\chi\theta\hat{\omega}\varsigma$) in Galilee between the villagers and residents of Sepphoris and Tiberias (*V* 375, 384). The villagers tried to burn both cities to the ground (*V* 375, 99). We must not forget also that Tiberias until only shortly before the war was the city where the debt records for Galilee were kept, which were subsequently moved to Sepphoris (*V* 38). Brunt concludes: "We may suppose that many of the peasants were burdened with debts to urban landlords and money lenders."[113]   Such widespread animosity toward the urban elite argues strongly that the urban centers of Palestine were "parasitic."

Further, the numerous references to the wealthy's exploitation of the poor also argue that the cities were parasitic on the countryside.   Jesus castigated the wealthy (Mk. 10:23, 12:40, Lk. 16:19-29) as did several other Palestinian teachers from this period.[114] The Similitudes of Enoch list not only kings, governors, and high officials among the wicked who will be judged, but also "landlords."[115]

Given the evidence above and the situation described in Chapter 2 of this monograph, Jones' statement of the relationship of cities to villages in the eastern half of the Roman empire would seem to be appropriate for Herodian Palestine as well. As more and more land came into the ownership of absentee landlords living in cities, the economic subordination of the village to the city or large town was increased. This is essentially the situation Jones is describing, although he is describing *poleis* in the technical sense. We can see no reason, however, to conclude that the situation was any different in Herodian Palestine. The surplus tended to flow to the city as rents and taxes. The luxury and splendor of the cities known to us from both the literature and now archaeology – the palaces, theaters, and other magnificent public buildings as well as large private houses – strongly support this conclusion. This economic relationship meant that peasants worked not just for their own subsistence but to maintain the standard of living of the wealthy.

Conclusion

The peasant lived within a network of social units which were the nuclear family, the courtyard neighbors, neighbors of the same alley, and fellow villagers. Most peasants probably lived in villages of a few hundred or towns of a thousand to two thousand people, but many also lived in small hamlets and on the estates of wealthy landowners.

We can only speculate about the changes in kinship relations brought on by the Hellenistic and later Roman changes in land tenure. First of all it seems likely that the extended family, the *beth av*, began breaking up in the Hellenistic period, but the process may have lasted into the Mishnaic age. Second, we believe the clans or *mishpahoth* had already ceased by the first century A.D. to play a decisive role in peasant socio-economic relationships.

We can be more definite about the relationship between rural villages and urban centers. We can see no reason why Jones' description of the parasitic nature of large cities on the countryside should not also apply to Herodian Palestine. On the contrary, evidence seems conclusive from the account of the Jewish war that a strong animosity existed between city and country.

END NOTES

1.   See Dar, 1986, p. 1.

2.   *Ibid.* pp. 1-8.

3.   Applebaum in Dar, 1986, p. 257. *Cf* D. Hopkins, *The Highlands of Canaan* (Sheffield: Almond, 1985) pp. 251-261. - For *beth av* see Ex. 6:14, Num. 1:2, Josh. 22:14, 1Chron. 4:38.

4.   Dar, 1986, pp. 1-8.

5.   Yeivin and Edelstein "Excavations at Tirat Yehudah" *Atiqot* 6(1970) 56-67 Heb. with Eng. summary, and Dar, 1986, p.6.

6.   Yeivin and Edelstein, 1970, p. 6.

7.   Dar. 1986, pp. 10-12.

8.   See Day, 1932, 167-208; Rostovtzeff, 1957, p. 64.

9.   See the farms at Hirbet Basatin in western Samaria which had a work force probably of "several dozen hands" but no identifiable living quarters for them (Dar, 1986, pp. 24-26). On the other hand the farm at Hirbet Deir Sam'an also in western Samaria and dating from the Roman period may have had living quarters for the workers. Most rooms now are not well preserved and thus an identification of their function is impossible (Dar, 1986, pp. 26-30). Another isolated farm from the third to fourth century A.D. was found near Beth Shearim. See N. Avigad "Excavations at Beth Shearim, 1954" *IEJ* 5(1955) 205-239.

10.   See e.g., R. W. Hamilton "Excavations at Tel Abu Hawam" *Quarterly of the Department of Antiquities of Palestine* 4(1935) 1-69.

11.   Dar, 1986, pp. 230-245.

12.   *Ibid.*, pp. 80f.

13.   Y. Shiloh "The Four-Room House: Its Situation and Function in the Israelite City" *IEJ* 20(1970) 180-190. See also H. Rösel "Haus" in K. Galling, ed. *Biblisches Reallexikon* (Tübingen: Mohr, 1977) pp. 138-141.

14.   As Dar suggests (1986, p. 80).

15.   Yeivin, *Survey of Settlements in Galilee and the Golan from the Period of the Mishnah in Light of the Sources* (Hebrew University: Ph.D., 1971) pp. XIf. For floor plans see pp. 186-189.

16.   Dar, 1986, p. 83,

17.   H. K. Beebe "Domestic Architecture and the New Testament" *BA* 38(1975) 89-104, esp. p. 96.

18.   Beebe, 1975, 89-104. On lack of space see Safrai, 1976, p. 730. On insulae see also A. C. Bouquet, *Everyday Life in New Testament Times* (London: Batsford, 1953) pp. 36f.

19.   See J. W. Crowfoot, K. Kenyon, and E. L. Sukenik, *The Buildings of Samaria* (London: Palestine Exploration Fund, 1942) pp. 128 and 137; also Dar, 1986, pp. 42-46.

20.   V. Corbo, *The House of Saint Peter at Capharnaum*, trans. S. Saller (Jerusalem: Franciscan, 1972); and idem., *Cafarnao I* (Jerusalem: Franciscan, 1975). See also J. F. Strange and H. Shanks "Has the House Where Jesus Stayed in Capernaum been Found?" *BAR* VIII:6 (1982) 26-37.

21.   E. Meyers, J. Strange, and C. L. Meyers, 1981, pp. 25-51.

22.   Goodman, 1983, p. 30.

23.   Y. Tsafrir and K. G. Holum "Rehovot in the Negev: Preliminary Report, 1986" *IEJ* 38(1988) 117-127.

24.   M. I. Rostovtzeff, *Excavation in Dura-Europos* (New Haven: Yale University Press, 1943-1968).

25.   See Corbo, 1972, pp. 35-52, and Strange and Shanks, 1982, 26-37. See also the plan and artist's reconstruction of an insula in Meiron in Meyers, Strange and Meyers, 1981, pp. 25, 35.

26.   S. Safrai "Home and Family" *Compendia* I.2, p. 732. See Sotah 8:3 for mud-brick houses.

27.   Bouquet, 1953, p. 27.

28.   Peah 8:7. See Goodman, 1983, p. 39.

29.   Krauss, 1966, p. 27; Beebe, 1975, p. 101; Safrai, 1976, p. 732; Yeivin, 1971, p. XIV.

30.   Strange and Shanks, 1982, p. 34; Corbo, 1972, p. 37.

31.   See Safrai, 1976, p. 730; Krauss, 1966, p. 29; and Judith 8:5, Mk. 14:15, Acts 1:3, 20:8, Shab 1:4, BB 2:2f, Ned 7:4. For an example of a flat roof see Meyers, Strange, and Meyers, 1981, p. 40.

32.   Yeivin, 1971, p. XIV.

33.   Bouquet, 1953, p. 28 notes that poor Arabs of Palestine still live in only one room.

34.   Yeivin, 1971, p. XV. *Cf.* Stager. 1985, p. 18. This figure is close to the average family size (six) which we have accepted from Ben-David.

35.   Safrai, 1976, p. 733.

36.   Dar, 1986, p. 85. Thus Goodman's assertion (1983, p. 31) that the standard house sizes in the Mishnah are pure "theory" must be rejected.

37.   Krauss, 1966, p. 46. Krauss cites t.Maaseroth 2:8, 2:20, j.BB 2.7, j. Shab 6.1.

38.   Safrai, 1976, p. 729; Erub 7:1, BB 1:4, t.Erub 6:13f.   For archaeological evidence see e.g., Meiron in Meyers, Strange, and Meyers, 1981; and Corbo, 1972. See also Krauss, 1966, I, p. 45.

39.   Meyers, Strange, Meyers, 1981, p. 40.

40.   Danby understands the size to be 4 x 4 cubits.

41.   Meyers, Strange, Meyers, 1981, p. 40.

42.   *Cf* Arak 9:7, t. Maaseroth 2:20.

43.   Dar, 1986, p. 85.

44.   See Meyers, Strange, Meyers, 1981, pp. 33-37; Safrai, 1976, p. 729; Yeivin, 1971, p. XV; b.Pes 8a; Erub 8:4; BB 2.2f, 4:4.

45.   Krauss, 1966, I, p. 46. Se b.Yoma 11a, b.Pes 8a. Strange and Shanks suggest that the second courtyard in Insula I at Capernaum (see Plan 3) was for animals (1982, p. 34).

46.   Stager, 1985, p. 11.14.

47.   BB 3:5, Pes 1:1, Erub 8:6, Ohol 5:6, t. Maaseroth 3.8, 2:20, t.BB 2:16, t.BB 3:1, t.BB 2:13. See Safrai, 1976, p. 730; Krauss, 1966, I, p. 46; Strange and Shanks, 1982, p. 34; Yeivin, 1971, p. XVII.

48.   Hopkins, 1985, p. 225. See also N. Gottwald, *The Tribes of Yahweh* (Maryknoll: Orbis, 1979) pp. 285f; R. De Vaux, 1961, pp. 7f; A. Malamat, "Biblical Genealogies and African Lineages" *Archives Européennes de Sociologie* 14(1973) 126-136; D. A. Fiensy, "Using the Nuer of Africa in Understanding the Old Testament: An Evaluation" *JSOT* 38(1987) 73-83. The kinship group larger than the *beth av* was the *mishpahah* with the largest unit being the *shevet*.

49.   Gottwald, 1979, pp. 285-287.

50.   See Josh. 7:14-18, 1Sam. 9:1-4, Gen. 31:14, Num. 27:14, 1Kgs. 21:3, Ex. 6:14, Num. 1:2, Josh. 22:14, 1Chron. 4:38.

51.   See Hopkins, 1985, p. 253.

52.   Stager, 1985, pp. 18-22. *Cf.* Safrai, 1976, p. 732.

53.   Dar, 1986, pp. 84f.

54.   Translation in Danby.

55.   Translation in Neusner, *Tosephta.*

56.   Applebaum in Dar, 1986, p. 262.

57.   Rubin in *Essays in Honour of H. M. Shapira* (1972/1973), (Heb) summarized in Dar, 1986, p. 85.

58.   Goodman, 1983, p. 36.

59.   Goodman, *The Ruling Class of Judaea* (Cambridge: Cambridge University Press, 1987) p. 68.

60.   R. Hachlili and A. Killebrew "Jewish Funerary Customs During the Second Temple Period in the Light of the Excavations at the Jericho Necropolis" *PEQ* 115(1983) pp. 109-139, esp. p. 126.

61.   Goodman, 1987, pp. 68f.

62.   See Krauss, 1966, I, p. 45.

63.   Goodman, 1983, pp. 121f.

64.   Wolf, 1966, pp. 65-73.

65.   Golomb and Kedar, 1971, 136-140.

66.   Yeivin, 1971, p. XIII.

67.   Dar, 1986, p. 49. Dar gives the measurements of the width of the streets and alleys of Hirbet Najar, a Herodian village, as 2.5 meters and 3 meters. Presumably the smaller measurement was of the alleys. The Greek term was (ῥύμη) (Lk. 14:21, Mt. 6:2, Acts 12:10). See C. C. McCown "City" *IDB.*

68.   T.Erub 5:12-24; Erub 6:8.

69.   Erub 3:1, 6:8, 7:6; t.Erub 6:1-7. See also M. Friedlnder, "Erub" *JE*; Jastrow " (שתרוף)"; Danby, "Appendix I."

70.   Gottwald, 1979, pp. 261, 315f.

71.   Hopkins, 1985, pp. 257f.

151

72. See De Vaux, 1961, pp. 165f.

73. SVM II, pp. 201f. See Ezra 5:5, 5:9, 6:7, 6:14, 10:8, Neh 2:16, 4:8, 4:13, 5:7, 7:5.

74. Gottwald, 197, p. 261.

75. See esp. S. Nidith "Legends of Wise Heroes and Heroines" in D. A. Knight and G. M. Tucker, *The Hebrew Bible and its Modern Interpreters* (Chico, CA: Scholars Press, 1985) p. 451. She lists the arguments for and against the late date. Although the late date is now being challenged by some scholars, many still hold to it. E.g., W. H. Schmidt, *Einfhrung in das Alte Testament* (Berlin: de Gruyter, 1985) p. 316.

76. See W. Grundman "($\delta\hat{\eta}\mu o\varsigma$) " *TDNT*.

77. See H. J. Zobel "(משפחה)" in G. W. Anderson et. al., ed. *Theologisches Wörterbuch zum Alten Testament* (Stuttgart: Kohlhammer, 1984) Vol. V.

78. A. H. M. Jones, *Cities of the Eastern Roman Provinces* (Oxford: Clarendon, 1971) p. 283.

79. M. Harper "Village Administration in the Roman Province of Syria" *Yale Classical Studies* 1(1928) p. 106; N. Lewis, *Life in Egypt under Doman Rule* (Oxford: Clarendon, 1983) p. 66.

80. E.g., see Dar, 1986, Figure 43, (Hirbet Burqa). See also Ben-David, 1969, p. 49. *Cf.* also the results of the survey of the Golan by Urman, 1985, p. 93, who notes that most of the villages and towns had an agricultural economy. Cf. Lewis, 1983, p. 65.

81. See SVM II, pp. 86f; A. H. M. Jones "The Urbanization of Palestine" *JRS* 21(1931) 78-85; V. Ehrenberg "Polis" *OCD*.

82. Sherwin-White, *Roman Society and Roman Law in the New Testament* (Oxford: Clarendon, 1963) pp. 129f. *Cf.* SVM II, p. 188. The term ($\kappa\omega\mu o\pi\acute{o}\lambda\epsilon\iota\varsigma$) in reference to the villages of Galilee may indicate (Mk. 1:38) the same as the phrase ($\pi\acute{o}\lambda\epsilon\iota\varsigma$ $\kappa\alpha\grave{\iota}$ $\kappa\hat{\omega}\mu\alpha\iota$) (Mt. 9:35). See Goodman, 1983, p. 27. The term ($\pi o\lambda\acute{\iota}\chi\nu\eta$) which Josephus used frequently (*B* 1.33, 41, 334, 3.20, 134, 430, 4.84 etc.) seems to be a word for town or large village.

83. Krauss "City and Country" *He-Atid* 3(1923) 50-61; cited in Dar, 1986, p. 21.

84. Applebaum, 1976, p. 643; and Applebaum in Dar, 1986, p. 263.

85. Safrai, "The Jewish City in Eretz Israel" *City and Community*, pp. 227-236 (Heb) cited in Dar, 1986, pp. 21f; Goodman, 1983 p. 28. See Erub 5:6 and t.BB 3:5 on selling an (עיר) .

86.   Applebaum, 1976, p. 644.

87.   Erub 5:1, 5:3, 5:6, 5:8, Shek 1:1, Meg 1:1, 1:2, 1:3, 2:3, 3:1, Ket 1:1, Arak 9:6, Kelim 1:7. See SVM II, pp. 188f.

88.   Goodman, 1983, p. 28, affirms that the term (עיר) is used in the Mishnah over one hundred times, (כרך) only eleven times, and (כפר) twelve times.

89.   Yeivin, 1971, p. VI.

90.   Urman, 1985, pp. 87f, 93.

91.   Meyers, "The Cultural Setting of Galilee: The case of Regionalism and Early Judaism" *ANRW* II. 19.1 (1979) p. 700.

92.   Dar, 1986, pp. 51, 53, 42, 47, 36, 231.

93.   Yeivin, 1971, p. XV.

94.   Broshi, "The Population of Western Palestine in the Roman-Byzantine Period" *BASOR* 236(1979) 1-10; Shiloh, "The Population of Iron Age Palestine in the Light of a Sample Analysis of Urban Plans, Areas, and Population Density" *BASOR* 239(1980) 25-35.

95.   Dar often estimates the population however, at more than these amounts. For example, the population of Hirbet Najar would be at most 1000 people using Broshi's method, but Dar estimates the population at 1500 to 2000. See Dar, 1986, p. 51. The average village in Egypt may have been somewhat larger. Cf. Lewis, 1983, p. 68.

96.   See Meyers, Strange, and Groh, 1978, p. 7.

97.   Ben-David, 1969, p. 49. It is interesting that Ben-David's four categories harmonize well with the depictions of towns and cities in the Madaba Map. Small villages are depicted as buildings having two towers, larger villages with three towers, small cities with four or five towers (e.g., Jericho, Azotus) and large cities as aerial photographs showing actual walls and buildings (e.g., Jerusalem, Jamnia, Ascalon). See Avi-Yonah, 1954; pp. 21f.

98.   Z. Yeivin, "On the Medium-Sized City" *Eretz Israel* 19(1987) 59-71 (Heb. with Eng. summary).

99.   Dar, 1986, pp. 42-46.

100.   E.g., Dar, 1986, p. 49.

101.   G. M. Harper, 1928, 105-168; and Jones, 1940, p. 286.

102. See H. Shanks, *Judaism in Stone* (Jerusalem: Steimatzky, 1979) pp. 17-30.

103. Such as the building found at Nabratein by E. Meyers, J. Strange, and C. L. Meyers. See "Second Preliminary Report on the 1981 Excavations at en-Nabratein, Israel" *BASOR* 246 (1982) 35-54.

104. The market place was called (שׁוק) in the rabbinic literature (see Jastrow) and (ἀγορά) in the Gospels (Mk. 6:56). See also Goodman, 1983, p. 54.

105. Applebaum, 1976, p. 687.

106. The pre-Mishnaic market day was Friday. See Applebaum, 1976, p. 687 and Goodman, 1983, p. 54.

107. *B* 3.54f. *Cf.* Pliny's list of toparchies in Palestine in *N.H.* 5.70. See SVM II, pp. 190-196.

108. Jones, 1940, p. 268.

109. Goodman, 1983, p. 133; idem., 198f, pp. 419-421.

110. Applebaum, 1977, pp. 370f.

111. Horsley and Hanson, 1985, pp. 220-226.

112. Cornfeld, 1982, pp. 186. See further Chapter 1 on the class conflict evident in the Jewish rebellion.

113. P. A. Brunt "Josephus on Social Conflicts in Roman Judaea" *Klio* 59(1977) 149-153. Cf. S. Frayne, *Galilee, Jesus and the Gospels* (Philadelphia: Fortress, 1988) p. 146.

114. See CD 8:12, 9:15, T.Judah 21.7, TDan 5:7, Assumption of Moses 7:6, 2Enoch 10:5 and Cronbach, 1944, p. 144; 1Enoch 94:4-10, 97:8-10 and G. W. E. Nickelsburg, "Riches, the Rich, and God's Judgment in 1Enoch 92-105 and the Gospel According to Luke" *NTS* 25(1979) 324-344.

115. See E. Isaac's new translation in *POT*, I, on 1Enoch 62:1, 3, 6, 12, 63:1, 12. Literally landlords are "those who hold the land." On the date of the Similitudes see J H. Charlesworth, "The SNTS Pseudepigrapha Seminars at Tbingen and Paris on the Books of Enoch" *NTS* 25(1979) 315-23, esp. 322.

CHAPTER 5
THE SOCIAL STRUCTURE OF PALESTINE
IN THE HERODIAN PERIOD

From top to bottom, from the monarch or ethnarch to the "expendables", everyone knew his place. The peasant villager stood socially over against other groups located on a different rung of power and prestige, even as he was culturally differentiated from the urbanite. Palestine was a stratified and bifurcated society.

To be avoided in our investigation in this chapter is the attempt to describe the social structure by referring mainly or exclusively to the religious sects (Sadducees, Pharisees, Essenes, Zealots) as if every individual Jew adhered to one of them.[1] Nor shall we consider the rabbinic sages as a social class as many scholars do[2] since there were both rich and poor, priests and laity, as well as high government officials and day laborers among them. They could hardly have constituted a homogeneous social class. We shall also refrain as much as possible from treating the am ha-aretz as an asocial class. No doubt many people belonging to this group were poor peasants and the term probably meant originally "peasant,"[3] but there were also in the Mishnaic period wealthy am ha-aretz. The term mainly, as used by the rabbis, indicates a religious distinction between the rabbinic sages and certain groups of other people.[4]

We must also be cautious of the uncritical use of sociological theories which may really only apply in a modern industrial society.[5] On the other hand, to ignore any contribution to this discussion which sociology-anthropology can make is simply to invite both naiveté and ethnocentrism. What we need is a model which is true both to the historical conditions of ancient agrarian societies and informed by sociology.

The model we have selected is a composite of those suggested by G. E. Lenski and G. Alföldy.[6] Lenski's work is important because he not only sought to combine the insights of both the Functionalist and Class-conflict schools of sociological theory, but also because he deals with societies according to the anthropological classification of cultural development: bands, tribal societies, agrarian societies, and industrial societies. Alföldy's contribution is his clear demarcation of not only the upper and lower classes in ancient Roman society, but also the demarcation between rural and urban life. The graph given below, then, is mainly an adaptation from Lenski's similar graph with features added from Alföldy.[7]

The graph indicates by its shape the social structure of Palestine in the Herodian period. The long, thin rectangle at the top of the figure which stands over the diamond shape at the bottom represents the upper portion of society. As Lenski pointed out from his graph the height of this section indicates the social and economic gap between the upper and lower classes and the width of this part of the graph shows the numerically small size of this portion of the population. MacMullen, Alföldy, and Rillinger estimate that the upper classes of the Roman empire as a whole (the Senators, Knights, and Decurions) comprised no more than 1% of the total population.[8] The percentage in Palestine of the elite groups – the Herodian nobles, the High Priestly families, and the wealthy lay aristocracy – may have been similar.

Note that all of these upper classes according to the graph are urbanites. Yet in spite of the fact that most of these wealthy aristocrats lived in one of the main Palestinian cities (Jerusalem, Sepphoris, Tiberias, Caesarea Philippi) or in one of the towns or large villages (e.g., Gischala, or Gamala) their wealth was probably exclusively or mainly derived from land as we attempted to show in Chapter 2. These wealthy urbanites and their learned and cultured underlings formed structurally (but not numerically) one half of agrarian society in Palestine. They comprised the Great Tradition which stood over against the rural masses (as well as the urban lower classes), the other half of agrarian society, called the Little Tradition.

Secondly, one should note that these upper class groups are both wealthy and politically powerful. Indeed their class status is based primarily on possessions (i.e., land). Since Rome always entrusted the rule of its subjects to local wealthy people, political power always means wealth and wealth often means political power. There were no poor or middle class political rulers in the Roman empire.[9]

It is important to emphasize the essential bifurcation of peasant society into aristocrats and peasants. This structure was endemic to most ancient agrarian societies and was certainly present in the Hellenistic kingdoms and later in the Roman Empire. J. H. Kautsky's definition of aristocrats in such societies also accurately describes Herodian Palestine:

> ...the Aristocracy can be initially defined simply as consisting of those in an agrarian economy who, without themselves engaging in agricultural labor, live off the land by controlling the peasants so as to be able to take from them a part of their product. Of course, only a small percentage of the population can be aristocrats, because each peasant produces only a relatively small surplus and the average aristocrat consumes far more than a peasant.[9a]

At the very top of this society during the period of time we are considering sat the king (Herod the Great, Agrippa I and Agrippa II), the procurator (when Rome ruled all or part of Palestine directly), or the tetrarch/ethnarch (Archelaus, Antipas, Philip). These leaders exceeded all other members of the elite class not only in political power, but probably also in wealth. Because these political overlords enriched their top government officers and other friends with large land grants, controlled appointments to the High Priesthood, commanded the army, and levied taxes, their power even over the other aristocrats was enormous.

The Herodians in this graph are members of Herod's extended family and their descendants. Most of them (and not just his political heirs) must

TABLE C

Palestinian Social Structure
in the Herodian Period

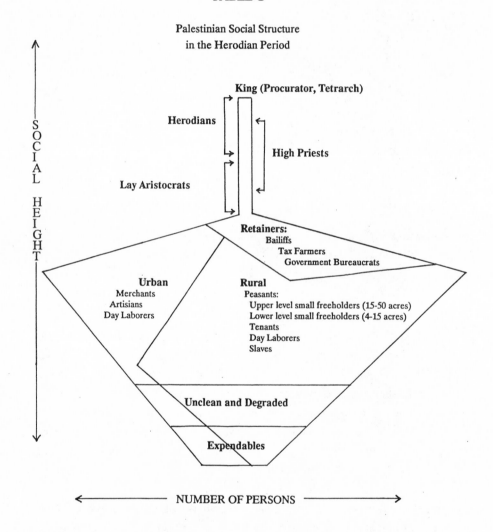

have inherited great wealth, as the estates of Salome and Berenice (see Chapter 2) would indicate. In addition to the family members we should include the upper echelon government administrators such as Ptolemy of Rhodes (see Chapter 2) to whom Herod granted a large estate in Western Samaria. Perhaps also in this category would have been Joseph, Herod's chief treasurer (A 15.185) and Corinthus his chamberlain (A 17.55f; B 1.576) who presumably also would have been given estates from the royal domains. Perhaps Herod's distinquished friends such as Nicolas of Damascus (A 17.225, B 2.21) also were enriched from the royal lands.[10] The evidence also indicates that Agrippa I and Agrippa II did the same for their trusted officials (see Chapter 2). Thus these officials have wealth, political power, influence, and prestige and must be included in this group. The lower level government officials, however, would be included in the retainer class described below.

The Herodians lived mainly in the cities of Palestine such as Jerusalem, Caesarea, Sebaste, and later Tiberias, Sepphoris, Caesarea Philippi, and Bethsaida Julias where they built royal palaces for themselves.[11] The palaces both of Herod and his successors must by all accounts, have been lavish displays of wealth.[12] But Herod also owned many other residences which were scattered throughout Palestine (e.g., Jericho, Masada, Herodium, Machaerus) and presumably, his successors and descendants had other residences built as well.

The next group in the class of the elite is the High Priests. Following SVM[13] we are using the term High Priests (ἀρχιερεῖς) as "members of the noble families from which the High Priests were selected," (Acts 4:6, B 6.114). Thus the High Priests were not only a social group but a caste into which one had to be born. Admission could be gained no other way.

We have described this social group in Chapter 2 as in many cases wealthy landowners. Some of their wealth may have derived, it is true, from the tithes and other temple perquisites which they received (some of them by force)[14] and Jeremias[15] may even have been correct when he suggested that they took money from the temple treasury. But we also showed above that many Priests were large landowners (Chapter 2)[16] However they gained their wealth, it seems likely that many were wealthy before they became High

Priests since, it appears, in many cases, they bought the priesthood (2Macc 4:7f, 4:24, b. Yeb 61a).[17]

Most of the High Priests in the Herodian period as we pointed out above came from one of four (or possibly five) families. These are the families listed in the lament passage of the Talmud (b.Pes 57a): The houses of Boethus, Hanan, Kathros, and Phiabi.[18] The sons or sons-in-law from these dynasties probably entered the High Priesthood already from a high social standing both as far as the wealth and prestige of their families. Goodman[19] has suggested that since Herod chose two of the High Priests from families in Alexandria or Babylon (A 15.22, 320), that Herod made them wealthy in Palestine by granting them lands so that by his death there existed a wealthy, landed priestly class. But one should also consider the possibility that at least one of these families (Boethus) already possessed some wealth before being appointed High Priest. At any rate by the first century A.D. these families were certainly wealthy and powerful, as were also most likely the other two families from which new High Priests were appointed. The fact that these four families were able to maintain a virtual monopoly on the High Priesthood shows their extraordinary power and influence.

Most of the members of this caste must have lived in the upper western part of Jerusalem.[20] Ananias, the High Priest when the revolt began in A.D. 66, had a house there, evidently near the palace of Agrippa II and Berenice (B 2.426f). This section is also where the "Burnt House" was found by the archaeological team of Avigad. From an inscription on a lead weight which read (בר קתרס) "son of Kathros," Avigad concluded that the house belonged to a scion of the house of Kathros. The House was destroyed in A.D. 70 (B 6.8-10). This is also the area where the other large and lavishly decorated houses were found by Navigad and here in this neighborhood is the traditional location of Caiaphas' house.[21]

The next social group within the elite class is the group of lay aristocrats. They are called "elders" (πρεσβύτεροι) (Mk. 15:1, Acts 4:5), "leaders" (προεστῶτες) (V 194), "first men" (πρῶτοι) (V 9, 185), Mk 6:21, "notables" (γνώριμοι) (B 2.410, 318), "powerful ones" (δύνατοι) (B 2.316, 411), "those first in rank (τίμη) and birth (γένος)" (A 20. 123), and "honored men" (יקירין) (Yoma 6:4). The three extraordinarily wealthy men of Jerusalem who could allegedly supply Jerusalem for twenty-one years (see Chapter 2) were called "the greatest of the land" (גדולי מדינה) (Gen R 42.1).[22]

These men were the non-priestly and non-royal members of the elite class who because of their wealth, influence, and achievements were leaders of their communities. Some of them were perhaps on the Sanhedrin either in Jerusalem or a smaller town (B 2.405, Mk. 15:1) and some were local magistrates (B 2.237=A 20.123, V 134; cf. V 134; cf. V 246, 278).[23] These aristocrats apparently had to assist the tax farmers in collecting the taxes (A 20.194, B 2.405).[24]

Most of these wealthy citizens in Jerusalem must have lived in the same high classed quarter as the High Priests. The aristocrats not only left behind evidence of their wealth in Jerusalem in the remains of their luxurious mansions (see Chapter 2)[25] but also in extravagant tomb complexes.[26]

We find this same social group in Tiberias as well. Josephus says (V 32-39) there were three groups in Tiberias at the outbreak of the war: a group of the most insignificant persons, a group led by Justus, and the "respectable citizens" (εὐσχημόνων) among whom were Julius Capellus, Herod son of Miaris, Herod son of Gamalus, and Compsus the son of Compsus. T. Rajak[27] surmises that the first man listed by Josephus was a Roman citizen, judging by his name; that the next two are from the Herodian family, and notes that Compsus' brother Crispus was the former prefect of Agrippa I (V 33). These men are clearly from the upper class of Tiberias.[28]

Apparently this social group also existed at Sepphoris. We do not possess information about the leaders of Sepphoris from the Herodian period, but the later rabbinic material about Sepphoris indicates a class of aristocrats similar to what we already have seen in Jerusalem. Bchler[29] affirmed that these leading citizens were called "the great ones," "the great of the generation," and "Parnasim" (i.e., leaders or managers). These great ones were evidently large landowners. In a Talmudic passage quoted by Bchler, a sage from the third century A.D. distinguishes three social classes based on wealth: the landowners, the peasants (am ha-aretz), and the "empty ones (ריקנים) (i.e., the poor).[30]

Probably also every town of good size had its wealthy and influential citizens such as John of Gischala (*V* 43-45) or Simon of Gabara (*V* 123-125). Thus this social group which forms part of the elite class was scattered more widely than the High Priests and Herodians.

As the graph indicates the power and prestige of these three groups overlapped. The High Priest certainly had more power than the lower individuals among the Herodians and the upper lay aristocrats must have enjoyed greater influence and respect than the lower members of the High Priestly families. In general, however, we should say that the Herodians, as royalty and with the closest ties to Rome, were the most powerful social group in Palestine. The High Priests who enjoyed not only wealth but religious prestige would have been second. The lay aristocrats had only their wealth and perhaps their own natural abilities to commend them and so must have been as a group socially lower than the High Priests.

These three groups, then, constituted the class of the elites, small in number – perhaps only one percent of the population – and socially, extremely elevated over the rest of the people.

The next class, termed by Lenski[31] the Retainers, stands between the elite and the peasants. Lenski maintains that most agrarian societies have employed Retainers to mediate between the common people and the ruling class. Lenski suggests that Retainers deflected some of the hostility which the lower classes would have felt toward the elite, since the peasants and small craftsmen could never be sure whether their trouble came mainly from the Retainers or higher up.

The Retainers administered the financial and political affairs of the upper class and enforced their goals. For this service, says Lenski, they "shared in the economic surplus." That is to say they were elevated economically above the ordinary mass of people. As with nearly all social distinctions, however, the line between the lower aristocrats and upper Retainers was fuzzy, just as the line between the lower Retainers and upper peasantry.

Tax collectors are the obvious first example of retainers, whether one speaks of the small tax farmers – who F. Herrenbrck[32] maintains were mainly responsible for collecting the revenue – or of toll collectors. John the tax collector who resided at Caesarea (*B* 2.287), Zacchaeus the chief tax collector who lived at Jericho (Lk. 19:1-10), and Levi of Galilee (Lk. 5:29) belonged to this class. The first two examples indicate that the Retainers could become quite wealthy.

In light of the results of Chapter 2 we should expect the bailiffs to have played a very significant role in Palestinian society in the Herodian period. The office of bailiff was known all over the empire and was termed in Greek (οἰκονόμος) , in Latin *vilicus*, and in Hebrew (בן בית), (איקונומוס) (a loan word), or (סנטר).[33] These important officials are mentioned twice in Lk (Lk. 12:42-48, 16:1-8). The example in Lk. 16:1-8 of the dishonest bailiff is especially revealing. Here we see the far reaching authority which the bailiff exercised over his master's economic affairs. Since bailiffs were often slaves or freedmen,[34] the slaves referred to in Mk. 12:2 and Mt. 24:45 are probably also bailiffs.[35] In spite of the lowly origins of many of the bailiffs their skills at administration must have made them invaluable to absentee landlords. Columella (first century A.D.) describes at length the characteristics both the bailiff and his wife should possess (XI.1.3-29, XII.1.1-6). He must be a man of sober and non-indulgent disposition who works hard. He must by example and by use of authority ensure that everyone does a full day's work.[36]

Dar thought he had identified the living quarters of a bailiff in western Samaria. The medium-sized estate at Qasr e Lejah (see above Chapter 4) has a residence which he terms "the manager's house."[37]

The third type of Retainer[38] would be the judicial magistrate whom Freyne finds in *B* 2.571 and Lk. 12:58 (=Mt. 5:25). Lk. 18:2 may also refer to this official. They evidently judged legal disputes and served in nearly every town of any size.

To these officials we should also list soldiers, both Roman and Herodian, and perhaps High Priestly.[39] Also the lower officials of the royal court would be Retainers.[40]

The aristocrats and their Retainers stood over the common people both in the city and in the country. In the city were small merchants, artisans and day laborers whose standard of living could range from comfortable to very poor. Wealthy merchants would presumably have entered eventually into the aristocratic class. The small merchants would include what Jeremias calls the "retail traders" and perhaps others who engaged in either foreign or local trade on a small scale.[41] Craftsmen could be quite well off–as the temple builders were[42]–but were always at any rate better off than the unskilled day laborers who often lived in poverty just above the level of beggars.[43]

The various levels within the rural peasant class have already been explored in the previous chapter. We would consider upper level peasants to be those who needed no outside income to maintain their subsistence. They owned enough acreage to feed their families and to live fairly comfortably. Dar may have found some examples of this level of peasantry in Samaria. In two villages he discovered a house that had a larger compound than the others and a more elaborate tomb than the rest.[44]

Lower level peasants received most of their living from their piece of land, but had to supplement this income in one of the various ways suggested in Chapter 3. The tenants and day laborers owned no land or very little land (less than four acres) and so received most if not all of their income from land owned by someone else. Thus they had even less control of the means of production than the lower level small-freeholder. Slaves were similar to tenants and day laborers financially, but had the additional disadvantage of lack of personal freedom.

The unclean and degraded classes were found both in the city and the country. These consist of people "inferior to the masses of common people" due to occupation, heredity, or disease.

The occupations which were scorned were prostitutes, dung collectors, ass drivers, gamblers, sailors, tanners, peddlers, herdsmen, and usurers among others.[45]

Those groups inferior to the common people due to heredity would have included mainly those born illegitimately. Kiddushin 4:1 lists a hierarchy of births ranging from priests to the lowly four: bastards,

Gibeonites, those that must be silent when reproached about their origins, and foundlings.[46] The word usually translated bastard, (ממזר), was actually not the equivalent of that English word meaning illegitimate child. The (ממזר) is the child of an adulterous or incestuous union (as defined by Lev. 18 and 20). A (ממזר) could not "enter the congregation of the Lord" (Dt. 23:3).[47] That is, they could not intermarry with Israelites. The (נתין) was a descendant of the Gibeonites whom Joshua (Josh. 9:27) made temple slaves. They were also according to later rabbinic law (b.Yeb 78b) excluded from the Israelite community as far as intermarriage.[48] Whether this group actually existed in the Herodian period might be questionable. The (שתוקי) must be silent when reproached about his descent because he does not know who his father was (Kidd 4:2).[49] The (אסופי) is a child taken up from the street whose father and mother are unknown (Kidd 4:2).[50]

Yeb 4:13 indicates that records were kept of one's ancestry. R. Simeon b. Azzai (120-140 A.D.) reports that he found a family register in Jerusalem which said "such a one is a bastard...."[51] The precise definitions of these terms were often debated by the sages but the stigma attached to them was not. It "marked every male descendant...forever and indelibly...."[52] One Mishnaic passage e.g., demands that an Israelite be scourged who marries a bastard or Gibeonite (Makk 3:1).

P. Laslett has shown by sociological study of bastardy that those born illegitimately tend also to bear and beget children illegitimately. They, therefore, maintains Laslett, tend to form a "sub-society" marked off as outcasts from others and perpetuating themselves as sub-society through successive generations of illegitimacy.[53]

Finally, are those included in the unclean and degraded class due to disease. We should think here especially of the lepers who seem to have abounded in Palestine.[54] Such people were declared unclean by a priest (Lev. 13:11, 25) and had to remain apart from everyone else crying out from a distance "Unclean!" (Lev .13:45f). Lepers lived then, a life of social ostracism.

At the very bottom of the social structure, according to Lenski, were the "expendables." This group consisted of "criminals, beggars, and underemployed itinerant workers." Lenski remarks concerning this class:

"Agrarian societies usually produced more people than the dominant classes found it profitable to employ." Lenski estimates, based on statistics from Europe from the sixteenth to the eighteenth century, that most agrarian societies contained about five to ten percent of the population in this class.[55]

We should list first of all the bandits as expendables. Hengel was one of the first scholars to describe bandits in Palestine in sociological terms. Banditry was a problem throughout the Greco-Roman world in the time period we are considering. The ranks of bandits were swollen by runaway slaves, deserting soldiers and impoverished peasants.[56] One sociologist, E. J. Hobsbawn, has described the phenomenon of banditry in agrarian societies generally as "a primitive form of organized social protest."[57] This thesis has been most recently taken up by R. Horsley and J. S. Hanson[58] in their work on Palestine in the first century A.D.

That banditry in the ancient world was rooted in social and economic factors is hardly deniable.[59] We also find examples in Palestine of banditry originating with poverty and hardship. But we must be cautious in attributing to bandits the "Robin Hood" heroic stature that Horsley and Hanson describe.[60] They attempt to show that bandits often enjoyed the support and protection of the peasant villagers and were even their heroes. Their two examples of such a phenomenon are Hezekiah and his men, who were executed by Herod the Great (*A* 14.168) and Eleazar ben Dinai to whom the Galileans turned to get justice on a group of Samaritans for murdering some pilgrims (*A* 20.118-36, *B* 2.228-31). Horsley and Hanson point out that the execution of Hezekiah and his men brought a storm of protest. But we must remember that those protesting in the case of Hezekiah were the relatives of those slain and their protest was more against Herod's summary execution of these men without trial. Even the Sanhedrin, certainly no lover of bandits was appalled by Herod's handling of the matter (*A* 14.165-167). Further, Josephus writes that they sang Herod's praises in the villages and cities because in getting rid of Hezekiah he had granted security and peace to the region (*A* 14.160). Possibly Josephus is stretching the truth here and in reality presenting the viewpoint of the urban elite rather than the peasant villager, but it is also possible that many peasants honored bandits as much out of fear than hero worship and that there was general relief when Hezekiah was executed.

Further, we must remember in the case of Eleazar ben Dinai that the peasants turned to him as a last resort only after Cumanus dallied about giving them justice. The Mishnah on the other hand (Sota 9:9) remembers ben Dinai as a murderer. Perhaps he was a local hero or even a "freedom fighter" or Zealot,[61] but this is hardly provable.

Even if one could then, produce a few examples of bandits as social protesters representing the will of the common people it would not change the verdict on banditry in general. Bandits were generally considered objects of dread and animosity in the Jewish sources. They were dangerous, ruthless criminals who preyed on innocent people. The rabbinic sources, Josephus, and the New Testament reflect this attitude.[62]

Beggars also appear frequently in Palestine. They are lame (Acts 3:2, Jn. 5:3, Shabb 6:8, Lk. 16:20) or blind (Jn. 9:1, Mt. 21:14, Mk. 10:46) and sit along the roadside in the country (Mk. 10:46), or along the streets and alleys in the city (Lk. 14:21). A favorite place for beggars was the temple (Acts 3:2) since almsgiving was considered especially meritorious when done there.[63]

We shall now make four concluding observations concerning the social structure of Herodian Palestine. First, the numerical difference between rich and poor was enormous. We have already indicated that perhaps only about one percent of the population belonged to the elite class. What percentage of the population lived in extreme poverty? Again we can only estimate based on statistics from other societies. These statistics may or may not be valid for the Greco-Roman world in general and for Palestine in particular. MacMullen notes that in Europe in the fourteenth and fifteenth centuries, one-third of the population lived in "habitual want." He defines habitual want as: one "devoted the vast bulk of each day's earnings to his immediate needs and accumulated no property or possessions to speak of."[64] MacMullen estimates that the poor in the Roman empire equaled the same percentage. This figure does not seem out of line for Herodian Palestine. The figure would include not only the Expendables but most of the day laborers among the urban and rural workers and probably many of the tenant farmers. Thus, the statement by R. Ishmael (A.D. 120-140) regarding the poverty in Palestine may have an element of truth in it: "...the daughters of Israel are comely but poverty destroys their comeliness."[65]

The second observation is that the economic and social distance between the elite class and the lower classes was incredibly great. As Lenski notes in his comments on his graph characterizing the social structure of a typical agrarian society, the part of the graph depicting the elites should actually be far higher and far thinner than one can represent on one page.[66] Lenski continues: "One fact impresses itself on almost any observer of agrarian societies, especially on one who views them in a broadly comparative perspective. This is the fact of the *marked social inequality*."[67] A. N. Sherwin-White observed that in the Gospels we basically find two classes: very rich and very poor.[68] This social inequality resulted, to a great extent, says Lenski, from the "proprietary theory" of government which was that the state was a piece of property which its owner could use for his own personal advantage. Lenski notes that the Ptolemies, Seleucids, and Roman emperors are the best examples of those who adhered to this theory of government.[69] The social and economic distance, then, between Herod the Great and the lame beggar on the street is probably now beyond our ability fully to comprehend.

The third observation is that there existed a large cultural gap between urban and rural peoples. Alföldy represents this in his pyramidal graph[70] and many other historians have also noted this condition. The rural population in the eastern Roman empire for the most part seems to have maintained their native language and customs[71] whether Coptic in Egypt,[72] Lycaonian or Celtic in Asia Minor,[73] or Aramaic in Syria and Palestine.[74] On the other hand in the cities people spoke Greek, many were literate, and most were in touch to some degree with the great institutions and ideas of Greco-Roman society. This was especially true of the aristocrats, but to some extent even true of the urban poor, according to de Ste. Croix, since the urban poor may have "mixed with the educated" in some way.[75] Such mixing could take place in Palestinian cities not only in synagogues but in theatres amphitheatres and hippodromes, as well as in the courts of justice.[76] Thus there was a gulf even between the peasants and the urban poor. As L. White has observed for medieval agrarian societies: "Cities were atolls of civilization...on an ocean of primitivism."[77]

The natural result of such a cultural gap was the strong sense of superiority on the part of the urbanite over the country peasant. Lenski shows that in agrarian societies in general the urban elite have viewed peasants as subhuman.[78] Rostovtzeff observed that city residents in the Roman empire regarded the (γεωργός) or *paganus* as an inferior uncivilized being.[79] MacMullen writes that the urbanite regarded the peasant as an "unmannerly, ignorant being."[80] Finkelstein maintained that all the residents of Jerusalem – both wealthy and poor – would have agreed in their contempt for the provincials (country peasants).[81]

The rabbinic attitude toward the rural people of Palestine is an example of this contempt. Here we shall cautiously allow some statements made about the am ha-aretz to inform our inquiry.[82] Though certainly not all am ha-aretz were poor (Demai 2:2f, t.Demai 3:6f), many must have been.[83] Thus disparaging comments about the am ha-aretz by the rabbis probably reflect not only their religious, but also their social differences. In this case then we shall regard the am ha-aretz as peasants. The am ha aretz in the rabbinic literature are equated with the crude and unlearned people, called (בור) in Hebrew which means basically "outside (the city)".[84] They are consistently represented as ignorant and unteachable and their wives are "like reptiles."[85]

One can also detect this contempt in Josephus. He has the High Priest in *B* 4.239, 241 refer to the Zealots – many of whom came from the rural districts of Palestine[86] – as "slaughtered things" (θύματα) and "offscourings" (καθάρματα). Cornfeld's translation captures the tone of these words: "the dregs and scum of the whole country."[87] Either these words are fairly close to the High Priest's or are Josephus' own words but either way they represent the words of someone from the elite class describing the lower rural classes. Josephus himself in *B* 5.443 calls the Zealots "slaves, rabble (συγκλύδες), and bastards" which Cornfeld renders, "slaves, the dregs of humanity and bastard scum."[88] Whether we should take the term bastard (νόθον) literally here or only as a pejorative metaphor is uncertain, but we should at least not rule out the possibility that many

many participants in this rebellion came from the outcast class. At any rate Josephus demonstrates his contempt for the peasant classes with these words.

The final observation we should make is that most of the population in ancient agrarian society belonged to the rural peasantry. Rostovtzeff[89] affirmed that rural peasants must have been overwhelmingly in the majority in antiquity, but offered no percentages. Ramsay MacMullen suggests 70 to 75% of the people in ancient Italy were peasants.[90] De Ste. Croix accepts the figure of L. White the medievalist who estimated that ten people were needed in the country to produce enough food to enable one person to live away from the land.[91] If this estimate is reasonably accurate for Palestine – and the relative lack of large cities would argue that it is – then over 90% of the population lived outside the cities, in small villages or towns engaged in agriculture.

This society, structurally, was in most respects probably much the same as societies scattered throughout the Roman empire. The three groups in the elite class correspond to the elites in Roman cities (Senators, Equites, Decurions) who had almost absolute control of both political power and wealth. Indeed the two (wealth and power) almost always went hand-in-hand. Beneath the elites was a class of semi-elites who discharged the wishes of the aristocrats and served as a buffer against the resentment aimed at the upper-class by the common folk. Further down the social and economic scale were the peasant freeholders who eked out a subsistence but at least owned a piece of land. At bottom were those living in "habitual want." Palestinian society was divided. It was divided horizontally by the enormous chasm between the wealthy and the common masses and vertically by the cultural gap between the urban and rural populations.

END NOTES

1. P. Alfaric, *Die Sozialen Ursprünge des Christentums* (Darmstadt: Progress, 1963; French 1959); E. Lohmeyer, *Soziale Fragen im Urchristentum* (Leipzig: Quelle und Meyer, 1921) pp. 53-55. To some extent also F. Houtard, *Religion et Modes de Production Précapitalistes* (Brussels: University of Brussels, 1980) pp. 232-238, is guilty of this although he attempts to place the sects into a broader social framework.

2. See e.g., E. E. Urbach, "Class-Status and Leadership in the World of the Palestinian Sages" *Proceedings of the Israel Academy of Sciences and Humanities* 2(1968) pp. 38-74, esp. pp. 47 and 61; Büchler, *Political and Social Leaders of the Jewish Community of Sepphoris in the Second and Third Centuries* (London: Jews' College); and Stern, 1976, pp. 619-621. Goodman, 1983, p. 118, criticizes considering the sages a social class.

3. Finkelstein, 1962, pp. 24f, 754-761; Moore, 1954, vol. I, p. 60; II, p. 72. See also Jer. 34:19, Ezra 4:4, 2Kgs. 24:14 and BDB.

4. See especially A. Oppenheimer, 1977, pp. 18-21.

5. E.g., J. Gager, *Kingdom and Community* (Englewood Cliffs, New Jersey: Prentice-Hall, 1975) pp. 39-41 on the theory of cognitive dissonance as seen in a flying-saucer cult in the United States. This book contains otherwise, however, many interesting insights.

6. Lenski, *Power and Privilege* (New York: McGraw-Hill, 1966); Alföldy, *Die römische Gesellschaft* (Wiesbaden: Steiner, 1986). The critique of Alföldy made by R. Rilinger "Moderne und zeitgenössische Vorstellungen von der Gesellschaftsordnung der römischen Kaiserziet" *Saeculum* 36(1985) 299-329, does not seem applicable for Palestinian rural society.

7. Lenski, 1966, p. 284; Alföldy, 1986, p. 10.

8. MacMullen, 1974, p. 89; Rilinger, 1985, p. 302; Alföldy, *Römische Sozial-geschichte* (Wiesbaden: Franz Steiner, 1975) p. 130.

9. P. A. Brunt, "Local Ruling Classes in the Roman Empire" in D. M. Pippidi, ed. *Assimilation et Résistance a la culture Gréco-romaine dans le Monde Ancien* (Paris: Academiei, 1976) pp. 161-170; Goodman, 1987, pp. 34, 44.

9a. Kautsky, 1982, pp. 79f.

10. On Herod's court officials and friends see Jeremias, 1969, pp. 88f.

11. See SVM II, pp. 115-118, 169-176, 178-182 on these cities. For the Herodian palaces see SVM I, pp. 304-308.

12.   See *B* 5.176-183 for Herod's palace in Jerusalem. The Herodians apparently later owned other mansions in Jerusalem: *V* 46, *B* 2.426f. On the palace of Antipas at Tiberias see *V* 64-67.

13.   SVM II, p. 235. As SVM (II, 235f) note the arguments of Jeremias, that "High Priests" really refers to a class of upper level priests and not necessarily family members, may be superfluous since so much nepotism seems to have been practiced. See Jeremias, 1969, pp. 160-181f and b.Pes 57a, t.Zeb 11:16.

14.   See *A* 20.181, b.Pes 57a; and Jeremias, 1969, p. 98. For wealth through tithes see *V* 12, 15; *A* 20.181, 206f and Safrai, 1976, p. 823.

15.   Jeremias, 1969, p. 99. Jeremias also suggests landownership and commerce as the means the High Priests used to enrich themselves, as well as taking bribes.

16.   See also Kreissig, 1970, p. 82; Finkelstein, 1929, p. 189.

17.   Jeremias, 1969, p. 98; Kreissig, 1970, p. 82.

18.   See Stern, 1976, pp. 605-609; Smallwood, 1962, pp. 14-34; Jeremias, 1969, p. 194.

19.   Goodman, 1987, pp. 40-44.

20.   Finkelstein, 1962, p. 12.

21.   Avigad, 1983, pp. 66-72.

22.   For the collection of these and other titles see Jeremias, 1969, pp. 224-226; Finkelstein, 1962, vol. I, p. 16, and Goodman, 1983, p. 33.

23.   Jeremias, 1969, p. 224.

24.   *Ibid.* p. 228; Baron, vol. I, p. 274.

25.   Avigad, 1980, passim.

26.   See N. Avigad, "The Burial-Vault of a Nazarite Family on Mount Scopus" *IEJ* 21(1971) 185-200. The tomb is richly decorated like the royal tomb of Queen Helene of Adiabene and the family tomb of Herod. Thus the tomb belonged evidently to "one of Jerusalem's aristocratic families." Perhaps also to be included here is another tomb found on Mt. Scopus. See L. Y. Rahmani "A Jewish Rock-Cut Tomb on Mt. Scopus." *Atiqot* E.S. 14(1980) 49-54.

27.   Rajak, "Justus of Tiberias" *Classical Quarterly* N.S. 23(1973) pp. 345-368; esp. 351. Cf. Kippenberg, 1978, pp. 129f.

28. Goodman seems correct, 1983, p. 33, that Mk. 6:21 refers to the aristocrats of Galilee. This reference would probably more specifically refer to Tiberias.

29. Büchler, *The Political and Social Leaders of the Jewish Community of Sepphoris in the Second and Third Centuries* (London: Jews' College, no date) pp. 7-10.

30. B. Hull 92a; Büchler, *ibid.* p. 35.

31. Lenski, 1966, pp. 243-248.

32. Herrenbrück, 1981, pp. 178-194. *Cf.* also M. Stern "The Province of Judea," 1976, p. 333.

33. See Jones "Colonus" in *OCD*; LSJM; O. Michel " (οἰκονόμος)" *TDNT*; Jastrow. For the wide distribution of the Greek term see E. Ziebarth "Oikonomos" Pauly-Wissowa XVII, 2, Col. 2118f. For the term in the rabbinic literature see: Lev R 12, Pesikta Rabbati 10, b. Shabb 153a, t. BM 9:14, t. Yom Tob 4:9, t. BB 3:5, BB 4:7.

34. Jones, "Colonus" *OCD*.

35. See Michel in *TDNT*.

36. *Cf.* Cato, de *Agricultura* CXLIIf.

37. Dar, 1986, p. 10.

38. See Freyne, 1980, p. 198. These local judges appear also in the rabbinic literature. See b.Shabb 139a and Urbach, 1968, p. 67.

39. Roman soldiers: Mt. 8:9, Acts 10:1; Herodian: *A* 17:156, *B* 1.652, *B* 2.8, *A* 19.315, 353 and Jeremias, 1969, p. 89; High Priestly: Jn 18:3, 12.

40. Jeremias, 1969, pp. 88-90 for a description of these officials.

41. *Ibid.*, pp. 100, 35-51.

42. See the family buried in the tomb at Givat ha-Mivtar north of Jerusalem headed by "Simon the Temple Builder." This tomb and its contents are described by V. Tzaferis "Jewish Tombs at and near Givat ha-Mivtar, Jerusalem" *IEJ* 20 (1970) 18-22; N. Haas "Anthropological Observations on the Skeletal Remains from Givat ha-Mivtar" *IEJ* 20(1970) 38-59; J. Naveh "The Ossuary Inscriptions from Givat ha-Mivtar" *IEJ* 20 (1970) 33-37. This is evidently a family of craftsmen who did hard manual labor but obtained a measure of financial success.

43. See above Chapter 3 on day laborers.

44. Dar, 1986, pp. 46f.

45.   Lk. 7:37-39, Mt. 21:31, Kidd 4:14, Ket 7:10, b Kidd 82a, b.Sanh 25b, and Jeremias, 1969, pp. 303-312. Also see Sanh 3:3.

46.   See Danby's translation and notes here. *Cf.* also Horayoth 3:7f.

47.   L. N. D. Dembitz "Bastard" *JE.*

48.   See Jastrow.

49.   *Ibid.*

50.   *Ibid.* B.BM 87a says a man should not marry a female foundling.

51.   Danby's translation.

52.   Jeremias, 1969, p. 342. For the definition of these terms see *ibid.*, pp. 337-344.

53.   P. Laslett, "The Bastard Prone Sub-Society" in P. Laslett, K. Oosterveen, and R. M. Smith, *Bastardy and Its Comparative History* (London: Edward Arnold, 1980) pp. 217-246.

54.   Mk. 1:40, 14:3, Lk. 17:12, Meg 1:7, Moed Katan 3:1, Sotah 1:5, Zeb 14:3, Pseudo Philo 13:3, Apocryphal Syriac Psalm 155 (see *POT* II, p. 624). The word seems to have been generally used for infectious skin diseases. See Lev 13.

55.   Lenski, 1966, pp. 281-283.

56.   Hengel, 1961, pp. 34f.

57.   Hobsbawm, 1959, p. 13.

58.   Horsley and Hanson, 1985. They refer to the banditry of Palestine as "social banditry." Isaac, 1984, p. 177 calls it "political banditry."

59.   See Chapter 3. On bandits in the ancient world see also R. MacMullen, *Enemies of the Roman Order* (Cambridge: Harvard, 1966) pp. 255-268; B. D. Shaw "Bandits in the Roman Empire" *Past and Present* 102(1984) pp. 3-52.

60.   See Horsley and Hanson, 1985, p. 74, who refer to the bandits of Palestine as "Jewish Robin Hoods."

61.   H. Bietenhard, *Sota* (Berlin: Töpelmann, 1956) pp. 153-155, regarded Eleazer b. Dinai as a Zealot freedom fighter.

62.   See e.g., Mk. 14:48, Lk. 10:30, Jn. 10:1, 2Cor. 11:26; Shab 2:5, t. Taan 2:12, BM 7:9; *B* 2.253, 4.135, 406, *A* 14.159, 17.285, 20.185, 20.256. Also see Hengel, 1961, pp. 42-46. On the other hand some authors in antiquity could romanticize the brigand and pirate leaders into heroic figures. This should

not cause us to lose sight of the fact, however, that the bandits caused untold hardship on the general population. See Hengel, 1961, pp. 34f.

63.   Jeremias, 1969, pp. 116f.

64.   MacMullen, 1974, p. 93.

65.   Nedarim 9:10. Translation in Danby.

66.   Lenski, 1966, p. 285.

67.   *Ibid.*, p. 210. Emphasis is Lenski's.

68.   Sherwin-White, 1963, p. 139. Sherwin-White cites Lk. 16:1-6 and Mt. 18:23-34 = Lk. 7:41.

69.   Lenski, 1966, p. 214.

70.   Alföldy, 1986, p. 10.

71.   De Ste. Croix, 1981, pp. 10, 13; Rostovtzeff, 1957, pp. 193 and 346; MacMullen, 1974, p. 46.

72.   MacMullen, 1974, p. 46; Jones, 1940, p. 293.

73.   See Acts 14:11 and Jones, 1940, p. 290.

74.   SVM II, p. 26, "...The prominence of Aramaic at every level as the main language of Palestinian Jewry is now solidly backed by evidence...." The same was true for the native languages of North Africa, Britain, Gaul, Spain and others. See Rostovtzeff, 1957, pp. 193f; Jones, 1940, pp. 29Pf; Brunt, 1976, pp. 170-172. For Aramaic as the nearly exclusive language of Upper Galilee, see E. M. Meyers, "Galilean Regionalism as a Factor in Historical Reconstruction" *BASOR* 221(1976) 93-101. For Greek in Galilee see Rajak, 1973, p. 368, and *A* 20. 264.

75.   De Ste. Croix, 1981, p. 13.

76.   See SVM II, pp. 46, 48, 54, 55. As the authors say (p. 55) even though Josephus (*A* 15.268) declared that theaters and amphitheaters were alien to Jewish custom, "...it should not be assumed that the mass of the Jewish population did not frequent them." For the benefits of the urban proletariat in living in the city see Jones, 1940, p. 285.

77.   White quoted in de Ste. Croix, 1981, p. 10.

78.   Lenski, 1966, p. 271.

79.   Rostovtzeff, 1957, p. 192.

80.   MacMullen, 1974, p. 32. See also Jones, 1940, pp. 295f.

81.   Finkelstein, 1962, p. 24. For Palestine see also Applebaum, 1977, pp. 370f, and Theissen, 1978, pp. 47-58.

82.   Oppenheimer, 1977, pp. 18-21, for a caution against viewing the am ha-aretz as a social class.

83.   See Finkelstein, 1962, pp. 24f, 754-761.

84.   Avoth 2:6. See G. R. Driver "Notes on the Text of the Psalms" *HTR* 29(1936) p. 172. See also Mikvaoth 9:6 and Num R 3. Also see Jastrow ad loc.

85.   Moore, 1954, I, p. 60; II, pp. 72f, 157; G. Vermes, *Jesus the Jew* (London: Collins, 1973) pp. 54f. *Cf.* also b.BB 8a and Urbach, 1968, p. 71, where Rabbi would open his storehouses during the famine but not for the am ha-aretz; and Heinemann, 1954, p. 267.

86.   This conclusion is convincingly argued by Horsley and Hanson, 1985, pp. 220-223. See e.g., *B* 4.135, 419-439, 451.

87.   Cornfeld, 1982, p. 277.

88.   *Ibid.*, p. 388.

89.   Rostovtzeff, 1957, p. 346.

90.   MacMullen, 1974a, p. 253.

91.   De Ste. Croix, 1981, p. 10; L. White, "Die Ausbreitung der Technik 500-1500" in C. M. Cipolla and K. Borchardt, ed. *Europäische Wirtschaftsgeschichte: Mittelalter*, Bd. I (Stuttgart: Gustav Fischer, 1978) p. 92. *Cf.* Kautsky, 1982, p. 269.

CONCLUSION

The social history of Palestine in the Herodian period is the history of the concept of land in the Little Tradition over against the Great Tradition. Land was viewed in a more traditional sense according to the Little Tradition, but in a more entrepreneurial, capitalistic sense according to the newer concept which had made its way into the Great Tradition. The new economic concepts which Hellenism and Romanism brought to Palestine were bound to lead to sharp tensions between the Jewish common folk and their political masters.

The traditional concept of the land of Israel had been – and remained so among the peasantry – that the land belonged to Yaweh with Israel as his tenants. The implications of this starting point were that, first, everyone ought to share roughly equally in the use of the land. Second, no one should be permanently displaced from the use of the land, especially that piece of land (his patrimony) which had been in use by his forebears. Revived interest in the Jubilee during the Herodian period seems to stem from a longing among the common folk for its enforcement.

With the coming of Hellenism and later Romanism the socio-economic egalitarian ideal in which everyone would sit under his own vine and fig tree – an ideal which admittedly had never been completely realized – became an even more remote possibility. Under Ptolemy and later the Seleucids, Herods and Roman Emperors, the large royal estates gobbled up huge chunks of the land of Israel. In the Herodian period these estates – many of which first began as royal estates under Ptolemy – stretched along the Coastal Plain and Shephelah, in the Judean and Samaritan Hill Country, along the lower Jordan Valley, in the Hill Country of Galilee, the Golan, Perea, and Idumea. Later, especially under the Romans, the aristocratic Jews developed a capitalistic view of the land and built their own large and medium-sized estates.

Such a movement in land ownership must have cost many peasants their farm plots. The result was a class of tenant farmers and day laborers who barely stayed at the subsistence level in the best of times. The peasants who were able to hold on to their patrimony were undoubtedly burdened under taxation, farm plots that were too small, and simply the vicissitudes of life in the ancient Mediterranean world. Yet economic conditions in Herodian Palestine seem to have been about the same for the peasants as elsewhere in the Greco-Roman world. Great economic changes came to almost all the lands conquered by the Hellenists and later Romans.

Such profound changes economically inevitably had their impact on kinship and social relationships. The basic socio-kinship units for a peasant in Herodian Palestine were the nuclear family, the extended family, and the village. The extended family was under stress during the period we have considered. The extent of the stress seems to have varied from region to region and depended also on the extent of economic change the family experienced. Yet in general one can detect a trend toward the break-up of the *beth av* in Jewish society. The medium social unit became then the neighbors of the courtyard, many of whom were probably not relatives. The old larger units, the clans or *mishpahoth*, had completely ceased to function as effective socio-kinship units. Thus the village became the largest social unit. The villages – or larger towns – stood over against the urban centers. The urban centers were typically parasitic and exploitative of the peasant village, the same pattern found in general in the eastern half of the Mediterranean world.

The picture one gets when one puts all this together is of a society divided both vertically and horizontally. Horizontally, the society was divided between the "Haves" and "Have-nots." The aristocrats – Herodians, High Priestly families, and lay aristocrats – were large estate owners who exploited the labor of the peasants. Vertically, the society was divided between urban and rural. Since most of the aristocrats lived in the urban centers and owned large estates, the urban centers were essentially exploitative of the rural areas. Yet the division was more than economic; it was cultural as well. Even the urban proletariat would have felt a difference between themself and the rustic.

What this understanding of Jewish society means for our interpretation of history is a question only time will answer. The great events of the first century A.D., the sect-formation of Judas of Galilee, the preaching of John the Baptist, the ministry of Jesus, and the Jewish War, among others, await further re-examination from the perspective of socio-economic conditions, especially the conditions among the peasantry. We must not neglect the religious motivation and ideas behind these movements, for surely the actors in these events were very religious and in some sense the leaders of these movements were "theologians." Yet both the leaders and the followers were very much aware that they were addressing, in their message and by their actions, life in its socio-economic reality.

Most of the Jewish peasants of the Herodian period died in historical obscurity. Those few that attained some individual notoriety usually suffered terrible deaths as a result of the attention focused on them, either because they were actually dangerous or only perceived as much. But we must not forget them as a class. In the first place we need to appreciate the way of life of a significant number of the human race. But also we cannot claim any longer rightly to study history merely by examining the deeds of the rich and famous.

SELECT BIBLIOGRAPHY

Abel, F. M.
1927   "Sappho et Arous" *Journal of the Palestine Oriental Society* 7, 89-94.

1967   *Geographie de la Palestine.* Paris: Le Coffre.

Alfaric, P.
1959   *Die Sozialien Ursprünge des Christentums.* Darmstadt: Progress, (French, 1959)

Alfölfy, G.
1986   *Die römische Gesellschaft.* Wiesbaden: Steiner.

Alon, G.
1980   *The Jews in their Land in the Talmudic Age.* Jerusalem: Magnes.

Alt, A.
1959   *Kleine Schriften.* München: Beck.

Amiran, D. H.
1950-51   "A Revised Earthquake Catalogue of Palestine" *IEJ.* 1, 223-246.

1952   "A Revised Earthquake Catalogue of Palestine II" *IEJ.* 2, 48-65.

Applebaum, S.
1971   "The Zealots: the Case for Reevaluation" *Journal of Roman Studies.* 61, 155-170.

1976   "Economic Life in Palestine" *Compendia.* I.2, 631-700.

1977   "Judaea as a Roman Province: the Countryside as a Political and Economic Factor" *ANRW.* II.8, 355-396.

1986   "The Settlement Pattern of Western Samaria from Hellenistic to Byzantine Times: A Historical Commentary" in S. Dar. *Landscape and Pattern.* Oxford: BAR.

1987   "The Problem of the Roman Villa in Eretz Israel" *Eretz Israel.* 19, 1-5.

Avigad, N.
1971   "The Burial-Vault of a Nazarite Family on Mount Scopus" *IEJ.* 21, 185-200.

1976   "How the Wealthy Lived in Herodian Jerusalem" *BAR.* 2, 22-35.

1980   *Discovering Jerusalem.* Oxford: Basil Blackwell.

Avi-Yonah, M.
1954   *The Madaba Mosaic Map.* Jerusalem: Israel Exploration Society.

1962a   *Geschichte der Juden im Zeitalter des Talmud.* Berlin: de Gruyter.

1962b   "Scythopolis" *IEJ.* 12, 125-134.

1975   *The Herodian Period* (Editor). London: Allen.

1977   *The Holy Land.* Grand Rapids, Michigan: Baker

Baron, S. W.
1952   *A Social and Religious History of the Jews.* New York: Columbia University.

Baumbach, G.
1965   "Zeloten und Sikarier" *Theologische Literaturzeitung* 90, 727-739.

Beebe, H. K.
1975   "Domestic Architecture and the New Testament" *BA* 38, 89-104.

Bell, H. I.
1948   *Egypt from Alexander the Great to the Arab Conquest.* Oxford: Clarendon.

Ben-David, A.
1974   *Talmudische Ökonomie.* Hildesheim: Georg Olms.

Ben-Horin, U.

1952   "Official Report on the Earthquake of 1837" *IEJ* 2, 63-65.

Bickerman, E.
1938   *Institutions des Seleucides.* Paris: Libraire Orientaliste Paul Geuthner.

Bouquet, A. C.
1953   *Everyday Life in New Testament Times.* London: Batsford.

Broshi, M.
1979   "The Population of Western Palestine in the Roman-Byzantine Period" *BASOR* 236, 1-10

Broughton, T. R. S.
1938   "Roman Asia Minor" in T. Frank, Editor. *Economic Survey of Ancient Rome.* Baltimore: Johns Hopkins.

Brunt, P.
1971a   *Italian Man Power.* Oxford: Clarendon.

1971b   *Social Conflicts in the Roman Republic.* New York: Norton.

1977   "Josephus on Social Conflicts in Roman Judaea" *Klio* 59, 149-153.

182

Büchler, A.
1904   "Die Schauplätze des Bar-Kochbakrieges" *JQR* 16, 143-205.

1906   *Der galiläische 'Am-ha' Ares des zweiten Jahrhunderts.* Vienna: Alfred Hölder.

1912   *The Economic Conditions of Judea after the Destruction of the Second Temple.* London: Oxford University.

No date   *Political and Social Leaders of the Jewish Community of Sepphoris in the Second and Third Centuries.* London: Jews' College.

Clark, C. and M. Haswell
1966   *The Economics of Subsistence Agriculture.* New York: St. Martins.

Conder, C. R., and H. H. Kitchener
1882   *The Survey of Western Palestine.* London: Committee of the Palestine Exploration Fund.

Cornfeld, G.
1982   *Josephus: The Jewish War.* Grand Rapids, Michigan: Zondervan.

Corbo, V.
1972   *The House of Saint Peter at Capharnaum.* Translated S. Soller. Jerusalem: Franciscan.

1975   *Cafarnao* I. Jerusalem: Franciscan

Cronbach, A.
1944   "The Social Ideals of the Apocrypha and the Pseudepigrapha" *HUCA* 18, 119-156.

Dalman, G.
1964   *Arbeit und Sitte in Palästina.* Hildesheim: Olms.

Damaschke, A.
1924   *Bibel und Bodenreform.* Berlin: Mann.

Dar, S.
1986   *Landscape and Pattern.* Oxford: BAR.

Davies, W. D.
1974   *The Gospel and the Land.* Berkeley: University of California.

Day, J.
1932   "Agriculture in the Life of Pompeii" *Yale Classical Studies* 3, 167-208.

Derrett, J. D. M.
1963   "Fresh Light on the Parable of the Wicked Winedressers" *Revue internationale des droits de 1' antiquité* 10, 11-41.

Dyson, S. L.
1975   "Native Revolt Patterns in the Roman Empire" *ANRW* II.3, 138-175.

Finkelstein, L.
1929   "The Pharisees: Their Origin and their Philosophy" *HTR* 22, 185-261.

1962   *The Pharisees.* Philadelphia: Jewish Publication Society of America.

Finley, M. I.
1973   *The Ancient Economy.* London: Chatto and Windus.

Fitzmyer, J.
1971   *Essays on the Semitic Background of the New Testament.* London: Chapman.

Frank, T.
1936-1938   *Economic Survey of Ancient Rome.* Baltimore: Johns Hopkins.

Frayn, J. M.
1979   *Subsistence Farming in Roman Italy.* London: Centaur.

Freyne, S.
1980   *Galilee from Alexander to Hadrian.* Wilmington, Delaware: Michael Glazier.

Garnsey, P., Editor.
1980   *Non-slave Labour in the Greco-Roman World.* Cambridge: Cambridge Philological Society.

Golomb, B., and Y. Kedar.
1971   "Ancient Agriculture in the Galilee Mountains" *IEJ* 21, 136-140.

Goodman, M.
1983   *State and Society in Roman Galilee,* A.D. 132-212. Totowa, N.J.: Rowman and Allenheld.

1987   *The Ruling Class of Judaea.* Cambridge: Cambridge University.

Gottwald, N.
1979   *The Tribes of Yahweh.* Maryknoll: Orbis, 1979.

Grant, F. C.
1926   *The Economic Background of the Gospels.* London: Oxford University.

Haas, N.
1970   "Anthropological Observations on the Skeletal Remains from Givat ha-Mivtar" *IEJ* 20, 38-59.

Hachlili, R.
1979   "The Goliath Family in Jericho: Funerary Inscriptions from a First Century A.D. Jewish Monumental Tomb" *BASOR* 235, 31-66.

Hachlili, R., and A. Killebrew
1983   "Jewish Funerary Customs During the Second Temple Period in Light of the Excavations at the Jericho Necropolis" *PEQ* 115, 109-139.

Hachlili, R., and P. Smith
1979   "The Genealogy of the Goliath Family" *BASOR* 235, 67-71.

Hamel, G. H.
1983   *Poverty and Charity in Roman Palestine, First Three Centuries.* University of California, Santa Cruz: Ph.D.

Harper, M.
1928   "Village Administration in the Roman Province of Syria" *Yale Classical Studies* 1, 105-168.

Heichelheim, F. M.
1938   "Roman Syria" In T. Frank, Editor. *Economic Survey of Ancient Rome.* Baltimore: Johns Hopkins.

Heinemann, J. H.
1954   "The Status of the Labourer in Jewish Law and Society in the Tannaitic Period" *HUCA* 25, 163-325.

Heinisch, P.
1935   *Das Buch Leviticus.* Bonn: Hanstein.

Hengel, M.
1961   *Die Zeloten.* Leiden: Brill.

1968   "Das Gleichnis von den Weingärtnern Mc 12:1-12 im Licht der Zenonpapyri und der rabbinischen Gleichnisse" *ZNW* 59, 1-39.

1974   *Judaism and Hellenism.* Translated J. Bowden. Philadelphia: Fortress.

Herrenbrück, F.
1981   "Wer waren die 'Zöllner?' *ZNW* 72, 178-194.

Herz, J.
1928   "Großgrundbesitz in Palästina im Zeitalter Jesu" *Pälastina Jahrbuch* 24, 98-113.

Hirschfeld, Y.
1985   *Archaeological Survey of Israel: Map of Herodium.* Jerusalem: Department of Antiquities.

Hobsbawm, E. J.
1965   *Primitive Rebels.* New York: Horton.

Hopkins, D.
1985   *The Highlands of Canaan.* Sheffield: Almond.

Horsley, R. A. and J. S. Hanson
1985   *Bandits, Prophets, and Messiahs.* Minneapolis. Winston.

Houtard, F.
1980   *Religion et Modes de Production Précapitalistes.* Brussels: University of Brussels.

Isaac, B.
1984   "Bandits in Judaea and Arabia" *Harvard Studies in Classical Philology* 88, 172-203.

Isaac, B., and I. Roll
1982   *Roman Roads in Judea: The Legio-Scythopolis Road.* Oxford: BAR.

Jeremias, J.
1962   *Jerusalem in the Time of Jesus.* Philadelphia: Fortress.

Jirku, A.
1966   *Von Jerusalem nach Ugarit.* Graz: Akademische.

Johnson, A. C.
1936   "Roman Egypt to the Reign of Diocletian" In T. Frank, Editor. *Economic Survey of Ancient Rome.* Baltimore: Johns Hopkins.

Jones, A. H. M.
1938   *The Herods of Judea.* Oxford: Clarendon.

1940   *The Greek City from Alexander to Justinian.* Oxford: Clarendon.

1964   *The Later Roman Empire.* Oxford: Blackwell.

1971   *Cities of the Eastern Roman Provinces.* Oxford: Clarendon.

de Jonge, M., and A. S. van der Woude
1966   "11Q Melchizedek and the New Testament" *NTS* 12, 301-326.

Kaplan, J.
1969   *Two Groups of Pottery of the First Century A.D. from Jaffa and its Vicinity.* Tel Aviv/Jaffa: Museum of Antiquities.

Kippenberg, H. G.
1978   *Religion und Klassenbildung im antiken Judäa.* Göttingen: Vandenhoeck und Ruprecht.

Kippenberg, H. G., and G. A. Wewers
1979   *Textbuch zur neutestamentlichen Zeitgeschichte.* Göttingen: Vandenhoeck and Ruprecht.

Klausner, J.
1975   "The Economy of Judea in the Period of the Second Temple," In M. Avi-Yonah, Editor. *The Herodian Period.* London: Allen.

186

Klein, S.
1912   "The Estates of R. Judah Ha-Nasi" *JQR* N.S. 2, 545-556.

1923   *Neue Beiträge zur Geschichte und Geographie Galiläas.* Vienna: Menorah.

1933   "Leqorot Haarisit Hagedolah Beeretz Israel," *Bulletin of the Jewish Palestine Exploration Society* I.3, 3-9.

1938   "Leqorot Haarisit Hagedolah Beeretz Israel," *Bulletin of the Jewish Palestine Exploration Society* 3/4, 109-116.

1939   *Eretz Yehudah.* Tel Aviv: Debir.

Kochavi, M.
1972   *Judea, Samaria, and the Golan: Archaeological Survey.* Jerusalem: Carta.

Krauss, S.
1964   *Lehnwörter.* Hildesheim: Georg Olms.

1966   *Talmudische Archäologie.* Hildesheim: Georg Olms.

Kreissig, H.
1969   "Die Landwirtschaftliche Situation in Palästina vor dem Judäischen Krieg" *Acta Antiqua* 17, 223-254.

1970   *Die sozialen Zusammenhänge des judäischen Krieges.* Berlin: Akademie.

Lambert, G.
1950   "Jubilé Hébrue et Jubilé Chrétien" *Nouvelle Revue Theologique* 72, 234-251.

Lance, D.
1967   "Gezer in Land and in History" *BA* 30, 34-47.

Landau, Y. H.
1966   "A Greek Inscription Found Near Hefzibah" *IEJ* 16, 54-70.

Lehmann, M. R.
1963   "Studies in the Murabaat and Nahal Hever Documents" *Revue de Qumran* 4, 53-81.

Lenski, G. E.
1966   *Power and Privilege.* New York: McGraw-Hill.

Lewis, N,
1983   *Life in Egypt Under Roman Rule.* Oxford: Clarendon.

Lohmeyer, E.
1921   *Soziale Fragen im Urchristentum.* Leipzig: Quelle and Meyer.

MacMullen, R.
1966   *Enemies of the Roman Order.* Cambridge: Harvard University.

1974   *Roman Social Relations.* New Haven, Conn.: Yale University.

Maisler, B.
1952   "Beth Shearim, Gaba, and Harosheth of the Peoples" *HUCA*
            24, 75-84.

Malina, B.
1981   *The New Testament World: Insights from Cultural Anthropology.*
            Atlanta: John Knox.

May, H. G.
1974   Editor. *Oxford Bible Atlas.* London: Oxford University.

Meyer, E.
1921   *Ursprung und Anfänge des Christentums.*   Stuttgart/Berlin:
            Cotta.

Meyers, E.
1976   "The Cultural Setting of Galilee: The Case of Regionalism
            and Early Judaism" *ANRW* II.19.1, 368-702.

1979   "Galilean   Regionalism   as   a   Factor   in   Historical
            Reconstruction" *BASOR* 221, 93-101.

Meyers, E. M., J. F. Strange, and D. E. Groh
1978   "The Meiron Excavation Project: Archeological Survey in
            Galilee and Golan, 1976" *BASOR* 230, 1-24.

Meyers, E., J. F. Strange, and C. L. Meyers
1981   *Excavations at Ancient Meiron, Upper Galilee, Israel 1971-72,*
            1974-75, 1977. Cambridge, Mass: BASOR.

Momigliano, A.
1966   "Herod of Judea" *CAH*, Volume X. Edited S. A. Cook, F. E.
            Adcock and M. P. Charlesworth.   Cambridge: Cambridge
            University.

Moore, G. F.
1954   *Judaism.* Cambridge: Harvard University.

Naveh, J.
1970   "The Ossuary Inscriptions from Givat ha-Mivtar" *IEJ* 20, 33-37.

Netzer, E.
1975   "The Hasmonean and Herodian Winter Palaces at Jericho" *IEJ*
            25, 89-100.

Neusner, J.
1960   "The   Fellowship (חבורה   ) in   the   Second   Jewish
            Commonwealth" *HTR* 53, 125-142.

1973   *From Politics to Piety.* Englewood Cliffs, N.J.: Prentice Hall.

Newman, L. E.
1983   *The Sanctity of the Seventh Year: A Study of Mishnah Tractate*
            Shebiit. Chico, CA: Scholars Press.

North, R.
1954   *The Sociology of the Biblical Jubilee.*   Rome: Pontifical
            Institute.

Oakman, D. E.
1986   *Jesus and the Economic Questions of His Day.*
            Lewiston/Queenston: The Edwin Mellen Press.

Oppenheimer, A.
1977   *The Am Ha-aretz.* Translated I. H. Levine. Leiden: Brill.

Puech, E.
1987   "Notes sur le manuscrit de 11Q Melkisedeq" *Revue de Qumran*
            12, 483-513.

Raban, A.
1982   *Archaeological Survey of Israel: Nahalal Map.* Jerusalem:
            Archaeological Survey.

von Rad, G.
1961   *Theologie des alten Testaments.* München: Kaiser.

Rahmani, L. Y.
1980   "A Jewish Rock-Cut Tomb on Mt. Scopus" *Atiqot* E.S. 14, 49-
            54.

Rajak, T.
1973   "Justus of Tiberias" *Classical Quarterly* N.S. 23, 345-368.

Redfield, R.
1956   *Peasant Society and Culture.* Chicago: University of Chicago

Ringe, S. H.
1981   *The Jubilee Proclamation in the Ministry of Jesus: A Tradition
            Critical Study in the Synoptic Gospels and Acts.* Union
            Theological Seminary, N.Y.: Ph.D.

Rosenfeld, B. Z.
1988   "The 'Boundary of Gezer' Inscriptions" *IEJ* 38, 235-245.

Rostovtzeff, M.
1922   *A Large Estate in Egypt in the Third Century B.C.* Madison,
            Wis.: University of Wisconsin.

1941   *Social and Economic History of the Hellenistic World.* Oxford:
            Clarendon.

1957   *Social and Economic History of the Roman Empire.* Revised by
            P. M. Fraser. Oxford: Clarendon.

Safrai, S.
1976   "Home and Family" *Compendia* I.2, p. 728-792.

1976   "Religion in Everyday Life" *Compendia* I.2, p. 793-833.

Safrai, S., and M. Stern
1974-1976   *The Jewish People in First Century.* (Editors)
            Assen/Amsterdam: Van Gorcum. (Compendia Rerum
            Iudaicarum).

Sanders, J. A.
1975   "From Isaiah 61 to Luke 4" In J. Neusner, Editor. *Christianity,
            Judaism, and other Greco-Roman Cults.* Leiden: Brill.

Schalit, A.
1969   *Herodes.* Berlin: de Gruyter.

1976   "Domestic Politics and Political Institutions" In A. Schalit, Editor. *The Hellenistic Age.* London: Allen.

Schlatter, A.
1897   *Die Tage Trajans und Hadrians.* Gütersloh: Bertelsmann.

Schottroff, W., and W. Stegemann
1984   *God of the Lowly* (Editors) Translated M. J. O'Conell. Maryknoll, N.Y.: Orbis.

Schürer, E., G. Vermes and F. Miller
1973-1987 *The History of the Jewish People in the Age of Jesus Christ (175 B.C.-A.D. 135).* Edinburgh: T. and T. Clark

Shanks, H.
1979   *Judaism in Stone.* Jerusalem: Steimatzky.

Sherwin-White, A. N.
1963   *Roman Society and Roman Law in the New Testament.* Oxford: Clarendon.

Shiloh, Y.
1970   "The Four-Room House: Its Situation and Function in the Israelite City" *IEJ* 20, 180-190.

1980   "The Population of Iron Age Palestine in the Light of a Sample Analysis of Urban Plans, Areas, and Population Density" *BASOR* 239, 25-35.

Smallwood, E. M.
1962   "High Priests and Politics in Roman Palestine" *Journal of Theological Studies* 13, 14-34

Smith, P., E. Bornemann, and J. Zias
1981   "The Skeletal Remains" In E. Meyers, J. F. Strange and C. L. Meyers.

Smith, P. E. and J. Zias
1980   "Skeletal Remains from Late Hellenistic French Hill Tomb" *IEJ* 30, 109-115.

Sperber, D.
1965   "Costs of Living in Roman Palestine I" *Journal of the Economic and Social History of the Orient* 8, 248-271.

Stager, L. E.
1985   "The Archaeology of the Family in Ancient Israel" *BASOR* 260, 1-35.

de Ste. Croix, G. E. M.
1981   *The Class Struggle in the Ancient Greek World.* Ithaca, N.Y.: Cornell University.

Steckoll, S. H.
1968   "Excavation Report in the Qumran Cemetery" *Revue de Qumran* 6, 323-336

Stenger, W.
1988   *Gebt dem Kaiser was des Kaisers ist.* Frankfurt: Athenäum.

Stern, M.
1974   "The Province of Judea" *Compendia* I.1, p. 308-376.

1974   "The Reign of Herod and the Herodian Dynasty" *Compendia* I.1, 216-307

1975   "The Herodian Dynasty and the Province of Judea at the End of the Period of the Second Temple" In M. Avi-Yonah, Editor. *The Herodian Period.* London: Allen.

1975   "The Reign of Herod" In M. Avi-Yonah, Editor. *The Herodian Period.* London: Allen.

1976   "Aspects of Jewish Society: The Priesthood and other Classes" *Compendia* I.2, p. 561-630.

Strange, J. F., and H. Shanks
1982   "Has the House Where Jesus Stayed in Capernaum been Found?" *BAR* VIII: 6, 26-37.

Tarn, W. W.
1952   *Hellenistic Civilization.* London: Methuen.

Taylor, J. E.
1979   *Seleucid Rule in Palestine.* Duke University: Ph.D.

Taylor, W. R.
1931   "New Gezer Boundary Stone" *BASOR* 41, 28f.

Tcherikover, V.
1937   "Palestine under the Ptolemies" *Mizraim* 4/5, 1-82.

1975   *Hellenistic Civilization and the Jews.* New York: Atheneum.

Theissen, G.
1978   *Sociology of Early Palestinian Christianity.* Translated J. Bowden. Philadelphia: Fortress.

Thompson, D. J.
1987   "Imperial Estates" In J.Wacher, Editor. *The Roman World.* London: Routledge and Kegan Paul.

Trocmé, A.
1961   *Jesús et la Révolution Non-violente.* Geneva: Editions Labor et Fides.

Tzaferis, V.
1970   "Jewish Tombs at and near Givat ha-Mivtar, Jerusalem" *IEJ* 20, 18-22.

Urbach, E. E.
1964   "Laws Regarding Slavery as a Source for Social History of the
            Period of the Second Temple, the Mishnah and Talmud"
            *Papers of the Institute of Jewish Studies, University College
            London* 1, 1-94.

1968   "Class-Status and Leadership in the World of the Palestinian
            Sages" *Proceedings of Israel Academy of Sciences and
            Humanities* 2, 38-74.

Urman, D.
1985   *The Golan.* Oxford: BAR.

de Vaux, R.
1961   *Ancient Israel.* Translated J. McHugh. London: Darton,
            Longman, and Todd.

Vermes, G.
1973   *Jesus the Jew.* London: Collins.

Wacher, J.
1987   *The Roman World* (Editor). London: Routledge and Kegan
            Paul.

Wacholder, B. Z.
1973   "The Calendar of Sabbatical Cycles during the Second Temple
            and the Early Rabbinic Period" *HUCA* 44, 153-196.

Wallace, S. L.
1938   *Taxation in Egypt.* Princeton: Princeton University.

White, K. D.
1967   "Latifundia" *Bulletin of The Institute of Classical Studies* 14, 62-
            79.

1970   *Roman Farming.* London: Thames and Hudson.

1977   *Country Life in Classical Times.* Ithaca, N.Y.: Cornell
            University.

Wolf, E. R.
1966   *Peasants.* Englewood Cliffs, N.J.: Prentice Hall.

1969   *Peasant Wars of the Twentieth Century.* New York: Harper and
            Row.

van der Woude, A. S.
1965   "Melchizedek als himmlische Erlösergestalt in den
            neugefundenen eschatologischen Midraschim aus Qumran
            Höhle XI" *Oudtestamentische Studien* 14, 354-373.

Yadin, Y.
1965   "A Note on Melchizedek and Qumran" *IEJ* 15, 152-154.

1962   "Expedition D--The Cave of the Letters" *IEJ* 12, 227-257.

192

Yeivin, Z.
1971   *Survey of Settlements in Galilee and the Golan from the Period of
            the Mishnah in Light of the Sources.* Hebrew University: Ph.D.

1987   "On the Medium-Sized City" *Eretz Israel* 19, 59-71.

Yeivin, Z., and G. Edelstein
1970   "Excavations at Tirat Yehuda" *Atiqot* N.S. 6, 56.67.

Yoder, J. H.
1972   *The Politics of Jesus.* Grand Rapids, Mich.: Eerdmans.

Youtie, H. C.
1967   "Publicans and Sinners" *Zeitschrift für Papyrologie und
            Epigraphik* 1, 1-20.

REFERENCE WORKS

Bauer, W., W. F. Arndt, and F. W. Gingrich
1957   *A Greek-English Lexicon of the New Testament.* Chicago:

Brown, F., S. R. Driver, and C. A. Briggs
1968   *A Hebrew and English Lexicon.* Oxford: Clarendon.

Buttrick, G.
1962   *Interpreters Dictionary of the Bible.* New York: Abingdon.

Hammond, N. G. L.
1970   *Oxford Classical Dictionary.* (Editor) Oxford: Clarendon.

Jastrow, M.
1975   *A Dictionary of the Targumim, the Talmud Babli and Yershalmi, and the Midrashic Literature.* New York: Judaica.

Kittel, G., et al
1974   *Theological Dictionary of the New Testament.* (Editor) Grand Rapids, MI: Eerdmans.

Liddell, H. G., R. Scott, H. S. Jones, and R. McKenzie
1968   *A Greek-English Lexicon.* Oxford: Clarendon.

Singer, I.
1903   *Jewish Encyclopedia.* (Editor) New York: Funk and Wagnals.

194

PRIMARY SOURCES

a.)   DOCUMENTS FROM THE JUDEAN DESERT:

Benoit, P., T. J. Milik, and R. de Vaux
1961   *Les Grottes de Murabaat.* Oxford: Clarendon.

Beyer, K.
1984   *Die Aramäischen Texte vom Toten Meer.* Göttingen: Vandenhoeck and Ruprecht.

Fitzmyer, J., and D. J. Harrington
1978   *A Manual of Palestinian Aramaic Texts.* Rome: Biblical Institute.

Koffmahn, E.
1968   *Die Doppelurkunden aus der Wüste Juda.* Leiden: Brill.

Lohse, E.
1964   *Die Texte aus Qumran.* Darmstadt: Wissenschaftliche Buchgesellschaft.

Vermes, G.
1975   *The Dead Sea Scrolls in English.* New York: Penguin.

b.)   RABBINICAL SOURCES:

Albeck, A.
1952-58   *The Six Orders of the Mishnah.* Jerusalem: Bialeck.

Bauer, W.
1915   *Pea.* Giessen: Töpelmann.

Bietenhard, H.
1956   *Sota.* Berlin: Töpelmann.

Correns, D.
1960   *Schebiit.* Giessen/Berlin: Töpelmann.

Danby, H.
1933   *The Mishnah* London: Oxford University.

Epstein, I.
1948   *The Bablylonian Talmud.* (Editor) London: Soncino.

Goldschmidt, L.
1933   *Der Babylonische Talmud.* Haag: Martinus Nijoff.

Neusner, J.
1977-86   *The Tosephta.* Hoboken, N.Y.: KTAV.

Schwab, M.
1960   *Le Talmud de Jerusalem.* Paris: Maisonneuve.

Zuckermandel, S.
1954   *Tosephta.* Jerusalem: Gilead.

c.) OTHER JEWISH SOURCES

Charlesworth, J. H.
1985-87   The Pseudepigrapha of the Old Testament. (Editor) New York: Doubleday.

Frey, J. B.
1952   *Corpus Inscriptionum Iudaicarum.* Volume II. Rome: Pontificio Istituto di Archeologia Cristiana.

Thackery, H. St. J., R. Marcus, A. Wikgren, and L. H. Feldman
1961-65   *Josephus.* (LCL) Cambridge, Mass.: Harvard University.

d.) PAPR YI:

Bagnall, R. S., and N. Lewis
1979   *Columbia Papyri VII.* Missoula, Montana: Scholars Press.

Edgar, C. C.
1971   *Zenon Papyri.* Hildescheim: Georg Olms.

Hengstl, J.
1978   *Griechische Papyri aus Ägypten.* München: Heimeran.

Hunt, A. S., and C. C. Edgar
1934   *Select Papyri.* (LCL) Cambridge, Mass.: Harvard University.

Husselman, E. M.
1971   *Papyri From Karanis.* London: Clowes.

Preisigke, F.
1916   *Antikes Leben nach den ägyptischen Papyri.* Leipzig: Teubner.

Tcherikover, V., and A. Fuks
1957   *Corpus Papyrorum Iudaicarum.* Cambridge, Mass.: Harvard University.

STUDIES IN THE BIBLE AND EARLY CHRISTIANITY